Dear Daddy,
Here is my
first hard cover
published work.
Love,
Chippy

# America the Beautiful

# America the Beautiful

### A Modern Guide to Sex, Security and the Soft Buck

EDITED BY **JOEL LIEBER**

*DAVID WHITE* NEW YORK

First Edition

Published in the United States of America by
David White, Inc.
60 East 55th Street
New York, N. Y. 10022

Library of Congress Catalog Card Number: 68-29588
Copyright © 1968 by David White, Inc.

Manufactured in the United States of America

# Contents

vi

# Introduction

I can hear some Statesman emeritus out there reading these pieces and saying, "Ah'm tahd ah people runnin' down ah country." But this great horn of plenty that is America—this "big barbecue," as the Statesman once called it—is a damn funny place. (As Lenny Bruce said, the State has no sense of humor.) It is a country as easily profaned with words as it is glorified by them, as easily laughed at as taken seriously. For, depending on where you sit—high or low, in or out—either you are the reality and *America* is the fantasy, or *you* are the fantasy and America is the reality.

Of this country, our children are told at an early age, anybody can do anything and anybody can be anything, and that's democracy. It's not true, of course. But anybody can sell anything here. That *is* true. And in selling even the most preposterous commodities, anybody can pretend he's in it for the common good, not for profit.

Selling is what this book is about—selling things and services for a lot of money. The products and services described in these pages—and the attitudes toward them—are peculiarly American. They are not pushed with the same passion in other countries, nor pursued by the public with the same abandon. The salesmen, scoutmasters and tour guides are everywhere about us, telling us what we need, exploiting insecurity, greedy with the ease with which they can perform their outrages on the masses.

When it comes to money, American excesses are at their most rampant. When it comes to money, we are never commonplace. What to one seems like healthy, uniform prosperity, to another smacks of compulsive materialism. One thing is certain: we are extravagant. We indulge ourselves with purchasables. We are lavish. We crave the security of costly services and possessions. We crave the security of security for no other sake but security's. We chase after a security that cannot be bought with dollars.

We have manufacturers presenting baby dolls to make children wise, more sophisticated and more secure; we have big business offering the graduate lifetime job security; we have promoters heralding the end of the how-boy-meets-girl dilemma; we have friendly folks offering

vii

terminal security to the aged. Along the way, experts can relieve the anxieties of the overweight among us, and group therapists can put the out-of-touch back in touch. We have more insurance agents in this country than the rest of the world put together; in fact, we have become, as a nation, a whole tribe of insurance specialists.

Love (or at least meaningful sex) seems to rank highest among the securities that cannot be bought—judging at least by the amount of attention sex receives from America's salesmen and tour guides. In many inimitably American ways, pleasure and commercialism have become confused. Scarcely even noticeable, since it goes on all around us, the soft sigh manages to sound the same as the click of a cash register. Day in and day out, we are victimized by a perversion of romantic themes into income-producing sexuality.

And yet we know how to be so cheerful and affable while being ridiculous about all this. We have a certain complacency going for us. We casually give the appearance that everything is all right. Yet, not far under our appearance we are galloping in circles, anxious, war-whooping, engaged in madness and absurd dances.

This book, then, is about money and sex, American-style. It is also about selling, and about security and its more prevalent enemy, insecurity. Every article that follows touches a different aspect of these themes. In these times, to publish a book about American excesses and say nothing about war and politics and race would be unbecoming. But in various subtle ways these overriding concerns appear between the lines in several of the articles, even though they are not the focal point. More important, I believe, is the fact that out of these relevant observations of the American scene there emerges a certain mood—a loneliness and frustration on the part of a public that is easily herded, an anesthetization of human feeling on the part of the ringleaders—that makes the disturbing American attitudes in these other realms more easily appreciated, more predictable.

Each of the authors here seems to ask a variation of the same question: Are we all going crazy? What happened? How did we ever get ourselves into such a fix? Not many people remember the answers anymore. Certainly the authors of the articles that follow are guilty of not providing the answers. Their reports illuminate and astonish, and make us sad while we laugh. Each, in his own way, fell victim to the highest kind of cool, amusing, penetrating journalism. That way, without the roadblocks of essay and editorial, the reader is free to travel the same roads the authors took, through America the Beautiful—north to Security, south to Sex, and east and west to the Soft Buck.

JOEL LIEBER

# America the Beautiful

W E *are seeing children who are excited and disturbed by dolls like Barbie and her friends. With baby dolls, girls can play at being active, nurturing mothers and housewives; with Barbie, girls learn to expect to be valued for an ever-increasing wardrobe and their ability to manipulate their fathers and, later, husbands, into buying clothes and more clothes. Boys are being seen in the clinic who use Barbie for sexual stimulation, a fact which might trouble the same parents who are scandalized by comic books and pin-up magazines, were it not for the fact that Barbie masquerades as a child's toy. Both boys and girls are introduced to a precocious, joyless sexuality, to fantasies of seduction and conspicuous consumption. This reflects and perpetuates a disturbing trend in our culture, which has serious mental-health complications."*

—A statement by Dr. Alan F. Leveton, director of the Pediatrics Mental Health Unit, University of California Medical Center, San Francisco, in *Ramparts* Magazine, April 1965.

# Barbie, Go Home, or
# Bring Back Teddy Bears

*Chauncey Howell*

FANTASY #1:

Smiling, singing Julie Andrews is leading the kids across an edelweiss-suffocated Alpine meadow . . . the Wide Screen is oozing marshmallow. Somewhere back in the warm womb-gloom of the loges, Ken gulped. He had been thinking about something for a long time, as all boys will.

1

His vinyl plastic hand reached over and nervously came to rest on Barbie's lovely knee (vinyl plastic, too, and an "articulated joint," to boot). She was wearing her "Beau Time" Ensemble Pak, so Ken had assumed she wouldn't mind a little knee action.

Barbie stirred, visibly annoyed. With a brisk but gentle gesture she brushed Ken's quivering hand from her knee. "You must never touch me," she whispered firmly but understandingly.

"You'll have to wait until after I've worn my 'Here Comes the Bride' Ensemble Pak—and you've worn your 'Here Comes the Groom' EP, which, incidentally, wholesales at fifty cents more than my own wedding EP. Think of the big markups possible on both: and you wanted to spoil it all!"

Suddenly Ken felt a new, a finer, deeper feeling toward Barbie surging through him. She was really a wonderful girl. He was so lucky! Shyly, he squeezed her lovely hand. Though vinyl plastic, it felt warmer and more comforting than ever before.

Barbie smiled her marvelous smile, that special little smile of a girl who knows what it's all about—fashion, boys, good grooming, you name it! Well, that "touching" business was finally settled, she thought to herself. You have to know how to handle boys. They don't really know what they want. You have to be firm with them. They need understanding. Dear, foolish Ken.

Barbie hoped that someday she could be as understanding as Julie Andrews. She tried to smile like Julie Andrews. It was hard, when your lips are permanently set in a smug pout that even Sandra Dee would envy. Ken had already forgotten the episode just past. He was happily nibbling on a plastic pretzel from his "Party Fun" Fashion Pak Assortment. He'd just have to wait. But Barbie is wonderful, isn't she?

FANTASY FULFILLMENT FOR YOUNG AND OLD! Now! The rich, wonderful, merchy World of Barbie lies open and beckoning to all! No longer are Barbie and her charming, clothes-conscious friends the sole property of the pre-pubies. Now, NOW, older, more experienced voyeurs, fetishists, overreachers, sexual fantasists and perjured romantics can join in the fun. They too can enjoy and cherish the delicious, fashionable, "fun" World of Barbie.

Thirty-five-year-old divorcees, grandmothers in gift shops, tired insurance executives, decorators—imaginative adults everywhere—can now identify with Barbie and her swinging, carefree, teen-age world. Why should nasty seven-year-old pre-pubies have all the fun and fantasy? Let them go back to their teddy bears and baby dolls that wet, their stuffed plush platypuses and Raggedy Anns and Andys. Barbie's too good for them. Yeahh!

Barbie is the perfect expression of materialist America in all its groovy greed for consumer goods. And, she's made by Mattel, Inc. ("If it's Mattel, it's swell"), which is located in California, that fab Lotus Land where all good things are possible. Like Barbie.

Since 1959 when Mattel introduced Barbie to the waiting world, the astounding growth of her popularity and of the company itself have almost kept pace with the galloping strides of the Teen Takeover. Although Mattel does not release figures, it can be reasonably estimated that the Barbie bit accounts for nearly $100 million in gross sales per year. Today, Mattel is the biggest toy company in the world and Barbie, who is responsible for most of the company's success, is the most popular doll in history. Shirley Temple dolls and Sparkle Plenty dolls don't even rate in the big Barbie sweepstakes.

This year, Mattel enrolled the one-millionth little girl in the Barbie Fan Club, which is the second largest girls' organization in the world—after the Girl Scouts. In the national *Barbie* Magazine (25 cents per bimonthly copy), space normally allotted to fatuous stories about Barbie, her problems, and her wardrobe is devoted to pictures of the one-millionth little girl, eleven-year-old Mary Lou Ray, of Belmont, Mass., being shown around New York City and the Mattel national marketing meeting. In every shot Mary Lou is holding her Barbie as though it were a garlic talisman against vampires. Such is the power of Barbie.

Mattel peddles advice from Barbie (acne never had so kindly an apologist!) to girls in the seven to twelve age range on radio and television programs all over the country—and in more than 250 daily and 200 weekly newspapers. Mattel also has a "public service" program, called "Pigtails to Ponytails," that includes commentary and a film on how mothers can use fashion dolls (like Barbie, of course) to encourage their pre-pubies to stop acting like tomboys and adorable little realgirls and start acting like up-tight teen-age clotheshorses long before their time.

Subtly and with seeming altruism, Mattel has masterminded one of the most remarkable jobs of *agitprop* in modern times—and this, above and beyond their huge annual expenditure for conventional advertising. Barbie is a vinyl plastic Ronald Reagan: she's got so much cleverness and power behind her now, she can't help but win big—and bigger.

CAST OF CHARACTERS IN "THE WORLD OF BARBIE" (a biased view):

BARBIE herself. Chief honcho. Miss Teen Tough. Presumed to be about seventeen or eighteen years old by the little twelves-and-unders who own her. Eleven and a half inches tall and stacked (5¼-3-4¾). Barbie's little orphan annies are the burgeoning delight of perverts and the despair of little girls who are not yet as well fixed—thus encouraging pectoral *Angst* among pre-pubies, thus in turn encouraging sales of that loathsome threat to the fast-fading spirit of Louisa May Alcott, TRAINING BRAS!

Barbie's hair is set in the bitchy mode of the season. Her do and color can both be easily changed, but if a child has no aptitude for hairburning with Dynel, she can easily fit Barbie with one of the "hi-fashion" wigs in Barbie's wig wardrobe. Barbie's eyes are heavy-lidded: you have your choice of finding them either cruel or sensuous. Above the lashes runs a mean streak of blue mascara, applied with the bold expertise of a showgirl.

In the current Mattel catalog, Barbie has her choice of almost seventy different smart teeny outfits, most of them fully accessorized. These include "fun" dresses (everything Barbie does is "fun"), soignée evening gowns, lacy, humpy "underfashions," and a riding costume complete with boots and crop just in case Barbie wants to make like Barbara Stanwyck in some old movie. Barbie has every imaginable accessory from jewelry and TV sets up to automobiles and a perfect little "dream house" (the decor is gauche but looks expensive, which, after all, is more important).

Mattel has everything for Barbie and, naturally, she will want it all. Mattel estimates that a father can spend up to $100 on his daughter's

Barbie; other sources say $200. Yes, Barbie has everything but a diaphragm or a pill kit. With a boyfriend like Ken she doesn't need them.

KEN is Barbie's walking-stick and eventual husband. Stands slightly taller than she and, beyond a short haircut, no mascara, no nubbins and heavier legs, displays no visible sexual difference. Ken comes with a complete line of costumes and accessories, too. In recent years his clothes have been embarrassingly fey (Barbie could have worn some of them herself). This year they are more masculine and less frivolous. The only touch of fashion madness left him is a black Beatle wig in his "Ken a Go Go" Ensemble Pak.

MIDGE is Barbie's best friend. Plainer, and with freckles on her snub nose, Midge is to be loved for her imperfection just as Barbie is to be loved for her perfection. Midge is typical of the less attractive women good-lookers like Barbie are reputed to gather about them: Midge sets Barbie off.

In *Barbie* Magazine stories, Barbie is always putting silly Midge straight on Barbie's own hard, narrow path. Midge can wear all of Barbie's exciting clothes, but she never wears them as well as Barbie does, if you know what I mean.

Simulated black patent leather carrying cases are available for carrying Barbie and Midge—with their little costumes—to and from grade school. Amusingly, they're reminiscent of cases hookers carry on 8th Avenue—to and from work.

Midge and Ken have their own accessories, but their main function in the World of Barbie is to act as accessories to Queen Bitch Barbie.

FRANCIE is Barbie's fifteen-year-old Mod cousin, who has just arrived this season with her own rooted eyelashes and eyelash brush—and, you guessed it, a complete wardrobe: Mod clothes that Barbie can wear, too! Imagine confident Barbie in dykey vinyl? Easy.

ALLAN has been deleted this year. He was Ken's best buddy and poor Midge's boyfriend. His main virtues were his uncanny resemblance to Dwayne Hickman and his ability to wear Ken's clothes. Allan has been driven from the gates of Barbie's teen paradise. Apparently, Mattel figures that Midge can share Ken with Barbie, if Barbie will let her. Doubtful.

SKIPPER is Barbie's little sister, presumably the same age as the little girls who own Barbie. Skipper, too, has a complete wardrobe of expensive clothes which can be worn by her best friend, SKOOTER. Both girls share a boy friend in common, little RICKY, who comes with a complete collection of boychik duds. Natch, Mattel knows what they're doing. Skooter is Skipper's Midge, and although their relationship is not yet as tense and sado-masochistic as Barbie and Midge's, it has interesting possibilities.

TUTTI is Barbie and Skipper's baby sister. Among her accessories is a twin brother TODD. Barbie can change her outfits for her, feed her "bendable and posable" dog for her, and baby-sit for her—that is, if Barbie's not too busy changing her own clothes, running for school offices, or giving befuddled Ken and Midge tough-minded advice in the form of Barbie-Think.

Other toy firms have tried to cash in on the Barbie Bonanza, but dolls like American Character's "Tressy" and "Mary Makeup" (sic) just can't stand up to Barbie, who could stare down any competitor with those hard little eyes of hers.

One firm, though, has cashed in on the Barbie Syndrome very nicely—but in a curious, unexpected way. Hasbro has a doll for boy pre-pubies that has been shockingly successful: G.I. Joe, Action Soldier!

In addition to his regulation dog tag (just one) and Army-style field manual, Joe has such an array of military costumes, equipment, and impedimenta in his wall locker that only the most jaded of uniform fetishists would fail to be impressed.

Joe comes in white or black; his right cheek is scarred; he can soldier in any branch of the service; he can carry every imaginable hand-held death-dealing device recognized by the Pentagon. Hasbro supplies them all—for a price.

Joe can change allegiances, too, and, if he pleases, become an Aussie or British commando, a Red Army ground-pounder, an "Imperial Japanese Soldier," or, most horrifying of all, a Nazi Storm Trooper complete with Luger and Iron Cross.

Hasbro is the trade name of the parent firm, Hassenfeld Bros.

"Hassenfeld," curiously, means "field of hate" in German, which of course is the language Joe would speak when he is wearing his cunning little SS outfit.

The sensibilities and malleable minds of male pre-pubies are also open to attack by another line of war dolls: "The Tigers" (Topper Toys). Each "Tiger" is fully outfitted for combat and each has a specific character and squad position. They include "Sarge," with a cigar and .45, "Combat Kid," with Molotov Cocktail, and "Pretty Boy," who would rather salute than kill and looks like a swish Richard Egan.

Barbie and her friends, G.I. Joe and his comrades-in-arms, supply material for a child's playtime microcosm of selfishness, narcissism, and savagery. In spite of the hysterical yawpings of the toy industry's flacks, these dolls do not encourage maturity in their owners, they do not set up "creative play situations" except in the worst sense, and they do not make a child more responsible to himself, his parents, or others.

Barbie and Joe are the stuff that dreams are made of—nightmares.

If, dear reader, after wearying it so far you are still unimpressed with the Fantasy Fulfillment Potential in the Wonderful, Willful and Wicked World of Barbie, or you are too stunned by facts and observations to imagine any further taste-tempting titillations on the standard Barbie-cue, then pause and consider two more fantasies:

FANTASY #2:

Last season, Barbie and Ken both had nurse and doctor outfits, completely accessorized. This season, Mattel dropped them from the line and, instead, is supplying a Pan Am stewardess uniform for Barbie. Ken gets nothing new to replace his old hospital whites, but, inexplicably, Mattel has left his doctor's kit in the catalog. Naturally, Ken can't accompany Barbie on her exciting cross-country stints as big-deal Waitress-in-the-Sky, and he is miffed. M-I-F-F-E-D! First spunk he has shown in a long time.

The Pan Am flight from glamorous L.A. has just touched down at Kennedy. Barbie, still Miss Efficiency, is frankly pooped after a long flight of serving meals, fluffing pillows, and putting down fresh hardware salesmen. The usually vigorous rat-tat-tat of her spike heels has a slower beat now as she walks into the darkened, deserted Hostess

Lounge—I'll just touch up my face, she thinks. There, lurking behind a plastic rubber plant is Ken, still very miffed. He has a wild look in his eyes and his doctor's kit in his hand . . .

FANTASY #3:

Ken has been drafted. Fortunately, G.I. Joe's uniforms fit him. After some training, he has been sent to Vietnam where, in either his Lockheed Hercules C-130B (made by Revell, Inc., $1) or his Republic F-105 "Thunderchief" (made by Aurora Plastics Corp., 98 cents), he drops defoliation chemicals or Napalm (made by Dow Chemical Co.; prices available on request) on hapless Vietnamese villages. He is troubled at first, but when an Air Force information officer tells him that VC are known to be concentrated in those villages, he is relieved, then pleased to be able to serve his country so well after all—and, of course, keep the world safe for Barbie.

One hot, steamy day, as Ken's plane, loaded with defoliants and Napalm, dipped low over a rice paddy, suddenly BLAM!, it was shot down by a "Tiger Cannon" (Topper Toys), which had fallen into the hands of the VC. Somehow, a badly wounded and unconscious Ken was pulled from the paddy by a United States patrol which carried him back to a field hospital in Da Nang. Fortunately, Ken had been wearing his G.I. Joe "Scramble-Parachute-Pack" when he leapt from the burning plane.

When Ken awoke from his coma, who should he find sponging his feverish brow but BARBIE! Wonderful, understanding Barbie! Almost a year had passed and Mattel, eager to get in on the growing market for patriotic "hawk" toys, had restored Barbie's Nurse Ensemble Pak to the catalog, but with an important difference: Barbie is now a Combat Nurse—and she has her own suture kit and plastic M-14. Barbie has also been taught to kill with her hands, just in case. We knew it all along. Good old Barbie.

Slowly and with understanding, Barbie nurses Ken back to health. Ken never tries to touch her. He's learned. He can wait until it's all over and until they've worn their high-mark-up wedding EPs. Barbie is so good.

Late one night, Barbie is especially tuckered from changing Ken's bandages and her own costumes and hair color—and under combat conditions, no less. The familiar, brisk, matter-of-fact slosh-slosh-slosh of her combat boots has a slower beat now as she walks into the darkened, deserted Nurses' Tent. There, lurking behind a plastic chemical-toilet is a G.I. Joe "Viet Cong" doll. He has a wild look in his eyes and his rapist kit in his hand . . .

We'll never know if Barbie could really kill with her hands.

Exhausted with fantasizing? Disgusted with Barbie? Disgusted with yourself? Relax and be soothingly reassured. Multiple Toymakers of New York has the Final Solution to the Barbie Question: their spectacularly evil toy "Stretch 'Em Wheel" ($1), an accurate model of the medieval rack.

Multiple Toymakers leeringly describes this plaything of theirs as "a real scream," and promises that it will break the back of the toughest doll—even Barbie.

Y OU *are a city-slicker observing a teenie beauty contest: the finalists are a throng of really beautiful little girls (ages thirteen to seventeen). At stake is a crown and a convertible, a Caribbean cruise and a "chest full" of sneakers—a scholarship, triumph, and lots of tears.*

# The Neatest Teener

### by Dan Wakefield

The Miss Teen Age America Pageant at Dallas, which threatens to become a permanent annual rite, brings together nearly a hundred girls between the ages of thirteen and seventeen who have been selected as "America's most representative teen-agers." After an arduous week of smile-ridden competition they participate in an hour-and-a-half nationwide television spectacle which features the coronation of the most "representative," or "ideal," teen-age girl of all. In the world of Miss Teen Age America, the words "representative," "typical," and "ideal" are all synonymous, and represent the highest goal attainable. Each hopeful contestant is faced with the same challenging question as she goes through her rounds of interviews, talent performances, and modeling tests: "Mirror, mirror on the wall, who is the most representative of all?"

This new contribution to our culture was of course the brainchild of a Texas "merchandising expert" who was dazzled by the potential of the Teen-age Market and its ten billion dollars annual purchasing power. The corporation founded to tap this tender mine, Teen America Associates, Inc., has had its ups and downs and changes of ownership, but in the darkest hours of crisis new men of vision have arisen from the ranks of Dallas financiers to keep alive the dream, and the major national advertisers have signed up to have their products blessed by the Teen

Queen. The first "coronation pageant," held in Dallas in 1961 and televised locally, inspired CBS to guarantee Teen America Associates up to $55,000 annually for the rights to televise the show on a nation-wide hookup for the next seven years. A national audience estimated at thirty million watched the crowning of the second Miss Teen Age America in October 1962.

With the promise of getting a "backstage" view of this new ritual I flew down to Dallas on coronation eve last October and proceeded directly to rehearsals at the State Fair Music Hall. In that vast auditorium the eighty some contestants were going through their paces with a top CBS production crew flown in from New York and the Singing Cadets of Texas A. & M. College, a men's chorus "whose repertoire is as varied as their individual backgrounds." The press release which gave me this information on the Singing Cadets explained that their repertoire "consists of medieval liturgies, spirituals, classics, and novelty numbers or hit songs," but it did not go into their varied individual backgrounds and it was hard to guess what they might be, since all of the cadets wore identical blue blazers and gleaming smiles. As I entered the auditorium they were stationed in the pit crooning a melody with such hushed reverence that it might indeed have been a medieval liturgy, but the words were "You are bue-tee-full, proud and shyyyy. . . ." The curtains parted to reveal the massed Teen Queens in identical beige skirts and jackets and red blouses, staring out at the auditorium with practiced proud-shy smiles.

When the number ended, I located Paul Bradley, a New Yorker who was there to handle public relations for the pageant, and he ushered me backstage where I could talk with the girls. Bradley explained that the girls had been in Dallas for a week now and that the field had already been narrowed to twenty-five semifinal contenders. Out of that group six finalists had been chosen who would be the feature performers in the show. He motioned to a bright-eyed carbon copy of Debbie Reynolds who was standing nearby and informed me that she was a sixteen-year-old high-school girl from St. Louis and one of the lucky six finalists. He introduced us, and asked her to tell me about the kind of time she was having. She clasped her hands in front of her, pointed one foot forward in a modeling stance, and said in a breathless singsong:

"The nicest part has been meeting all the wonderful girls and making friends with them. The saddest part has been having the selections for the finals cut down, first to twenty-five and now to six. I'm just so sorry for all those girls who have already been eliminated."

I had no further questions to ask Miss Teen Age St. Louis, and so Bradley took me over to a brown-haired woman sitting quietly in the shadows and introduced her as the mother of last year's Miss Teen Age America winner. The mother explained to me that her husband was in the service-station business in Richmond, Virginia, and if it hadn't been for the wonderful scholarship that is the principal prize for the Teen Queen (it covers four years of tuition and all expenses at any college in the U.S. and is "valued at $14,000") they wouldn't have been able to send their daughter to the college of her choice, which turned out to be Colorado College, a small, liberal arts school in Colorado Springs.

"We couldn't have paid the expenses of our daughter traveling back and forth to school out there," the mother explained, "and without this wonderful scholarship she'd have had to go to school in the East."

Being saved from the fate of an Eastern education was evidently worth the year's difficult schedule for the seventeen-year-old daughter, who had to travel throughout the country during the school year making public appearances for sponsors of the Teen America contest, modeling for fashion shows and Teen endorsements of products, and giving talks to civic, charitable, and school groups.

"She traveled most every weekend, and the weekends usually began Friday morning and ended Monday night. But the school was very nice about it—and of course whenever she had a chance to talk to student groups she stressed the importance of studies and education."

Our chat was interrupted by a wave and a call from a dark-haired girl near the stage door who turned out to be Miss Teen Age America herself, and mother said sharply, "Dear, I'm having an *inter*view!" Miss Teen Age immediately threw her hands to her face and began to apologize profusely. I tried to assure both mother and daughter that I wasn't offended, and Miss Teen Age approached us, looking penitent in purple slacks and matching cashmere sweater. I had read in one of the press releases that the selection of Miss Teen Age was made "on the basis of a twelve-unit evaluation covering personality, talent, self-confidence, and an awareness of national, international, and local events. Her perception of the world she lives in has much to do with determining whether or not she is Miss Teen Age America." I had also read in a press release that this particular Miss Teen Age had "high hopes of a career in the diplomatic field—preferably working for the government in foreign countries."

She sat down on a folding chair beside me and explained that she was majoring in political science, and hoped someday to do "radio or TV news commentary" or perhaps "government work" as a career. She revealed that she admired Jacqueline Kennedy, but would not commit herself to any other political views. "Although I'm interested in politics, I'm not much of a politician," she explained. She was fiddling with the crown that comes with her office, shifting it from one hand to the other and pressing it over her purple-clad thigh, and I realized that as a representative of *all* teen-age America she probably did not want to align herself with any partisan views. I shifted the conversation to more general grounds and asked what people she admired in other fields. such as movies, theater, sports—anything—hoping to get an indication of who the current teen heroes and heroines might be. After some hesitation Miss Teen Age said, "I don't think I know that much about anyone's life to be able to judge."

Well, then, what was teen America reading? Did she have a favorite author?

"William Faulkner!" Miss Teen Age answered enthusiastically.

She smiled up at her mother who was perched on a stool a few feet away, like an ever-present prompting coach, and her mother smiled back. Heady with victory, Miss Teen Age plunged on to her reasons for being so fond of the chronicler of Yoknapatawpha: "He's kind of hard to keep up with, but he's a real good old Southerner."

Feeling quite at home now in the literary turn our discussion had taken, Miss Teen Age confessed that she loved reading though some-times her duties as Queen prevented her from reading as much as she'd like. For instance, she said that in the past week she had only had time to read one book.

"What book was that?" I asked.

"A history book."

"What kind of a history book?"

"A paperback."

I thanked Miss Teen Age America for her views and walked closer to

the stage to watch a scintillating sixteen-year-old in a pink-and-white gingham costume with long white bloomers belt out a song. She was Miss Teen Age Fresno, one of the six finalists, and for her talent performance on the program she was going to sing an updated version of "A Sweet Old-Fashioned Girl." The words, as close as I was able to transcribe them, went something like:
*"Howdya like ta meeta sweet ole fashun girl?*
*Scooble-dee-doo-bee-dum. . . . "*

When the song was finished with a rousing "Scooble-dee-doo-bee-doo-bee-dooooo: BOP!" and a matching gyration from Miss Fresno, the orchestra leader asked her to wait there for a moment. She stood beaming on the stage and winked down at the Singing Cadets with the superior *savoir-faire* of a Hollywood queen entertaining the troops.

When I walked back into the shadows of the stage corner, the current Miss Teen Age had disappeared and her mother was deep in conversation with Miss Joyce Selznick, a talent scout for Columbia Pictures. Miss Selznick was on hand to discover a teen-age girl to play the role of "Gidget" in *Gidget Goes to Rome*, a fresh teen-ager to replace Sandra Dee (*Gidget*) and Deborah Walley (*Gidget Goes Hawaiian*).

"I'm afraid she isn't a Gidget," Miss Selznick was saying to Miss Teen Age's mother.

"No, she isn't a Gidget," the mother admitted bravely. "She realizes herself that she isn't a Gidget."

"Well, we'll try to get something for her," Miss Selznick said consolingly. "Maybe something on TV in Denver she can do while she's at school. We'll try to get something to make her happy."

Mother thanked Miss Selznick and walked off with the look of a woman whose daughter was not going to be made happy by "something on TV in Denver." I introduced myself to Miss Selznick, a confident, friendly, no-nonsense woman who satisfactorily fulfilled my image of the Movie Scout.

"Poor kid," she said, referring to the outgoing Miss Teen Age. "The year's about up and she's afraid it will all be over. Well, we'll try to get something to make her happy."

A young man assistant came up and Miss Selznick said, "Did you get that boy we saw on the street?" The assistant said yes, he'd got him and the boy would be up to see Miss Selznick tomorrow.

"They all want to be in the movies," Miss Selznick informed me. "You can't tell me they still don't all want to be in the movies. I know."

Miss Selznick said that although she hadn't yet found a Gidget at the Miss Teen Age gathering, she had discovered some likely talent.

"These kids are still in the molding stage, and you can do a lot with them," she explained. "They've just filled out but they're still not sure of themselves. There's one really beautiful little girl from Los Angeles here, and I had her read for me several times. At first she was very shy, but now, after a couple of readings and interviews, she's beginning to get real aggressive. It's wonderful to see them develop."

I asked Miss Selznick about the movie she was casting for, and, tolerant of my ignorance of this box-office-smash series, she explained that it involved a teen-age girl named Gidget and her boyfriend, whose name was "Moondoggie." The Gidget movies had been so popular with the teen audience, she said, that Columbia Pictures was taking no chances in displeasing its young fans.

"This movie we're doing now was going to be *Gidget Goes to Paris*, but we started wondering if that's what the kids would like, and just to make sure we took a nationwide poll to see where the kids would like Gidget to go next. It turned out to be Rome by an overwhelming majority."

Miss Selznick had no idea why Rome was so popular among the teen-agers, but it was not her job to question the fact.

"The kids told us to go to Rome, so we go to Rome," she said conclusively.

A group of contestants had gathered off-stage around the current Miss Teen Age, and after making arrangements, to attend one of Miss Selznick's auditions the next day I wandered over to see what the talk was about. Three of the finalists were questioning the reigning monarch about her year as Teen Queen. One of them asked if she had been able to pick out her own Mercury Comet S-22 sports convertible that is one of the winner's prizes.

"Yes, but I waited to get it till this year so I'd get the '63 model," said practical Miss Teen Age America.

"Did you get to pick out your own *color*?" asked one of the aspiring ideal teen-agers.

Miss Teen Age nodded regally, and the aspirants sighed. The lucky one of them who would be chosen the next evening would win, in addition to the four-year-scholarship at the school of her choice and the Mercury Comet S-22 sports model (hardtop or convertible), a number of other equally essential components to the life of a typical teen-age girl: a year's supply of Coty "cosmetics and fragrances," a "chest full" of U.S. Keds sneakers, a ten-day "windjammer cruise" in the Caribbean, a diamond watch, a diamond pendant, pearls, a typewriter, and "many other valuable gifts." Showing the same practicality that the current Teen Queen had displayed, one of the aspirants asked her: "But did you make any more money besides? I mean for your personal appearances and all?"

"Oh, yes," the Teen Queen assured them. "They have to pay you for modeling, fashion show, and sponsor appearances."

I went on back to my hotel.

The next morning I rose early to breakfast with the Teen Queens, who had to eat at seven-thirty in order to get out early enough for the day of rehearsals at the Music Hall. The girls and their chaperones were dining in the large room of the hotel where they were being quartered by Teen America Associates. I chose a table near the back where two rather sleepy-eyed Teens and their chaperones were eating in gloomy silence. I soon learned that these girls had not been among the twenty-five semifinalists who would get to go up to the TV microphone and give their name and hometown; they were part of the larger herd who would serve as an animated backdrop to the show and the six featured finalists.

"My feet are killing me," said Miss Teen Age Wheeling, West Virginia, a red-haired girl who was dabbing halfheartedly at her scrambled eggs.

"These poor girls haven't seen anything since they've been to Dallas but the hotel and the Music Hall," said the woman beside her. "No sight-seeing, no entertainment, nothing but rehearsals."

"I haven't even seen Neiman-Marcus!" lamented Miss Teen Age Wheeling.

The woman with Miss Wheeling said to me, "You've heard of prison pallor? Well, these girls have hotel pallor."

I asked this lady if she were the girl's mother, and she said no, she was her chaperone. The girls whose mothers didn't come were assigned chaperones from their hometown.

"I guess I qualify particularly well as a chaperone," the lady explained. "You see, I'm a minister's wife and I also run a charm school."

Our pleasant little chat was interrupted by an unforeseen crisis. Mr. Charles Meeker, the director of the pageant, called for attention and said that he had a highly serious announcement to make; so serious that he didn't want to talk on the loudspeaker for fear that people might hear him outside the dining hall. The contestants and chaperones at the back moved closer to Mr. Meeker as he grimly revealed that he had received an anonymous letter that morning that he wanted to read. As well as I could reconstruct it, the letter was as follows:

"Mr. Meeker: There are fifty-four girls who have received no attention. Don't they deserve more recognition than the back row? A few of us mothers have gotten together to discuss this. If you don't give each of the fifty-four girls a chance to come to the mike you will be minus these girls and you can put it on with your twenty-five pets. We mean this and we are backing it up a hundred percent. We are not fooling so you better play ball or else."

It was signed, Mr. Meeker said, "Rejected Teen Agers Mothers."

There were gasps all around and Mr. Meeker quickly announced in firm tones that, when this meeting was over, "we will have a special person in the office of American Airlines to assist any mother and daughter who wish to check out of the hotel and return to their hometown today. He expressed deep sorrow that this crisis had arisen, and explained that life was full of disappointments and you had to "learn to take the bitter with the sweet." He was, however, making no concessions, and bravely took a firm final stand: "At eight o'clock tonight I can eliminate any number of people from the program simply by dropping the curtain at whatever point on the stage I want."

With hands on hips, Mr. Meeker looked around the room full of Teens, mothers, and chaperones, and said, "You pose no problem for us at all."

The revolt largely crumbled before Mr. Meeker's hard-line response, and only two or three of the girls were reported missing when the buses hauled the Teens to the Music Hall after breakfast. As I talked to more and more of the hometown Teen Queens backstage through the morning's rehearsal, my feeling was confirmed that the defection plot must be ascribed entirely to the irate mothers. It was impossible to imagine any of these girls challenging any aspect of any conceivable *status quo* or arriving at any opinion that might be termed "controversial." No doubt any such dangerous types had been eliminated earlier by the Teen-contest interview that had the candidates select their "philosophy of life" from a multiple-choice set. My feelings about the highly cooperative spirit of the girls seemed confirmed by an incident told me later in the morning by a CBS stage manager who had been brought in for the telecast of the pageant.

"These girls are amazing," he said with a shake of his head. "When I got here the first day I figured, well, these are just kids and I'd better let 'em know who's boss. I gave 'em my toughest speech. I told 'em, 'Look, from now on what I say goes. If I say stop, you stop; if I say move, you move. I hate to be tough on you, but that's my job and that's the way it's going to be.' When I finished, they all applauded. I felt like I had egg all over my face.

"But they're lovely girls," the stage manager said. "They're wonderful to watch. Just watch 'em. If you go get a Coke, most of 'em want to get a Coke."

At lunch I spotted a doll-like creature with large mischievous eyes and jet-black hair who seemed to hold some promise of surprise or novelty. I introduced myself to her—and her inevitable mother—and sat down to talk. The girl was Miss Teen Age Buffalo, and she explained gaily that she'd heard about the contest from a girl in her class at high school, and after she'd won the local contest the girl had stopped speaking to her. This frank, non-sweetened attitude buoyed my spirits, and I complimented Miss Buffalo on her beautiful black hair. She smiled and said, "I'm glad you like it," then took hold of the cute little curl that came down over her ear, lifted it upward, and, to my terror, seemed to be pulling her scalp off her head.

"See?" she said. "It's a wig. I'm blonde underneath."

I excused myself, and left the Music Hall building to try to sneak off for a drink. The sneaking part was necessary because the number-one "ground rule" for members of the press covering the Teen Pageant was that "we must insist on total abstinence while in the press room or in the

presence of our young contestants. . . ." Further measures for protection
of the Teen Queens against the lechers of the Fourth Estate included
"Ground Rule No. 5," which stated that "no interviews are allowed
above the fourth floor" of the hotel (the press room was on the fourth
floor), and "Ground Rule No. 6," which forbade the pageant staff from
giving out "the room number of the girls, nor their telephone number."
Actually, these protective measures were rendered superfluous, at least
in my own case, by the far more effective measures of the girls themselves: they addressed me as "sir" and referred to me as "the man from
New York."

The restrictions on the press were, of course, only part of the larger
"security measures" which the pageant sponsors solemnly adopted. The
TV show's producer, Paul Levitan, who has brought us such other
significant shows as the Miss Universe Contest, the Miss America
Contest, and the 1961 Presidential Inauguration, had told a reporter
several weeks before the Teen Age production that "security is just
tremendous at these things. You never hear a catcall or a wolf whistle.
Before a guy can open his mouth, an attendant ushers him out of the
hall." To keep the "grass roots" appeal of the production, the Teen
America people had ruled that the girls not wear bathing suits on the
grounds that they "aren't old enough." Although most of the girls were
fifteen or sixteen, the scattered fourteen-year-old contenders at Dallas
could hardly be spotted as juveniles. One of the finalists was fourteen-
year-old Miss Davenport, Iowa, a female of full poise and physical
endowment who could certainly wear a bathing suit with splendid
style. Although the contest was open to anyone from thirteen to
seventeen, there were no thirteen-year-olds on hand, but after seeing
the fourteens I decided this was probably not due to any lack of
full-blown thirteen-queens. More likely they were being saved for what
may be the next big attraction of our cultural scene: The Miss Pre-
Puberty American Pageant.

As a further security measure there were always policemen present
at the Music Hall during rehersals, and when I came back from having
two beers after lunch I walked quickly past a patrolman who stood at
the back of the auditorium with his arms folded, hoping he wouldn't
scent my secret, whip out his pearl-handled revolver and drop me in
the aisle for violation of Ground Rule No. 1. I was further leery of the

policemen that afternoon as I watched the rehearsal of the talent act of one of the finalists, a sloe-eyed seventeen-year-old Miss Teen Age Phoenix, who did a "modern dance" in blue tights to the exotic tune of cymbals and fluttery flute music. I looked up Miss Phoenix on my scorecard and found to my surprise that she "hopes for a career in literature, philosophy or psychology." With all that and the exotic modern dance I thought Miss Phoenix might well be the one *un*representative teen-ager of the flock, and I stopped her and her mother after rehearsal and asked if I might interview *them* (the policeman seemed to be eyeing me closely). Miss Phoenix had an appointment at the hairdresser's, but would be glad to talk to me there.

At the hotel beauty salon I found Miss Phoenix sitting under a dryer. She stuck her head out to answer questions, and politely began to explain about her hopes and interests. She said she had become interested in literature and philosophy through her school's Great Books course, but actually wanted to be a dancer. She had become interested in modern dance because "most of my friends were taking it." As if there were any further question of her "off-beat" or unrepresentative nature, she added that she was currently playing Emily in her school's production of *Our Town*. I thanked her and she ducked back under the dryer, looking quite representative after all.

It was almost five o'clock by then and Miss Selznick, the talent scout, had invited me up to sit in on an audition she was going to hold for five or six girls in the presence of Jerry Bresler, of Columbia Pictures, the producer who had done the first two Gidget movies and would also be handling *Gidget Goes to Rome*. When I arrived, there were a half dozen girls and three watchful Mothers assembled, and Miss Selznick was passing out Thermofaxed sample pages of Gidget dialogue. My old friend Miss Buffalo was there—without her wig—and she coyly asked if I recognized her as a blonde. I assured her I did, though I had the uneasy feeling there might be something else underneath *that*.

The producer was about forty minutes late, a restless time spent by the girls exchanging views on matters of teen concern, such as whether Mickey Mantle made more money than Bobby Rydell, a young crooner who, I was told, was "replacing Elvis Presley" in teen affections. There was also much speculation on what would replace the Twist, and Miss Teen Age Seattle insisted it would be "the Slop" rather than "the

Mashed Potato." To prove the virtues of "the Slop" Miss Seattle kicked off her shoes and got up to demonstrate it, scooting backward across the floor as if she were suffering from a series of hotfoots. During all this two of the mothers remained grimly silent, while a third, an enormous lady with a floppy hat that blessedly covered a good portion of her blank, massive face, discussed such problems as "what would you change your name to if you got into pictures?"

When Mr. Bresler finally arrived the girls and the mothers—except for the big one who seemed moored in her chair—jumped to attention and flashed their smiles. "My mouth is getting a twitch," one whispered, "from smiling so much." Mr. Bresler, an intelligent-looking, balding fellow in a dark suit and plain dark tie, surveyed the scene with an expert eye. After Miss Selznick had introduced the teens and said, "Those are the girls," Bresler looked toward the three cold-faced ladies in the corner and, smiling with the recognition of an anthropologist who has spotted a familiar breed, said, "And those are the mothers." Mr. Bresler said his plane had been delayed, and there would only be time for the girls to give their name, age, and hometown; then he would ask those whom he wanted to talk with further to come back tomorrow. The recitations of these vital statistics went off routinely except for the announcement of one girl that "my first name is Charmaine—but I prefer to be called Charm." Mr. Bresler took it all without flinching and the group was herded out, including one girl who had partially hidden herself in a corner cleaning ash trays in an effort to be left alone with the Movie People.

By this time I frankly felt that I'd seen enough of the Teen World at first hand and decided to go back to my hotel room to watch the pageant on television with my notebook and a bottle of bourbon. The production went smoothly, and the conclusion was appropriate. The crown of Miss Teen Age America was awarded to sixteen-year-old Miss Fresno, the *Sweet Old-Fashioned Girl* (scooble-dee-doo-bee-doo) with the professional wink. After shedding appropriate tears of victory—no doubt for the girls who hadn't been as fortunate as she—the new Miss Teen Age America was asked what her plans were. She said she guessed she'd be going to Detroit tomorrow (for her first sponsorship appearance) and she'd like to say "hello to all my friends out at Bullard High." Bud Collyer, the master of ceremonies, turned to the audience with a triumphant smile and said, "That sounded real normal!"

*So you want to meet the girl for you—the one with the big/medium/small breasts who prefers French/English/Hollywood movies and who sighs loudest on pink/yellow/white sheets. Three fine writing fellows will tell you all about it. All you have to do is answer the questions on the coded card and don't fold, spindle, or mutilate (it/her/him).*

# Boy . . . Girl . . . Computer

## by Gene Shalit

Out of computers, faster than the eye can blink, fly letters stacked with names of college guys and girls—taped, scanned, checked and matched. Into the mails speed the compatible pairs, into P.O. boxes at schools across the land. Eager boys grab their phones . . . anxious coeds wait in dorms . . . a thousand burrrrrrrings jar the air . . . snow-job conversations start, and yeses are exchanged: a nationwild dating spree is on. Thousands of boys and girls who've never met plan weekends together, for now that punch-card dating's here, can flings be far behind? And oh, it's so right, baby. The Great God Computer has sent the word. Fate. Destiny. Go-go-go. Call it dating, call it mating, it flashed out of the minds of Jeff Tarr and Vaughn Morrill, Harvard undergraduates who plotted Operation Match, the dig-it dating system that ties up college couples with magnetic tape. The match mystique is here: in just nine months, some hundred thousand collegians paid more than $300,000 to Match (and to its MIT foe, Contact) for the names of at least five compatible dates. Does it work? Nikos Tsinikas, a Yale senior, spent a New Haven weekend with his computer-Matched date, Nancy Schreiber, an English major at Smith. Result, as long date's journey brightened into night: a bull's-eye for cupid's computer.

22

"HOW COME YOU'RE STILL SINGLE? Don't you know any nice computers?"

Perhaps no mother has yet said that to her daughter, but don't bet it won't happen, because Big Matchmaker is watching you. From Boston to Berkeley, computer dates are sweeping the campus, replacing old-fashioned boy-meets-girl devices; punch bowls are out, punch cards are in.

The boys who put data in dating are Jeff Tarr and Vaughn Morrill, Harvard undergraduates. At school last winter, they and several other juniors—long on ingenuity but short on ingenues—devised a computer process to match boys with girls of similar characteristics. They formed a corporation (Morrill soon sold out to Tarr), called the scheme Operation Match, flooded nearby schools with personality questionnaires to be filled out, and waited for the response.

They didn't wait long: eight thousand answer sheets piled in, each accompanied by a three-dollar fee. Of every hundred applicants, 52 were girls. Clearly, the lads weren't the only lonely collegians in New England. As dates were made, much of the loneliness vanished, for many found that their dates were indeed compatible. Through a complex system of two-way matching, the computer does not pair a boy with his "ideal" girl unless he is also the girl's "ideal" boy. Students were so enthusiastic about this cross-check that they not only answered the 135 questions (Examples: *Is extensive sexual activity [in] preparation for marriage, part of "growing up?" Do you believe in a God who answers prayer?*), but they even added comments and special instructions. *Yale*: "Please do not fold, bend or spindle my date." *Vassar*: "Where, O where is Superman?" *Dartmouth*: "No dogs please! Have mercy!" *Harvard*: "Have you any buxom blondes who like poetry?" *Mount Holyoke*: "None of those dancing bears from Amherst." *Williams*: "This is the greatest excuse for calling up a strange girl that I've ever heard." *Sarah Lawrence*: "Help!"

Elated, Tarr rented a middling-capacity computer for $100 an hour ("I couldn't swing the million to buy it"), fed in the coded punch cards ("When guys said we sent them some hot numbers, they meant it literally"), and sped the names of computer-picked dates to students all over New England. By summer, Operation Match was attracting applications from coast to coast, the staff had grown to a dozen, and

Tarr had tied up with Data Network, a Wall Street firm that provided working capital and technical assistance.

In just nine months, some ninety thousand applications had been received, $270,000 grossed, and the road to romance strewn with guys, girls, and gaffes.

A Vassarite who was sent the names of other girls demanded $20 for defamation of character. A Radcliffe senior, getting into the spirit of things, telephoned a girl on her list and said cheerfully, "I hear you're my ideal date." At Stanford a coed was matched with her roommate's fiancé. Girls get brothers. Couples going steady apply, just for reassurance. When a Pembroke College freshman was paired with her former boyfriend, she began seeing him again. "Maybe the computer knows something that I don't know," she said.

Not everyone gets what he expects. For some, there is an embarrassment of witches, but others find agreeable surprises. A Northwestern University junior reported: "The girl you sent me didn't have much upstairs, but what a staircase!"

Match, now graduated to an IBM 7094, guarantees five names to each applicant, but occasionally a response sets cupid aquiver. Amy Fielder, eighteen, blue-eyed, blonde Vassar sophomore, got 112 names There wasn't time to date them all before the semester ended, so many called her at her home in New York. "We had the horrors here for a couple of weeks," her mother says laughingly. "One boy applied under two different names, and he showed up at our house twice!"

Tarr acknowledges that there are goofs, but he remains carefree. "You can't get hung up about every complaint," says Tarr. "You've got to look at it existentially."

Jeff, five feet seven, likes girls, dates often. "If there's some chick I'm dying to go out with," he says, "I can drop her a note in my capacity as president of Match and say, *Dear Joan, You have been selected by a highly personal process called Random Sampling to be interviewed extensively by myself.*" And Tarr breaks into ingratiating laughter.

"Some romanticists complain that we're too commercial," he says. "But we're not trying to take the love out of love; we're just trying to make it more efficient. We supply everything but the spark."

Actually, computer dating supplies more. According to Dr. Benson

R. Snyder, MIT's chief psychiatrist, it acts as a method that society condones for introducing a girl and a boy. "A boy knows that the girl has expressed her willingness to date by the act of joining. I think that's one of the most important things that it provides. It reduces the anxiety of the blind date; you know that the girl wants to go out with someone roughly like you.

"However," warns Dr. Snyder, "if this is taken too seriously, and it becomes institutionalized, it could be seen as a pressure for a safe, conformistic approach. In all relationships, there is a need for the unexpected; even that which is a little anxiety-laden."

With all the joys and ploys of computer dating, social life at sexually segregated schools in the Ivy League remains plenty anxiety-laden. At non-coed schools like Yale and Dartmouth, students lead lives of social isolation. Many are consumed by plans for weekend dates. "We try to pack a whole week into Friday and Saturday night," says a Princeton sophomore. "If we don't make out—if we don't sleep with the girl—the whole thing's a colossal failure."

Comments a distinguished New York psychoanalyst: "Ivy League students are forced to behave like monk-scholars. When they're freed on weekends, they seek emotional release. Almost all college boys are psychological adolescents, with an overpowering need for companionship, and they cannot be expected to live in seclusion. It's no surprise that sexual relations are more and more common among college-aged boys and girls."

"All-boy colleges create a climate for fantasy," says Carter Wiseman, a Yale sophomore. "Girls become unreal beings, so on the weekend you try to force the reality to fit into the fantasy you've created, and it *won't work!*"

Getting dates down here for the weekend is a terrible waste of time," said John de Forest, of Yale. "Hotel accommodations for the girl, expenses, arrangements . . . trying to find a girl in the first place. That's why Match is here to stay. I approve of it as a way to meet people, although I have no faith in the questionnaire's ability to match compatible people. The machine has no way of telling whether or not the girl has pazazz!"

But Wiseman insists, "The odds of getting along with a girl are better if she's been screened by a computer. Say you're interested in Renaissance art, and the machine gives you a chick who's interested in Renaissance art, you've got a basis to build on. You can't just go up to some girl on the street and say, 'Hello, do you like Botticelli?' "

"In midwinter, it's tough to meet a girl a couple of hundred miles away on any pretext whatever," says a snowbound Dartmouth senior. "Match is a great icebreaker; the girl will at least talk to you if you call."

Even before boys telephone their matches, most girls have a line on them through Ivy-vine sources—tipsters at boys' schools and upper-class girls who've dated extensively. Lists are passed through the dorms, where girls pencil comments next to familiar names: *cool; hang up when he calls; swings; fink.*

"What troubles me about all this computer jazz," says a sophomore at Connecticut College, "is my feeling that boys don't level when they fill in their questionnaires. I was honest with mine, but I wonder if some guys fill out theirs to see if they can get a first-nighter."

"Boys want one kind of a girl to date, but someone quite different to marry," says a Mount Holyoke senior. "Guys are just out for a good time, but I don't know any girl who goes on a date without marriage crossing her mind. When college kids are together, the girl thinks: 'I wonder what it would be like to be married to this fellow?' And the boy thinks, 'I wonder what it would be like to sleep with this girl?' "

"I don't see how the questionnaire can possibly result in compatible matches," says Ellen Robinson, of Connecticut. "Guys don't care about attitudes and interests. They all want a blonde with a great figure. But if you must fill out a questionnaire, I think the one from Contact is better."

She gets no argument from David De Wan, 22, the MIT graduate student who owns Contact, Match's principal rival in New England. "The Match questionnaire is unbeatable for national distribution," he says. "But in the Northeast, I can use a vocabulary that will be more effective than it would be in the Midwest. Phrases like *verbal fluency* and *aesthetic appreciation* sell far better at schools like Princeton and Harvard."

De Wan, a brilliant math and engineering student, does not have an organization as sprawling or yeasty as Tarr's. In fact, he has no organization at all. A frugal man, he runs deep in the black: he has no full-time employees. His office is a room in his grandparents' home near Cambridge. He uses a Honeywell 200 computer at three o'clock in the morning, when the rental is low. In one distribution of questionnaires, he drew eleven thousand responses at four dollars each.

De Wan has been going steady with a girl at Wellesley, so when he organized Contact, they put themselves to the test. Sure enough, the computer matched them. But the computer also matched her with an Amherst boy, who won her away. "It was very sad," says De Wan, "but it proved my system works. It found her a more compatible guy."

"I think that's a riot," says Dr. Snyder, who invited De Wan to discuss the computer project at a meeting of the MIT psychiatric staff. "I was a little bit appalled by its 1984 overtones, but was much less concerned after we talked. Contact provides students with a chance to get over the initial hurdle of knowing that they're not going to be immediately rejected. At their age, it's often difficult to make the kind of small talk that's so important at the initial stages of a relationship. My guess is that computer-matched people are more able to explore comfortably their interests. I think it's a useful social mechanism, but it would be misused if boys used it merely to make a connect for a sexual good time."

"I don't know that Match and Contact can really work," gainsays Dr. Morris S. Davis, astronomer and director of the Yale Computer Center. "Until body chemistry can be imputed into the computer to stimulate the actual reactions of two persons, I have my doubts concerning the efficacy of the method."

Dr. Snyder agrees that the computer can't predict compatibility. "But it's not just chemistry," he insists. "It's because you can't program something as complicated as the whole cluster of feelings and associations that surround a boy's notion of what a girl ought to be. What a computer *can* do is increase the probability of a satisfactory relationship by removing incompatible persons."

To test this theory, Christopher Walker, a senior at Yale, organized a dance for three hundred college boys and girls, who were selected at random, matched by computer and tested before and after the dance. They spent time with their matches, then with dates they "picked up" during the dance's designated free period. Preliminary findings: most had most fun with their "pick-ups." "If it turns out that way," says Walker, a psychology student who is a great admirer of Match, "it will be because a dance is only a one-night stand, where the only thing that counts is physical attraction."

Not everyone has faith in computers. At the University of Wisconsin two enterprising graduate students, Glenn Wisfeld and Michael Rappaport, have a service called SECS—Scientific Evaluation of Compatibility Service. They offer a short questionnaire, charge one dollar, provide one date, and somehow it works. Says Weisfeld, "We had our proudest moment when we were congratulated for making SECS a four-letter word."

Just the same, Tarr feels the future belongs to the computer. He's working on campus installations of hundreds of special typewriters, all linked to a centralized "mother computer." A boy, typing his requirements, will receive in seconds the name of a compatible girl on his campus who's free that night. Tarr is also organizing a travel service. On deck: a transatlantic cruise by an ocean liner packed with compatible couples. (Rejected name: *Ship of Fools*. Scene: night. The deck awash with moonlight. In the shadows a boy sings, "Come To Me, My Correlated Baby." Below decks, in the salon, a girl murmurs, "How do I love thee? Let me count the punchcards.")

Tarr already has outposts in New York, Chicago, Los Angeles, and will soon go international, providing students summer dates all over Europe.

Since collegians must fulfill each other's requirements, the questionnaire is designed to produce the profile of the applicant and the profile of the applicant's ideal date. Boys have discovered that there is more to getting the girl of their daydreams than ordering a blonde, intelligent, wealthy, sexually experienced wench. They must also try to guess what kind of boy such a girl would request. The future suggests itself: a boy answers the questionnaire artfully; a girl does, too; the computer whirs; they receive each other's name; breathlessly, they make a date; they meet; they stop short; there they are: Plain Jane and So-So-Sol. Two liars. But they are, after all, exactly alike, and they have been matched. It is the computer's moment of triumph.

# Matchmaker, Matchmaker, Compute Me a Match

*by Goodman* Ace

They tell a story that one morning down in Miami, Florida, a gigantic creature with three heads and eight legs crawled out of the ocean onto the beach, and a woman ran down to it and cried: "Have I got a girl for you!"

But according to a recent story in *Look,* that kind of matchmaking is all over and done with. Under the heading "The Big College Craze—Dating by Computer," there was described an operation known as "Operation Match," located in Cambridge, Massachusetts. It would seem that automation has struck a blow against women who arrange boy-girl meetings, object matrimony.

However, all is not lost. It is only a glancing blow, judging from some correspondence to this desk. The mother of the girl who subscribed to "Operation Match" sends it along with a note saying, "The enclosed is too good to keep to ourselves." It seems the young lady, Miss Jane Silberstein, of White Plains, New York, had read the *Look* story and had a go at it. She received this letter from "Operation Match":

Dear Participant:

We regret to inform you that we have been unable to find matches for you which satisfy the requirements you specified on your Operation Match answer sheet. The number of people whom it is impossible to match is a function of the difficulty of meeting certain standards of mutual compatability.

It is our policy to offer anyone who does not receive matches a card good for free participation in our next matching program.

Please find enclosed, therefore, a card which, when enclosed in an application for the spring 1966 match, will enable you to participate in our expanded program without further cost. We are sorry for any inconvenience you may have experienced, and we welcome your participation in the spring. . . .

Our heroine replied from her campus at the University of Pittsburgh:

Dear Sir:

I am enclosing the Operation Match card, which entitled me to an application without cost. You mailed this to me with a letter concerning the impossibility of matching me due to my diffiuclity in meeting certain standards of compatability.

I'd like a refund since I prefer not to participate in your program again.

I objected strongly to the implication in your letter of the "difficulty of meeting certain standards of mutual compatability." I have had quite a few dates with boys whom I have found compatible. I know that they have found me compatible since I have dated many of them several times. For those, and I do not include myself, who rely on your IBM-computed "matchmaker," I can easily understand how your letters could be a slight blow to their ego.

I expect to hear from you soon with my refund enclosed by check or money order. Thank you.

Of course Miss Jane has a case there. If it comes to the worst she can sue on grounds of incompatibility. And if the machine is any sort of a gallant gentleman he'll cough up the participation fee.

However, from the tone of her letter I feel the young lady is slightly peeved. Taking it out on a poor machine is an exercise in futility, although in retyping her reply it did help me, as I hope it did her, to remember definitely how to spell "compatibility."

But sending a letter back to a computer is not in the same league with handing a guy back a ring because he complains of your incompatibility. Miss Jane's neatly phrased and slightly sardonic letter is nowhere compared with "Marvin, here's your ring and your hat. Neither fits either of us."

That's the more satisfactory way to handle it. Why go through a middleman? Why IBM? It has that frantic look of I Wanna Be Married.

And while we're on the subject, why all this searching for a man who will be compatible? What happened to the girl who wants to mold a guy into what she is most compatible with? Has modern girl forsaken the challenges of molding for machine-made compatibility that lights up, tilts, spews out a little card that says, "Yes, dear"?

And what's so guaranteed about a computer-selected husband? What insurance is there he will always be up to his IBM? Even IBM stock is down fifty points or more from its high.

I've heard of shotgun marriages. But machine-gun?

# Computer Calculated Copulation

### by John Francis Putnam

Our world is where we like to keep on letting the machine do it for us. Almost everything. Take the time-and-money-saving bag of the computerized dating systems, with names like *Meet-a-Mate* or *Click* or *Data-Date*.

Who wouldn't really groove an effective short cut to the perfect sack scene, with the Machine speeding us right past all those boring preliminaries, especially when we know that the party we're being matched up with is willing because it's been *programmed* that way?

Anxieties end and the dawn is going to be rosy-fingered after all.

The big drag about these computerized systems is the corny style and content of the questions you are asked to fill in—questions that are supposed to present the real you, what you are like, who you are, etc.

It doesn't take long to find out that these questions are evasive, generalized and downright chickenshit. They're no better than the ones you find yourself asking at a party where there are the usual six guys to every girl, and you end up asking that tired old warhorse opener: "Well, what do *you* do?"

The data-computer questions are evading the real question: is it going to be *good* when you two finally hit the sack together?

Who cares whether you like foreign movies over Hollywood, or jazz over Mantovani and his strings; that detached, cool analytical power of the giant computer is getting short-circuited by a lot of chatter. Be-

sides, if these patterns are held to, the computer is liable to come up
with the *ideal* date for you . . . like your ex-wife.

Here are some samples of what a realistic questionnaire should be,
one that if fed into a computer would probably burn out a couple of
thousand transistors, but would still end up getting you happily, thor-
oughly, and beautifully laid. Don't be scared or embarrassed by these
questions. After all, the machine couldn't care less.

He/she is coming over to your apartment, probably to stay for the
night. Do you:

A. Frantically change those 6-week-old sheets and buy a new blanket?

B. Pile up records, guitar, magazines on the bed so that it won't look
so damned suggestively like a bed?

C. Play it cool and leave the apartment just as it is?

He suddenly brings out a set of dirty pictures and insists on showing
them to you. Do you:

A. Blush, but ask to see them a second time?

B. Treat it all as a bit of nostalgic and scabrous Americana, making
witty comments as to the staging, photographic quality, ambience and
technique?

C. Suggest that you both try some of the poses?

While talking to her, you pull out a handkerchief from your pocket
and a condom pops out and lands on the floor in plain sight. Do you:

A. Make a fast grab and hope she hasn't seen it?

B. Ask her to pick it up?

C. Observe something to the effect that "oh, yeah, there's been an
awful lot of clap around lately."

Realizing that you'll be staying at his place, in regard to your
wardrobe, do you:

A. Make sure to pick out a different dress (noncreasable) that you
can wear to work next day?

B. Rush out and buy funky bikini undies?

C. Just to be difficult, wear a bra that opens in the front?

In the heat of passion, you remember, too late, that she'll notice you're wearing dirty underwear. Do you:

A. Start an evocative bit on the erotic power of acrid male body smell?

B. Blame excessive, bourgeois fastidiousness on your respective mothers and take a shower together?

C. Decide to be dramatic and do it with all your clothes on?

As a female, you believe that birth control is your responsibility. Do you:

A. Drench yourself with strong perfume to kill that tell-tale Ortho-Creme odor?

B. Brazenly insert your diaphragm in full view of your partner?

C. Tell him how much your breasts have grown since you began taking Enovid?

She looks at her watch and says, "Oh, is it that late? I had no idea. Look, you can sleep over, but you have to promise that you'll behave." Do you behave by:

A. Starting with the touch-her-cold-toes-with-your-warm-toes ploy?

B. Come on spontaneously with "Oh, I forgot something—I didn't kiss you good night."

C. Assure her, "I'll only put it in a little way."

He suggests that you practice fellatio. Do you:

A. Make a request that he wear protection?

B. Tell him that you never suck off on the first date?

C. Ask him where he keeps the mouthwash?

She suggests that you practice cunnilingus. Do you:

A. Hint around to find out just how recently she took a bath?

B. Demand reciprocity of some sort?

C. Prepare the way with honey, mayonnaise, peanut butter . . . anything?

Your favorite music to make love by is:

A. Ravel's *Bolero?*

B. *Muddy Waters?*

C. Ravi Shankar?

D. Racing cars recorded live at Sebring?

During intercourse, how do you communicate to him verbally?
A. Call loudly upon the diety with remarks like, "Oh, my Gawd!"
B. Give full utterance to cherished Anglo-Saxonisms like "Oh, shit, honey, oh shiiiiiit!"
C. Keep repeating, "No, it's my fault! It's not you! It's me!"

During intercourse, how do you communicate to her verbally?
A. Indulge in a catechetical interrogation, like "What am I doin' to ya, baby, what am I doin', huh?"
B. Say, "Hey, aren't I great?"
C. Inquire with cold sarcasm, "Well, did you come yet?"

When it's over, do you:
A. Share the only remaining clean towel?
B. Urinate or defecate while leaving the bathroom door open?
C. Kiss your partner gently on the cheek and say, "Would you hate me if I had a cigarette now?"

He has had a fine ejaculation. Do you:
A. Pretend you have a bad cramp in your leg so that you won't have to tell him he's getting too heavy already?
B. Ask, "When will I see you again?" in a clinging tone of voice?
C. Subtly but emphatically move the scene over onto the dry side of the bed?

She has had a fine climax. Do you:
A. Fall asleep immediately?
B. Make a token display of affectionate gratitude, then fall asleep immediately?
C. Pretend to fall asleep immediately in order to recharge for more action?

In case of unwanted pregnancy and wanted abortion, do you believe:
A. He should pay?
B. She should pay?
C. Both should pay?
D. Medicare?

S*o if you're twenty-one, you'd better start thinking about a career and retirement benefits. Big
business, especially big scientific business, is dying to have you.*

# Through Connecticut with the
# Dow Recruiter

## *by Calvin Trillin*

NEW HAVEN
TUESDAY

Arthur Shaw arrived at the Yale Student Placement Bureau at eight-
thirty in the morning. He makes it a practice to arrive at a placement
office about half an hour before his first appointment, giving himself
time to arrange his forms in a convenient spot on the desk, place his
watch where he can glance at it quickly during an interview, and put
his nameplate—"Art Shaw, Dow"—where students can see it, so they
won't have to grope for his name. Also, he prefers to arrive before the
demonstrators do. He expected some demonstrators at Yale. In the
normal routine, a few days before a Dow Chemical Company recruiter
is scheduled to arrive on a campus Shaw's secretary phones the placement office to confirm the date and to find out how many students in
each discipline have signed up for interviews. These days, just as
routinely, Shaw, who is both a recruiter and the supervisor of recruiting
for the Northeast, gets on the telephone himself at one point to find out
if a demonstration is likely. He asks about the university rules that will
govern the demonstrators' behavior, he makes certain that the university president has been informed, and he says, as diplomatically as
possible, that although Dow will be happy to abide by any arrange-

35

ments the university makes, it has been the recruiter's experience that a demonstration often gets out of hand if the demonstrators are permitted inside the building. If it seems likely that there will be a particularly vehement demonstration, Shaw arranges for someone from Dow's public relations department to be present, thus permitting the recruiter to concentrate on his interviewing without distractions from reporters.

Three campus policemen were standing just inside the door of the Yale Student Placement Bureau when Shaw arrived, but there were no demonstrators. Ordinarily, demonstrators are not certain enough of Shaw's identity to say anything when he walks in anyway, although he looks suspiciously like a Dow recruiter. A serious-looking young man of twenty-five, with close-cropped red hair, he was wearing heavy horn-rimmed glasses, a neat three-button suit, a button-down shirt, and a striped tie. He had a wedding ring on one hand and a state university class ring on the other, and he was carrying a gray fibre-glass attaché case that looked almost too thin to hold anything. In the room assigned to him, on the ground floor of the placement office, Shaw and a university official cleared some supplies out so he could bring in a chair for the interviewers—the room considered least vulnerable to harassment from outside happened to be only five by eight—and Shaw arranged things on the desk to his satisfaction. Just before nine, a Student Placement official told him that pickets had gathered in front of the building; there were about thirty-five of them, huddled under umbrellas against a cold drizzle that had begun to fall, and holding signs like "Better Dying Through Chemistry." Shaw thanked his informant courteously, but he seemed only mildly interested.

In half-hour interviews from nine to eleven, Shaw talked with four students about working for Dow. He called each of the students by his first name, and he repeated the name often as—in a friendly but businesslike way—he asked about outside interests or outlined the first few years of a typical new employee in marketing or told of the pleasures of life in Midland, Michigan, where Dow has its corporate headquarters. The subject of demonstrations came up only at the close of an interview, when Shaw would smile and say that he hoped the student hadn't had too much trouble getting in.

Shaw's last appointment before lunch was with a young man who had been described to him as the undergraduate leader of the Yale chapter of Students for a Democratic Society, but the S.D.S. man did not appear. Shaw joined two or three placement officials in a larger office and spent some time going through résumés of prospective summer employees with a woman in charge of summer placement (who said that she had phoned the S.D.S. leader and informed him that not keeping appointments was bad manners). There were still campus policemen in the hall, but someone said that the demonstrators had been gone for an hour—they were driven away when the drizzle turned into a driving rain—and everyone seemed relaxed.

Suddenly, flames shot up in the hallway outside the office. The placement officials rushed to the door. A wastebasket had been placed in front of the door, and its contents were blazing. A few feet from the basket stood a young man—thin, blond, collegiately dressed. He had a book of matches in his hand. His face was slightly flushed. He looked rather frightened. "Why'd you do this?" a young assistant dean asked him, in a calm voice. "I'm curious about the symbolism." A campus policeman, looking perturbed, had dragged over an extinguisher and was putting out the fire. Shaw had remained inside the room.

"Fire and fire," the young man said. "I think the symbolism is pretty good."

At lunch, the assistant dean told Shaw and a recruiter from a management consultant firm that a talk with the young man had convinced him that the wastebasket fire had indeed been meant as a piece of symbolism, rather than as a way of harming anybody. "It was obviously an act of conscience," the dean said. "He just felt he had to burn some Dow literature. He's a nice kid."

Shaw did not seem as impressed by the symbolism as the dean was—a check before lunch had indicated that the fire consisted of all the mechanical and chemical engineering booklets he had placed in the waiting room—but he didn't disagree.

"It's funny," the recruiter from the consulting company said. "We do a lot of consulting for the Defense Department. I guess nobody knows."

"Don't let it out," Shaw said.

In the afternoon, Shaw began another series of interviews—
describing plant sites and travel requirements and salaries, and asking
if there were any questions about Dow.

"There's one thing," the first interviewee of the afternoon said,
somewhat hesitantly, at the close of the interview. "If I were in marketing, and so on and so forth, is there a chance for a draft deferment,
and so on and so forth?"

"Well, we've been real successful so far in getting our people de-
ferred, Dave," Shaw said. "Both technical and nontechnical. Of course,
no company can guarantee anything on this."

The student looked impressed.

Shaw's schedule showed that the second appointment of the afternoon was with a Miss Alexander, a graduate student in American
studies. She turned out to be a friendly-looking, dark-haired girl who
began the interview by commiserating with Shaw on the weather he
was having during his trip to New Haven. Shaw said he was just happy
to be there. Then Miss Alexander said she was wondering why bona-
fide, tuition-paying students had been refused entrance to the building
by campus police, and Shaw said she would have to ask the university officials.

"Could you tell me, Miss Alexander," he went on, "if you're interested
in Dow workwise?"

"I'd be more interested in working for Dow if it weren't doing
something criminal," she said. "I was wondering if a Dow employee
could be prosecuted as a war criminal ten or fifteen years from now,
under the precedent of Nuremberg." She didn't sound at all angry. She
had a slight smile on her face, like the fixed smile of a lady trying to be
polite while having tea with people she doesn't know very well.

"I assume you're talking about napalm," Shaw said.

"That, and crop defoliates," Miss Alexander said, almost pleasantly.

Shaw said that he didn't consider the situation analogous to that of
the manufacturers prosecuted at Nuremberg, and they spoke for a
while about whether a distinction could be made between napalm and
such weapons as tanks and guns—or between gas pellets for concentra-
tion camps and howitzers.

"We are supplying the government with material, and the government decides how to use it," Shaw said. "I guess I'm saying that Dow

made a decision to support our government and the long-term aims of our government, and I support this."

"Do you think this is what the German manufacturers thought?"

"I don't know what they thought," Shaw said. His voice was even, and he didn't sound offended. "Let's come back to Dow and you. Are you interested in Dow as an outlet for employment?"

"I'm interested in the moral position of working for Dow," Miss Alexander said, and she handed Shaw a picture of a burned baby. "I'm curious what goes through the head of a Dow employee when he sees some of these pictures."

Shaw said that while the picture was indeed horrible, war was horrible, and there was no pleasant way to die.

"Don't you think it's different?" Miss Alexander asked. "Don't you think there's a distinction when you use this against civilians?"

"I guess I'll have to say that the Secretary of Defense, Mr. McNamara, assures us that the product is used only against military targets," Shaw said.

"Does the company really believe this?" Miss Alexander asked. She still had a polite smile on her face.

"Well, Miss Alexander," Shaw said, "I guess I can only say that I feel as an employee of Dow that we're doing the right thing and that we've made the right decision. I'm proud to work at Dow."

Miss Alexander asked if there might ever be a time when Dow would dissociate itself from a government contract if the contract proved particularly repulsive, and Shaw said he couldn't speak for the company in that area, since he was at Yale only to discuss specific employment.

"Can you see any time that anything would be so repulsive to you personally that you couldn't work there?" she asked.

"Well, that hasn't come up," Shaw said. "I haven't thought of it. I'm not concerned about this possibility. I'm not concerned."

After about fifteen minutes, Shaw said that there seemed little more to discuss, and he asked Miss Alexander if she would be interested in an application.

"Yes, I would," Miss Alexander said, politely. "And, in case you don't have the S.D.S. statement, I'll leave you this." She smoothed out a mimeographed sheet that she had read from at one point during the interview—it was entitled "Dow's Four Horsemen: Destruction, Famine, Pestilence and Death"—and, apologizing for the fact that it had been smeared by the rain, gave it to Shaw.

"Real fine," Shaw said. "Thanks. Here's an application."

Miss Alexander took the application, thanked Shaw, and left the room.

GALES FERRY, CONNECTICUT<br>WEDNESDAY

Before driving out to the Dow plant at Gales Ferry, near Groton, Shaw called company headquarters in Midland from his motel to check on a recruiting trip scheduled for the New York State University at Buffalo the following week. Buffalo appointments had been postponed once, when there was reason to believe that recruiters might be in physical danger, and the university was still sufficiently concerned about maintaining order to request that Dow send an extra recruiter, so interviewing could be completed in one day. Shaw decided that he ought to consider sending a man from public relations with the recruiters to Buffalo.

Two of the plant managers at Gales Ferry had gone to the University of Connecticut as recruiters in October—the university had asked them to withdraw after students refused to let them enter the interviewing offices—and Shaw met with them in the morning to get their impression of the recruiting process in general and to "kick around a couple of ideas about napalm." One of the men gave a dispassionate account of being greeted by a mock funeral at Brown earlier in the week, and Shaw told about his interview with Miss Alexander. He predicted that more protesters might begin to show up on interviewing schedules—one recruiter at M.I.T. had been faced with seven in nine interviews— although most colleges are stricter than Yale about limiting interviews to students in the disciplines the recruiters are interested in, and radical chemical engineers are not easy to come by. He said a recruiter had no choice but to talk with a protester as long as employment was being discussed. "She was cagey enough not to ask why we're murdering babies," he said. "She was shrewd enough to ask questions like 'What moral decisions have you made about working at Dow?' or 'Could a person who works at Dow be prosecuted as a war criminal?'— really bordering on legitimate questions." The man who had been at

Brown said that newspapers in recruiting areas ought to be informed of the company's policy on napalm in advance, and Shaw said that all local newspapers were sent a press kit just before any Dow recruiting visit.

There was also a meeting with some young men who were about to be used as recruiters for the first time. Shaw, who wrote his master's thesis in business school on college recruiting, spoke about the advisability of going over résumés the night before, about how to fill out the interviewer's report, about the necessity of writing thank-you letters to placement officers, and, eventually, about napalm. "I think it's reasonable to assume that almost every campus will have a demonstration of some sort," he said. "Our approach as recruiters is, first of all, to avoid any direct confrontation. They want you to talk about Dow policy, but in my case I know I'm neither authorized nor qualified to discuss Dow policy. You should maintain a businesslike, professional attitude. Always be polite. If pressed by reporters, try to refer them to the corporate public relations group in Midland. Basically, your approach should be that you're there as the guest of the university and the only reason you're on campus is to recruit. Remember, they won't get a statement from you if you don't want to give them a statement. In the final analysis, the things you have going for you are common sense and a cool head. As these kids say, don't lose your cool."

STORRS, CONNECTICUT<br>WEDNESDAY

Late in the afternoon, John Powers, the student placement director of the University of Connecticut, gave Shaw the résumés of the students Dow would be interviewing the following day, and assured him that although demonstrators (or "the beatniks," as he called them) would probably be present, the university was now committed to the students' right to meet with bona-fide recruiters. "Let me tell you something," he said. "And I'm not going to be facetious. This is the best thing that ever happened to the placement office. You usually have to knock kids on the head to get them in here. Last year, we used to have six kids on a schedule. Now the schedules are full—twelve, thirteen people. The demonstration was not the only reason, but it was the biggest single reason. I'm beginning to think: give me publicity—good or bad, just so it's publicity. Maybe your company will find the same thing in the long run."

"Well," Shaw said, "we *are* less of an unknown quantity now."

THURSDAY

Shaw and another recruiter, who had flown in from Midland, chatted in an interviewing room until just before nine, and then Shaw went to the door to call in the other recruiter's first appointment and to leave for some courtesy calls on university officials. Shaw and the other recruiter planned to fly to Midland together in the afternoon. When Shaw opened the door, he found twenty or so demonstrators sitting on the floor of the hallway. Only one person seemed seriously intent on blocking the door—a thin young man with a blond mustache, who sat directly in the doorway, his back to the room. He had the look of somebody consciously not speaking, as if he had taken a vow of silence. The student with an appointment jumped over the young man into the room, and Shaw tried to leave. "Excuse me," Shaw said, but the young man with the mustache swayed in whichever direction Shaw tried to move, and two other people were tentatively blocking his path with a banner that said "Dow Lights the Way for L.B.J. in S.E. Asia." Shaw went back into the room. He makes it a practice not to push people out of the way. (At Boston University, not long before, when a student lie-in covered the entire floor space in front of the interviewing room, Shaw declined to leave until a dean advised that the only alternative was to spend the night. At that point, Shaw, after consultation with a Dow public relations man, removed his shoes and walked out on top of the students into several inches of snow; he was accompanied by the dean and two policemen, who, apparently working without benefit of public relations consultation, left their shoes on.)

A reporter for the campus paper had managed to get in with the interviewee, and began to ask Shaw questions while, a few feet away, the recruiter was asking the interviewee what type of job he was interested in. The door would not quite close, and the sound of conversation was coming in from the hallway.

"Did you expect trouble?" the reporter asked Shaw, holding a clipboard ready for the answer.

"We never expect any trouble," Shaw said, trying to keep his voice down. "We did expect a student demonstration."

In a few minutes, the provost and three other university officials arrived and picked their way through the demonstrators into the room. They greeted Shaw cordially, and he told them how happy he was to be at Connecticut. The other recruiter continued his interview. The provost led Shaw and the rest out of the room—everyone stepping over the young man in the doorway—and asked the dean of students to remain outside the door and make certain that students with appointments could get in. Shaw finished his task with the student reporter in another room—he said he was neither authorized nor qualified to comment on company policy—and then he went to make his courtesy calls.

# Aerospace Bonus Boys

### by Bob Elliot and Ray Goulding

Our nation's political and economic structures have undergone considerable change since the days when the simple credo "The business of America is business" provided an adequate picture of whatever we were muddling through. Currently, a more accurate appraisal of the situation in industry might be expressed by another equally thought-provoking homily: "The business of America is the business of recruiting enough fresh, young scientific talent to latch onto the business to stay in business."

Beyond doubt, a whole new pattern of events underlies much of the frenzied activity that now takes place behind the bland façade of belching smokestacks. In many industries, survival depends upon a steady inflow of government contracts, which, for reasons that are far from obvious, seems to depend, in turn, upon a steady inflow of new college graduates steeped in the gobbledygook of space-age technology.

As often occurs when demand outruns supply, matters quickly get out of hand, and the law of the jungle tends to prevail. The annual epidemic of "brain recruiting" by big business on college campuses is living proof of this newest form of *laissez faire* run wild.

However, the increasingy familiar sight of the scurrying recruiter on campus creates a false picture of purposelessness. Behind closed doors at every home office, strategic thinkers have laid careful plans that touch off the apparent frenzy. Day and night, dedicated men with the single-minded goal of building a winner are charting their course at just such gargantuan corporations as Complicated Aerospace Stuff, Inc.

*Fade in*

*Interior, executive conference room, Complicated Aerospace Stuff, Inc. The large walnut-paneled room is dominated by a long walnut-paneled conference table, around which are a dozen or so high-backed chairs upholstered in lush imitation domestic Naugahyde. There is a motion picture screen at one end of the room and a projector at the other. On a side wall hangs an ornately framed color photograph of a transistorized component, resplendent in a jumble of red, blue, green, and yellow wiring, all tastefully arranged to create the impression that the item is functional. A bronze plate at the bottom of the frame identifies the component as "Our Very First One Ever." At the open, the room is unoccupied except for* WARREN L. ("BUZZ") BODENHUME, *director of personnel manipulation for Complicated Aerospace Stuff, and* MELVILLE STERNBAUM, *by-lined columnist for "Diode Data, the Integral Devices Weekly."* BODENHUME *is clad in a sincere dark business suit and wears a nickel-plated whistle on a string around his neck.* STERNBAUM, *clutching a notebook and pencil, wears an inexpensive necktie loosened at the collar, a soiled felt hat with the brim turned up in front, and phosphorescent suede shoes. Both men are positioned informally, with* BODENHUME *crouched on his hunkers atop one of the conference chairs, while* STERNBAUM *sprawls in repose across three others.*

STERNBAUM: Well, it just figures that you'll be beating the bushes for new talent this spring, Buzz. After all, you finished a distant third in '67 behind Scientific Interplanetary Hardware and Unlimited Germanium Creations because you never displayed that front-line push to charge in there and pick off those government subcontracts when you needed them.

BODENHUME: Yes. But I've got a hunch this is going to be a season when you can throw the past-performance charts right out the window, Mel. Our rookie engineers can blitz the Pentagon with a lot more good, meaningless technical jargon in tight situations now. And, of course, Von Klegschmidt was on the sauce last year and only saw limited action. But the reports I get from the clinic indicate that he'll be back in top form for the opening of this season's government contracting.

STERNBAUM: Well, we've all seen how much territory a Nobel Prize hopeful like Von Klegschmidt can cover in Washington when he's sober. But some of the Pentagon procurement boys think it was bad strategy for you to let three veteran flow-charters go during the off-season in exchange for an untried utility physicist.

BODENHUME: Well, the way we look at it, a senile flow-charter can hurt team morale and cause you to wind up making the wrong product and all like that. The aerospace game's like anything else. If you start out to build a youthful organization, your best bet is to do it with young people.

STERNBAUM (*scribbling hastily in his notebook*): That's a concept in personnel I'm sure the whole industry will want to analyze, Buzz. And you see this rookie physicist playing a key role in your development program for the future, do you?

BODENHUME: That's right. He still hasn't got all the sophisticated moves you need for grabbing off those juicy defense contracts. But for a kid whose I.Q. will go maybe 210 or 215, he's real good at talking around in circles without saying anything that means much.

STERNBAUM: And, of course, when it comes to outlining proposals for government work, that's a big plus factor.

BODENHUME: Oh, absolutely. You can get in there with that low bid nine times out of ten if you never come right out and commit yourself to produce what the job calls for. (*The door opens, and the balance of Complicated Aerospace Stuff's top echelon tactical staff enters. The group is led by the firm's president,* NEWCOMB N. DIBBLEMAN, *a silver-thatched veteran of the Electronic Thing-a-Ma-Jig Industry whose stately bearing attests that he still feels pride in having gotten his start wiring faulty dirigible instrument panels in an abandoned interurban*

*depot. He takes his place at the head of the table, carefully guarding
the file folders jammed with papers that he carries. Following a respectful distance behind Dibbleman are his somewhat trustworthy,
but otherwise useless, assistants,* LUCAS BLETHERT, ORVILLE QUILLEN-
THAL, JR., *and* KNUTE L. FRATCH. *All three wear inoffensive gray suits and
vacant facial expressions.*)

STERNBAUM (*ignoring the others and continuing his interview with*
BODENHUME): But to make a smokescreen technique effective, you still
need that forward wall of Ph.D.'s.

BODENHUME: Yes. The Washington brass always puts a lot of stock in
counting those advanced degrees on your roster, especially when it gets
down to a toss-up decision on doling out the loot. But nobody pays any
attention to a guy's field of graduate study. That's how come we've
already signed four new Ph.D.'s in Portuguese literature. We can only
use them as file clerks, but they look good on paper.

STERNBAUM: Uh-huh. And I suppose you hope to beef up the team
even more by recruiting some of this year's graduates who are still free
agents.

BODENHUME (*angrily*): We don't go in for recruiting around here,
fellah. We just offer career opportunities with rapid advancement
incentives and liberal fringe benefits.

STERNBAUM: Well, I certainly didn't mean to imply—

DIBBLEMAN (*bellows*): Get that clown out of here, Bodenhume! You
know we don't let outsiders eavesdrop when we're going over scouting
reports from the recruiters.

BODENHUME: Right, N.N. *Beckons* QUILLENTHAL *and* FRATCH *as
Sternbaum cringes in dread anticipation, clutching his pencil and notebook to his bosom.* BODENHUME *and* FRATCH *begin efficiently trans-
porting* STERNBAUM *to an open window as* QUILLENTHAL *pries the notebook out of his clenched hand. Then the three assist him to exit in a
graceful half gainer down the air shaft.* BODENHUME *quickly closes the
window in an apparent move to stifle the sound of* STERNBAUM's *final
departing whinny, and all then take their assigned seats, with the
exception of* DIBBLEMAN, *who remains standing for reasons that he
would rather not discuss.*)

DIBBLEMAN: I don't suppose I need to recap the problems we're having with the J-27-dash-5 program. You all know we're completely tooled up for production, but we still don't have a first-rate man in research who can tell us why a solid-state gismo like that crank on the side is a vital component in a space capsule.

BLETHERT (*haltingly*): The answer must be there someplace, N.N. Integral Dynamics turns out funny-looking things a lot like the J-27-dash-5, and NASA's been grabbing them up at $38,000 a throw like they were going out of style.

(DIBBLEMAN *glares menacingly at* BLETHERT *as* QUILLENTHAL *stares hard at a coffee stain on the carpet in an effort to appear alert without seeming to pay too much attention.*)

DIBBLEMAN: I don't need to be reminded that Integral Dynamics is displaying the kind of fancy footwork that could push us out of the running, Blethert. And I hope you don't have to be reminded that they're doing it with the brains they recruited right under your nose at Carnegie Tech last year.

FRATCH: But you know the unethical tactics they threw at us there, N.N. Integral Dynamics never told those kids that the Edward Teller in their research department is just some old coot with the same name who hoses down the lab.

DIBBLEMAN (*icily*): That happens to be the type of inventive strategy that picks off the plums, Fratch. Only you didn't think of it first.

QUILLENTHAL: Excellent point, N.N. You can take your run-of-the-mill punk fresh out of engineering school, offer him twenty-five grand a year, and he'll jump at it. But it's the idea of rubbing elbows with an all-time great that hooks the whiz kids. Now, I've just found this osteopath in Cincinnati named Doctor Oppenheimer, and I thought—

DIBBLEMAN: Forget it. Might still be a little stigma attached there.

BODENHUME: Right! And any hint of controversy can kill you. The type of boy we're after is a clean-cut, loyal American who's just looking for a challenging career and money under the table.

FRATCH: True, but not such a loyal American that our essential-industry draft deferment pitch won't have a strong appeal.

BODENHUME: Don't start splitting hairs over terminology, Fratch.

When I say loyal, we all know I'm not talking about some kind of flag-waving fanatic.

(DIBBLEMAN *glares at* FRATCH *as* FRATCH *glares at* BODENHUME *as* BODEN-HUME *looks to* QUILLENTHAL *for support as* QUILLENTHAL *grabs a phone and begins dialing the recorded weather forecast number to indicate his firmly neutral position regarding all matters on which* DIBBLEMAN *has not yet made his feelings abundantly clear.*)

DIBBLEMAN: I wish all of you would stop wasting my time with chatter when we've got a pile of scouting reports to check out here.

QUILLENTHAL (*hangs up the phone with a sigh of relief*): I think we should all stop wasting N.N.'s time with chatter when we've got so many scouting reports to check out.

(*The others all stare at* QUILLENTHAL, *who reacts by nervously picking up the phone and dialing for another weather forecast.* DIBBLEMAN *takes a sheaf of papers from the table and begins flipping through them in a haphazard, but businesslike, fashion.*)

DIBBLEMAN: Now, I think we all know why we hit the skids in Washington during the last fiscal year. Soft landings on the moon were the big thing, and Scientific Interplanetary Hardware was three deep in retro-rocket component specialists. The only man we had to throw into the contracting fight was that nut from the branch plant who thought a rocket would soft land up there if you kept it attached to the earth with a long piece of string.

FRATCH: I've had my eye on a kid who shows a lot of promise in the retro-rocketry doodads, N.N. He'll be picking up his doctorate at Utah State this summer, and—

DIBBLEMAN: Utah! Fratch, you don't win the big ones in this league with untried kids from Utah State.

FRATCH: Well, his diction could pass for Ivy League. And I know he could figure out how to attach some of that old junk we've got in the warehouse onto retro-rockets and—

DIBBLEMAN: Forget it. If he was just going into the general Ph.D. pool, it might be OK. But for this job, a man's got to be able to name-drop an alma mater that'll open some important doors. Anything in this year's crop at M.I.T. or Cal Tech, Bodenhume?

BODENHUME: Well, most of Cal Tech's current strength is in civil engineering. I never saw so damned many experts on sewer-pipe seepage in my life. At M.I.T., we're still dickering with a young squirt who's number two in his class. But he's already got a $30,000 offer from Micro Intricate, and he wants us to match that and throw in a '68 Tornado and a carpeted office with color TV.

DIBBLEMAN: Humm. Well, I suppose we could open a spot on the roster by bouncing that guy who has the big corner suite on the third floor. I've never figured out what he does around here anyway.

QUILLENTHAL: I don't think we ought to mess with him, N.N. He's got an old picture of himself on his desk presenting Lady Bird with her first FCC television license in Austin.

DIBBLEMAN: Oh, is he the one? Well, then I remember how he got that corner suite and why we have to keep him. Any chance of making a trade for a retro-rocketry man, Fratch?

FRATCH: Well, I've put out some feelers to Scientific Interplanetary Hardware, but they only want to talk a deal for Haversham. And, of course, we can't give him up. He holds the patents on almost everything we make.

BODENHUME: I've been looking over a young professor at Michigan who's got a lot of style, N.N. I think it would be worth your time to see the action films we have on him.

DIBBLEMAN: Oh, all right. But those ivory-tower creeps never seem to get with it. They just sit around cooking up advanced theories to better mankind. And that kind of nonsense can disrupt a team's whole operation.

(BODENHUME *crosses to position himself at the movie projector as* QUILLENTHAL *rushes to draw the drapes, pretending not to notice the motionless remains of* STERNBAUM *still imbedded in the concrete at the bottom of the air shaft.*)

BODENHUME: I feel every bit as strongly about troublemakers as you do, N.N. But I'm sure this man would shape up fast. He's got a great little wife nagging him to jump to industry where the big money is. And his undergrad minor in political science is bound to give us a lift in this Washington game. He can move to his right or move to his left, all depending on how things go in November. Just catch this. (*Flicks on the projector.*)

(*Squiggly lines and upside-down numbers flash on the screen for a few seconds, prompting* QUILLENTHAL, FRATCH, *and* BLETHERT *to cough impatiently in a mass gesture of empathy with* DIBBLEMAN, *who is notorious for his lack of patience in regard to squiggly lines and upside-down numbers on movie screens. The coughing subsides when a grainy image of a young man scrawling a mathematical formula on a classroom blackboard comes into semi-focus.*)

DIBBLEMAN (thoughtfully): Maybe. Maybe not.

QUILLENTHAL: I don't like to make snap judgments, but that's the same intuitive reaction I get.

BODENHUME (*defensively*): Well, of course, he was just engaging in a light workout when we shot this footage. But notice how he's sprinkling all those Greek letters and square-root signs through that equation. Scribbles fast, too. Almost makes you think he's got a quick mind, if you don't notice he comes out with the wrong answer.

(*The figure on the screen turns from the blackboard and faces the camera with an arrogant smile, tossing the chalk casually in one hand as he utilizes the index finger of the other to punch emphatically at various undecipherable symbols on the board.*)

DIBBLEMAN (*contemptuously*): Nobody cares about that. But for Crissake, look at his bush-league summation style. He's right down to the nitty-gritty, and he's not even using a chrome-plated pointer to make his hard-sell pitch.

BODENHUME: Well, you understand we're seeing him in a low-budget operation here, and—

BLETHERT: But double-talking his way through scientific mishmash with no attention grabber but his finger?! He'd put a Pentagon contracting session to sleep, Buzz.

DIBBLEMAN: Or worse yet, show his inexperience in handling a pointer by fumbling it and blowing the ball game. No dice.

(*Accepting defeat,* BODENHUME *switches off the projector just as the figure on the screen is preparing to demonstrate his agility in erasing blackboard equations before their accuracy can be challenged. Fratch reopens the drapes as* QUILLENTHAL *clears his throat in a nervous manner which he hopes will be interpreted as a gesture of righteous indig-*

*nation by* DIBBLEMAN *and of understanding sympathy by* BODENHUME. *After a moment,* BLETHERT *rises and spreads his palms flat on the table with a studied air of confidence that is betrayed only by an unconfident quaver in his voice as he speaks.*)

BLETHERT: Boys, I hadn't planned to take the wraps off the greatest little deep thinker since Von Braun at this session because I know N.N. doesn't like to get in on the contract haggling with a kid who's playing holdout. But since he's virtually hooked, there's no reason why I should keep the good news to myself.

DIBBLEMAN (*coldly*): Blethert, I think you used the same identical buildup last year to sell me that bonus baby from Princeton. And if I'm not mistaken, he's now working out his option at $40,000 a year keeping track of our toggle-switch inventory in the Des Moines warehouse.

(BLETHERT *appears outwardly unmoved except for his knuckles, which whiten.*)

BLEHERT: Well, maybe he wasn't quite ready. But this boy's got greatness written all over him. Built an IBM 360 out of empty beer cans for his junior high science project, and he's been going like that ever since. They're giving him his Ph.D. at the University of Chicago next month, and from the dope sheet I've got, I'd say they're doing it because nobody can understand the thesis he turned in.

BODENHUME: Sounds good, N.N. It could mean he's got that inborn talent for being ambiguous. You can't teach a thing like that to a scientist. If the spark isn't there, he'll keep slipping back into saying something specific just when it can do you the most harm.

BLETHERT (*with renewed spirits*): Right. But this kid's shifty; a natural broken-field talker. Now, I've had him flown out here for the weekend to look over our operation with his dad, and I figure if we all go to work on 'em—

DIBBLEMAN (*explodes*): You let him bring his father with him! Blethert, you know what that can get us into. The old man's probably a frustrated semi-pro scientist himself with all kinds of wild dreams of glory for the kid.

BLETHERT: Now take it easy, N.N. The old guy's a stiff. Knows from nothing. Just let me call them in, and I promise you our troubles in retro-rocketry are over.

DIBBLEMAN: All right, but I don't like the setup.

(BLETHERT *moves hurriedly to the door and exits to the adjoining V.I.P. lounge and topless Whoopee Room.*)

QUILLENTHAL: Personally, with the old man hanging around to kibitz, I don't like the setup.

(BLETHERT *re-enters accompanied by* BRUNO COSKICHEKOWICZ, *a sullen youth clad in a University of Chicago letter sweater, emblematic of his four seasons of stardom in classified nuclear events under the football stadium.* BRUNO's *father,* VLADIMIR, *follows a pace behind. He wears a traditional coal miner's cap, even though it is obvious that his lamp has been out for a number of years.* BLETHERT *introduces the pair to his colleagues, and half-hearted greetings are ad-libbed by all.*)

DIBBLEMAN (*feigning human warmth*): Well, Bruno, Mr. Blethert tells me you may be trying out for a berth here at Complicated Aerospace. What do you think of our sprawling, multimillion-dollar little place?

VLADIMIR (*truculent and with too much of an accent to be possible*): He seen plenty better. How you fix, Bruno got to park car in middle of hot sun like anybody else. Even got to come up in same elevator with dumb people don't make much money. All very bad for fine boy with like what Bruno got inside his head.

(DIBBLEMAN *glares at* BLETHERT, *who looks beseechingly at* BODENHUME, *who shoots a sidelong glance to catch* QUILLENTHAL's *reaction only to discover that* QUILLENTHAL *is reacting by getting sick on the rug.*)

BODENHUME: Well, of course, we're chiefly concerned with blazing new trials to the future here. The twenty-first century lies just over the horizon, Bruno, and Complicated Aerospace has its feet planted firmly at the frontier of tomorrow—

BRUNO (*cutting in*): Sure, sure. And at least four other outfits are right there with you, giving me the same pep talk word for word. So let's change the subject. I figure thirty big ones a year will do for openers so I don't get killed taxwise. Now, Complicated Aero closed on the Big Board on Friday at 62 5/8, so let's say options to pick a thousand shares a year at 15. That makes a neat package without giving me those high-bracket blues.

DIBBLEMAN (*enraged*): It does more than that, Sonny. It also enables you to avoid being hired here. Even our top executives don't have stock arrangements like that.

VLADIMIR (*mutters*): *Drajna mirich zvdoga.*

DIBBLEMAN (*to Bruno*): What was that all about?

BRUNO: Nothing you don't already know. He just said that top executives are a dime a dozen, but you ain't got a single retro-rocket genius in this whole glassed-in birdcage. And once I walk out of here, you won't be seeing another one in a long, long time, Bubalah.

(DIBBLEMAN, *apparently undecided whether to strangle* BRUNO *with his bare hands or merely have him bushwhacked near the front gate, thoughtlessly pulls a pilot model of the J-27-Dash-5 component from his coat pocket and fingers it angrily for a moment. Then, in frustration, he slams it on the table and begins stomping back and forth across the room as* BODENHUME, FRATCH, QUILLENTHAL, *and* BLETHERT *look on with accumulating terror. Meantime,* VLADIMIR *brings forth a Hubbard squash from his overalls and calmly peels it with his pocketknife as* BRUNO *picks up the J-27-Dash-5 component and examines it with mild interest.*)

BRUNO (*to no one in particular*): Not bad. Needs a set screw next to the diode for a lead-in wire. But otherwise, it could do the trick.

(DIBBLEMAN *stops pacing and gallops to* BRUNO's *side as* BODENHUME, FRATCH, QUILLENTHAL, *and* BLETHERT *rise out of their chairs and instinctively crawl across the conference table toward the center of activity.*)

DIBBLEMAN: Do what trick? What trick is that? What can it do?

BRUNO: Well, nothing really—unless the last retro doesn't fire, and radio contact with J.P.L. is broken, too. That's a million-to-one shot, but if Uncle wants to throw away forty thousand bucks apiece on trinkets like this to backstop the main system, it ain't my worry.

DIBBLEMAN (*staring vacantly at the J-27-dash-5*): How much does it cost us to make these things?

BODENHUME: It depends. Like when we stamped out the pilot models on the Sunday graveyard shift and had to pay everybody double-double overtime, they ran us almost six dollars and a quarter apiece.

(DIBBLEMAN *nods to* BODENHUME *with what appears to be a stunned inability to comprehend the magnitude of it all. Then, head high though ashen, he crosses to the wall safe and begins removing bundles of currency and stock certificates which, with the assistance of* BODEN-HUME, QUILLENTHAL, BLETHERT, *and* FRATCH, *he stacks in neat piles on the table in front of* BRUNO. *Meanwhile,* VLADIMIR, *with one efficient sweep of his forearm, brushes the Hubbard squash peelings onto the carpet, and then carefully cleans his knife blade by rubbing it across a sooty trouser leg. The air of proud stoicism that has served him well through long years of misunderstanding born of abject confusion remains unbroken as he contemplates the sheer uselessness of a peeled raw squash.*)

*Fadeout*

*W*HEN *you are hunting for a husband, the strategy is grand and the approaches varied. You can stake your hopes and your wardrobe on a singles weekend. And even if you are bustless, hipless, lashless, and nailless, you are still not out of the running. From silicone shots to taxidermic surgery, a popular monthly shows a girl how to fake her whole body.*

# My Mother Said
# I Should Give It a Try

### by William Kloman

Resplendent in pink plastic curlers, forest green ski pants, and white angora sweater, Juliet Goldman stood surrounded by luggage. A sudden rain had left New York awash, and Juliet's feet were wet. "As if I don't have enough problems already," Juliet said. She had just read in a sociology text that after an American girl passes twenty her chances of getting married suddenly drop 50 per cent. Scientific proof of what Juliet's mother had always said. Once a girl is twenty-one, her mother often told her, she begins to lose her bloom. From there on, it's downhill all the way. Juliet would be twenty-two in just four months.

Standing in line, now, at Gate 101 of the New York City Port Authority Bus Terminal, Juliet pondered her mother's bloom theory. In line with her were about forty other girls, all of them, like Juliet, in their twenties, pensive—and single. Amid mounds of luggage they patiently waited for the Short Line bus to Grossinger's, where they were going to look for husbands.

"Here's your great chance for romance," the ad in the New York *Post* had said. "Your big weekend starts at Grossinger's this Friday." Later in the day, as business picked up, the buses would begin traveling in

convoys of two and three. By sundown nearly one thousand females
would converge on the twelve-hundred-acre Catskill resort, most of
them, like Juliet Goldman, passing through Gate 101 to board a Short
Line bus for the two-hour express run to the mountains. At Grossinger's,
as at most of the other big resort hotels in Sullivan County, New York,
"singles" weekends—during which a hotel offers special activities, and
sometimes special rates, for unattached men and women—have become
a big business.

Sullivan County, New York, situated in the gently rolling countryside
between the Shawangunk Mountains and the southern foothills of the
Catskills, has been a weekend and summertime playground for East
Coast city dwellers for three generations. The clientele of Sullivan
County's resorts has traditionally been Jewish, and their kitchens have,
for the most part, been kept kosher. For this reason the resorts of the
region are collectively called the "borscht circuit."

The archetypal Catskill success story is that of Grossinger's. In 1914
Selig and Malka Grossinger, who had been less than successful in the
restaurant business in New York City, moved to Sullivan County and
put $450 down on a small farm near the town of Liberty. Like other
farm families in the area, the Grossingers accepted boarders seeking
temporary relief from the city. The food was good and ample, the
climate bracing, and the rates nominal. As word spread, customers
came in increasing numbers. The Grossinger farm grew into a $10
million resort which now accommodates about 1,250 guests and has
nearly as many employees. Still owned and managed by the Grossinger
family, the hotel's reputation for excellent food and *heimischkeit*,
hominess, is world-wide.

About an hour after the Short Line bus had emerged from the
Lincoln Tunnel, billboards began to appear on snow-covered knolls.
HONEYMOONERS LIKE THE NEVELE . . . THE ALADDIN CONVENTIONS INVITED
. . . HOMOWACK LODGE DAY AND NIGHT SKIING ON PREMISES . . . BROWN'S
JERRY LEWIS SAYS MY FAVORITE RESORT. Each hotel touts its special at-
traction; the bigger resorts invoke their household gods. Jerry Lewis,
once a busboy at Brown's, now has a theater named after him there,
and regularly appears in Brown's advertising. Eddie Fisher was a band

vocalist at Grossinger's when Eddie Cantor discovered him and made him a star. With typical reserve, Grossinger's has dedicated an unobtrusive jukebox to Fisher's memory. Now, from the bus window, the Grossinger billboard came slowly into view. Graceful white lettering on a field of Wedgwood blue announced simply: GROSSINGER'S HAS EVERYTHING.

"This your first singles?" a girl named Beverly asked from across the aisle.

Juliet nodded. "How about you?"

"I've been to maybe a thousand of them."

Juliet smiled. "This is my first. My mother saw the ad in the *Post* and said I should give it a try."

"Welcome aboard," said Beverly.


By the early 1950's the Catskill resorts found themselves in competition with the increasingly accessible vacation spots of Florida, the Caribbean, and Europe. The middle-class shift to the suburbs made the quiet weekend or summer in the country unnecessary and, in some ways, tiresomely unattractive. Reliance on the Jewish-family trade was no longer sufficient, and efforts were made to attract conventions, Midwesterners, more gentiles, and young working people from New York and New Jersey.

In the old days at Grossinger's, guests busied themselves with berry picking, nature walks, or simply gazing at the scenery from rocking chairs on the front porch. Today Grossinger's boasts that it has something to fill every minute of its guests' day, "from dawn to yawn." The atmosphere has become distinctly citified. In most of the resorts, "casinos," or entertainment halls, furnished with wooden folding chairs, have given way to sleek nightclubs that feature big-name entertainers.

Happy family groups and shy honeymooners are much in evidence, but the backbone of the new trade in Sullivan County is conventions. The problem of how to keep the hotels' expensive facilities filled between conventions has been met with singular ingenuity. "You can't just say, 'We're open for business,'" says Mannie Halbert, one of the owners of the Raleigh. "Nothing will happen. What we do is look ahead on our calendar. If we find that we're not booked for a certain weekend,

we buy space in the New York newspapers about a month ahead
of time and start advertising a singles. I mean, we've built out to
*here*. You've got to do *something* to fill all those rooms."

As the Short Line bus came in sight of the rambling Tudor-style
"main house" of the vast Grossinger complex, passengers began collect-
ing their belongings and tending to their hairdos. A small flurry of
excitement ran through the bus. Juliet Goldman turned to Beverly and
Beverly's friend, whose name was Jan. "I hear they have a lot of
activities," Juliet said.

"True," said Beverly. "But they've got the system arranged so you
can't take advantage of all the facilities on the first day."

"I don't care," said Juliet, suddenly enthusiastic about the weekend.
"I want to do *everything*." Taking a small compact from her small purse
and checking her eye make-up, she added casually. "How were the
boys last time you were here?"

"What boys?" said Jan.

The average ratio at a singles is three or four females to one male, a
fact that disturbs the hotel owners, but doesn't seem to deter the girls
particularly. For the one thousand girls who responded to the Grossinger advertisement in the New York *Post*, a field of about three
hundred eligible men would be available. Plans are being made by
some hotels to even the odds a bit. Grossinger's reserves its least
expensive rooms for men. Its publicity flier asks the ladies' indulgence:
"Thank you for understanding and helping to send a man to the
mountains."

The Sullivan County Hotel Association disclaims fostering illusions.
"Nobody promises anybody they're going to find romance up here," says
Ben Kaplan, executive vice president. Still, in their ads, some of the
hotels *do* raise the possibility:

> The bookkeeper told the model
> the model told the receptionist
> the receptionist told the designer
> the designer told the secretary
> how much FUN they *all* had at the Waldemere.

The girls couldn't stop talking about all
the men, men, men, wonderful eligible men
they all met during their vacation at
wonderful Waldemere. . . .
Yes, the girls felt like queens every
minute of their vacation at the Waldemere
and now they feel like Cinderellas every
time the phone rings and another Prince
Charming calls to ask them for a date.
It happened to them. It could happen to
YOU, if you vacation at the Waldemere.

"Cupid to be busy," flashes a weekend news tip from Grossinger's. The
Concord (where "solitaire is a diamond, not a game") comes succinctly
to the point: REMEMBER THIS COULD BE YOUR LAST WEEKEND AS A SINGLE.

Juliet Goldman, in her attempt to "do everything" at Grossinger's,
managed, in her first afternoon, to take a beginners' skiing lesson, swim
in the indoor pool, observe a class in eye make-up at the hotel cosmetics
counter, take her first ride in a toboggan, and ice-skate. While skating,
she had met her first boy, an economics major from New York University, with whom she had made a date for dancing later that evening.

At supper, now, Juliet found herself at a large round table with five
other girls, all singles (two of them were Beverly and Jan, her friends
from the bus trip); three single men (two college students and one
grammar school teacher); and the mother of one of the girls. The
mother, by virtue of a recent divorce, was also a single.

Like hotel meals everywhere in Sullivan County, meals at Grossinger's are gargantuan. And at Grossinger's they are excellently
prepared, unlike some of the other hotels, where quantity is the main
attraction.

At dinner there was general agreement that the weather was beautiful and the food delicious. "My daughter is a teacher," the mother
announced, as her daughter attacked a side order of stuffed cabbage.

"Really?" one of the men replied. "I'm a teacher myself."

The daughter looked up from her cabbage and smiled.

"How interesting," the mother said. "You and my daughter should
discuss teaching."

After a brief silence, Beverly, the girl from the bus, opened a new topic. "Has anybody read *A Gift of Prophecy?* That book about Jeane Dixon?"

"She's that woman in Washington," answered the male teacher.

"The one who predicts things," said Beverly. "Well, I wrote her a letter."

"How interesting, dear," the mother said. "What did you write her about?"

"She's a very wise woman, really," Beverly said. "Some people think she's a fake, but she's not at all. I wrote her about some of my problems and asked her advice. Busy as she is, she condescended an answer."

Finishing her cabbage, the daughter joined the conversation. "What did she say?"

"She answered me. My problems. It was only a form letter, but she wrote some words at the bottom in handwriting."

"I hope you will try to follow her advice," said the mother.

"Yes," Beverly said. "I think everybody tries to follow advice, only we all don't have the will power. I hope I do."

"I'm following advice right now," Juliet Goldman announced. "My mother advised me to come up here for the weekend." One of the boys began coughing and had to be slapped on the back by the male teacher.

"You're *kidding!*" cried one of the girls. "You mean I'm not the *only* one?" Everybody laughed, except the girl teacher's mother, who took out pair of glasses and began reading the menu.

"Let me tell you about my mother," the girl continued. "The night of the big power blackout I was on my way to dinner with this boy from the office. Well, of course we had to get stuck in the subway. Like for five hours. So finally they came down after us, and we had to crawl along the side of the tunnel and up through this sewer grating. Right away I got to a telephone and called home. The first thing Momma said was, 'Are you engaged?' 'Momma!' I said. 'We were trapped in a *subway* car.' 'You're trapped in a subway car for five hours with an eligible man, and you're not *engaged?* Couldn't you be a little dependent, just for once? Couldn't you faint or something?' That's the way Momma is. The only thing I could say was, 'Mother, you *know* how I am in a crisis.'"

Singles—the people—aren't new to the Catskills. For years mothers have brought their daughters to such reputable resorts as Grossinger's in hopes of meeting a reputable young man of good family or other prospects who might have, or be induced to develop, marital intentions. "Where there are human beings," one hotelman says dreamily, "there is matchmaking. Singles weekends are as old as time." An entire mythology, bolstered by plays, novels, songs, and jokes, has grown up around the matchmaking customs of the borscht circuit. In the many years since Marjorie Morningstar fell in love with the social director at South Wind, the rules of the Catskill mating game haven't changed much. What *is* new is the high degree of organization which, within the past five years, has gone into transforming the matchmaking tradition into a lucrative business operation.

Guests at singles weekends feel the pressure of what they refer to variously as "the rat race," "the hunt," and "this damned jungle game." The girls especially. During the Friday night rock-'n'-roll party in the Terrace Room, Grossinger's nightclub, several paying guests alternated with two paid go-go girls in displaying themselves in tinsel cages beside the bandstand. "You've only got two days," one girl said. "You got to show what you've got."

At the bar, a man in his forties talked softly to a girl in her late teens "You're not the kind of a girl who belongs in a place like this. You belong at Stowe, or Sugarbush. I think you could even make it at Aspen."

At two o'clock Saturday morning, Juliet Goldman, in a pale empire gown, stormed into the Terrace Room to report to her friends, Beverly and Jan. "I've had it!" she said. "I've had it! I mean I've had it altogether!" She made a fist and shook it in the direction of the music.

"Ooo!" she said. "What's wrong with me? I mean *what*? Have I got two heads or something?"

"You look lovely," Jan offered.

"Everything was going great. I mean this guy I had the date with—David—we could *talk*. His father makes codfish or something. Nothing special, but OK. Then he runs into two of his buddies from school, and bang! All of a sudden I'm a boiled potato. What kind of a guy is that?"

Beverly looked worried. "Probably just immature," she said.

"Well, I'll tell you one thing," Juliet continued.

"I'll tell you this much. I don't *need* this damned place. I can pass for Italian."

As the ad in the newspaper had promised, on Saturday there was a "boy-meets-girl" participation program. It was called a "ski-ha" competition. Under the rules of the game, boys who could ski were supposed to seek out girls who could play the harmonica (and vice-versa) and enter the competition in teams of two. The contest was sponsored by the Hohner harmonica company, which provided the prizes—assorted items of skiing and harmonica-playing equipment. Hohner also gave each of the thirteen hundred singles who had come to Grossinger's for the weekend a miniature harmonica.

The first half of the contest, an amateur slalom run, was held Saturday morning. After lunch, the harmonica-playing competition was held in a room off the lobby. The master of ceremonies, Blackie ("the Heifetz of the Harmonica") Schackner, reminded the guests that the contest was strictly for amateurs. "It's not for virtuosos," he said. "In fact, we don't want any."

The first contestant, a lady who had entered the competition with her son, played "Jingle Bells." A girl named Marilyn next said she would try "a little ditty from the *New World* Symphony."

"Dat's written by Johann Sebastian Schmaltz," said a portly kibitzer in the rear of the room.

"What's your name, honey?" said Mr. Schackner to the third contestant, a pretty typist from the Bronx.

The girl said her name was Shirley and played "Home on the Range." The audience applauded.

"She gets a free trip to the Hohner factory," hollered the kibitzer, chewing on a ragged cigar, "in *Germany*."

The final contestant, a young girl, demurred, giggling. "This is really ridiculous," she said.

Mr. Schackner looked astounded. "No, honey," he said. "It is not ridiculous. It's *fun*."

For New Yorkers, fun in the Catskills isn't as expensive as a trip to Bermuda or Miami, but it still takes money. Figuring transportation costs and an allowance for new clothes, a young secretary or salesgirl can expect to invest a week's salary against the chance of meeting a few "men, men, men, wonderful eligible men" on a singles weekend.

Grossinger's famed *heimischkeit* is the most evident in periodic public discussions during which guests may air their grievances against the hotel and compare notes on common problems. Sometimes questions of policy are put directly to the guests. "How many prefer round-robin seating, which allows you to change tables at each meal and thus meet a maximum number of people?" asks Nat Fleischer, who, when he isn't running the Grossinger Forum, as these discussions are called, entertains guests with hypnotism experiments. "How many prefer the security of always knowing where their seat is going to be?" Most preferred the opportunity of meeting the maximum number of people.

The Forum met on Sunday morning, after breakfast, and guests were encouraged to exchange useful tips and discuss their weekend experiences. Sarah, a single in her early forties, told a true-life success story: "Girls, I did it once. I was once in the Terrace Room with a married couple of my acquaintance, and in came a man who was very attractive to me. Beautiful music was playing, and I was very anxious to dance. I said to my friend's husband, 'I wish I could meet that man,' and as it happened, my friend's husband knew the gentleman in question. Well, he introduced us, and the man asked me to dance. We spent that evening together, and the next afternoon and evening, and at the end of the weekend the gentleman offered to drive me back to the city. As a matter of fact, he's here again this weekend, and he's taking me home again."

The audience—about fifty guests of various ages—applauded warmly, and Mr. Fleischer commended Sarah for taking the "direct approach" to the matter of meeting a stranger.

"I will not say that Sarah used a direct approach," a lady named Edna objected. "I will say that she took advantage of a situation. Not all of us know a couple who can introduce us to their friends. And I will say that, should a woman want to dance, it is not possible for her to *ask*. Such a behavior is not acceptable in our society."

Fleischer attempted a compromise. "There is a way. There is a way. Let me suggest this. Is there a person in the world who doesn't like the feeling that he knows something somebody else doesn't know? Is there a person who is not complimented by being made to feel that he can be of assistance, especially to a lady? Of course, the male in our society is supposed to be aggressive, forceful. The male animal. But this is not always the case. That being so, what is wrong with the woman getting to know the man by asking him a question? 'Pardon me, but do you happen to know the name of the band leader?' Something of that nature."

"I don't intend to force my attentions on any man by pretending to be stupid," a lady called out.

"It's not forcing your attentions, madam," Fleischer replied. "It's just asking a question. *There's nothing wrong with asking a question in the Terrace Room.*"

A woman to Fleischer's right interrupted: "In our society a female shouldn't *have* to do anything!" The audience groaned with exasperation.

Fleischer: "*No!* A female doesn't *have* to do *any*thing. This is a democracy! But if she doesn't do anything, sometimes nothing's going to happen, either."

Beneath the applause which greeted Fleischer's declaration, the "fwee, fwee" of several miniature harmonicas was audible.

"Madam," Fleischer continued, "at the present time I am working on a doctoral dissertation in psychology. Take my word for it."

"I'd like to change the subject," said a young man, standing and raising his hand simultaneously. "This whole place closes down by three-thirty in the morning. I like to stay up till five. Couldn't you have a jukebox, or *something?* Records we could play after the bar closes? I mean for my age group?"

Fleischer took a small black notebook and a pen from his coat pocket and began writing. "Mmm," he said, looking up. "I'll tell you what I'm going to do. I'm going to make a note of your suggestion and submit it to the hotel management. This is not a decision I can make, or we can make here this morning." He began writing again. "Mmm. Something for people . . . of that age group . . . to do . . . after three. Mmm."

Putting his notebook away, Fleischer began to close the meeting. "Out of thirteen hundred people," he said, "all you have to do is meet that one person, ladies and gentlemen. Let's all remember: Yesterday is a canceled check. Tomorrow is a promissory note. But today is ready cash. Right now, today, is there the chance of meeting the right one today? *Right now?* Maybe not. But we say, if the chances of meeting *the* one are small, why not enjoy the journey? Thank you for being such a wonderful, wonderful audience, and teaching me so much about meeting, American style."

The audience applauded lustily. "Fwee! Fwee! Fwee!" went several miniature harmonicas, strongly and in unison.

"Our hotels have various images," said Ben Kaplan of the Hotel Association. "You go to Grossinger's expecting warmth, graciousness, and hospitality. The Concord, on the other hand, is known for its thrust."

In 1935, when Grossinger's was just beginning to move into the big time, the owners of what was then the Kiamesha Ideal Hotel defaulted on a mortgage held by Arthur Winarick. Winarick had already made a fortune in the hair tonic business and took over the operation of the Kiamesha Hotel—which he renamed the Concord—as a lark. Because of his outside interests in hair tonic and cosmetics, Winarick had the capital to build to his heart's content. As he added swimming pools, golf courses, and rooms, and hired expensive talent to entertain his guests, neighboring hotels began to work hard to keep up with the Concord.

As the largest and undoubtedly the richest hotel in Sullivan County, the Concord is often subjected to intramural criticism. The owners of some of its more staid rivals consider it a vulgar upstart, a parvenu. It is important to the Concord, then, to prove that Grossinger's isn't the only place in the mountains that has class. The story is still told of the vast white marble lobby the Concord built after World War II. When guests complained that the lobby lacked the warmth and hominess that Grossinger's offered, the Concord's owner ordered the marble covered over with wooden paneling.

Nowhere in Sullivan County are singles managed more efficiently—or taken more seriously—than at the Concord. For its annual "April in Paris" singles weekend, the Concord hires strolling violinists to sere-nade guests while they check in. It offers lectures on European wines: "Reek with *savior-faire*!!" invites a publicity release.

The motor force behind the Concord's singles program is Rose Ahrens, the hotel's chief social hostess. "I make from singles doubles," Rose says, "and they come back next year triples."

Today, the Cordillion Room is maintained especially for Rose's singles mixers and dances. When the room is in use, an armed guard is posted at the entrance to notify guests that the party inside is for singles only. Even with the guard there, marrieds often try to crash the affairs, at which free champagne (New York State Chaumont) is traditionally served.

Since singles and marrieds tend to look alike to the untrained observer, the best Rose can do, she says, is "appeal to their consciences." At the opening of each singles party she mounts the bandstand and says, "We're here to help the needy, not the greedy. So will all married people please leave the room and not come back?"

As the guests in the Cordillion Room mill about, eating and meeting, they are entertained. A singer, all but hidden by a four-foot-high ice-carving replica of a basket, and flanked by two pelicans of similar size and composition, sings "Give Me the Simple Life." Part of the Catskill tradition is to ignore all entertainers except big-name stars.

From the bandstand, Rose periodically tries to create an appropriate atmosphere. "Remember, gentlemen," she says, "if you ask a lady to dance it may be your chance for a new romance." And, "If you mingle, your spine will tingle, your pockets will jingle, and you won't stay single."

This summer Grossinger's had a full week of singles events, and hired a computer to match guests according to their individual requirements. At the Concord, a singles sanctuary is marked off at poolside. Rose Ahrens patrols the boy-meets-girl area, shooing away the greedy and guiding the needy with blasts on a bosun's whistle, signaling when it is time to change lounges and meet new people. Headquarters for the younger set, however, is the Laurels, a training ground for singles who someday will move on to Grossinger's, or even the Concord.

The atmosphere there is casual in the extreme. In the Laurels' dining room, Catskill informality is reduced to what must be its irreducible essence.

Bernie Weiss, student and waiter, a size too large for his starched white jacket, lounges against a wall nibbling string beans from an idle tray. A few yards away a foursome of intense girls eat slowly, conscious of Bernie's painstaking appraisal.

"Hmmm," Bernie says, addressing the chubbies of the four. "How 'bout you and me go on weight-watchers till Labor Day. Maybe then . . ."

"*Meshuginah*," mutters the fat girl.

"Not at all," says Bernie, pulling up a chair to join the girls. "Bernie the Waiter, soon to be Bernie the Lawyer, is a prince in disguise."

"Your disguise works," says a second girl, whose name is Shirley.

"*Touché*," Bernie says, and then gets up to clear the table.

"For all we're paying, you'd think they'd give us matching dishes," says Shirley. "This noon I had a fork from Lindy's, a salad bowl from some hospital, and a plate marked GM Training Center. Next time I want to go some place classy, I'll stay home."

Bernie returns to the table with three large servings of strawberry shortcake, which he serves to everyone but the fat girl. "We take the best care of you at the Laurels," he says. "So don't grouse. Besides, here you can have bacon for your breakfast." He leaves again to attend to other patrons.

"That's *some*thing," says a third girl, Barbara. "At the Pines, God forbid you should ask for milk in your coffee, never mind bacon."

"OK, bacon's *some*thing," says Shirley. "But it's not everything. Where are all the rich young eligibles you promised us?"

Barbara looks to make sure Bernie is out of earshot. Then she says hoarsely, "The waiters, you dopes. The *waiters*. Do you think they're here because they like the food?"

Shirley looks stunned. Squinting, she says, "*Bernie?*"

"Bernie," says Barbara, nodding somberly.

Love in the Catskills knows no season. Short Line buses transport their wistful cargo to the mountains twelve months a year. Several years ago the Concord blurred the seasonal distinctions entirely by freezing its outdoor skating rink and, in the midst of a heat wave, invited its guests to skate in their bathing suits.

At Grossinger's it was early Sunday afternoon and Juliet Goldman sat in the lobby, surrounded by luggage. She was blowing softly into a miniature harmonica. Across the lobby, a line of guests waited patiently to pay their bills. Near a staircase leading up from the main entrance, workmen set up tables to receive members of a convention due to

arrive later in the day. WELCOME BILT-RITE BABY CARRIAGE. REGISTER
HERE said a sign attached to one of the tables. "Fwee, fwee, fwee," went
Juliet's harmonica. Around her, people said good-byes. Everyone
agreed that the weekend had been happy and successful. "You know
what?" Juliet said. "This place has possibilities. Next time I'm simply
going to have to try harder."


# Sex and the Single-minded, or Manhunting as a Military Science

### by Ralph Schoenstein

For many years, the American girl who yearned for a husband had to
put all her faith in Palmolive and prayer; but since 1965, she has had a
magazine that does for manhunting what Moshe Dayan's memoirs did
for war. Today's marriage-starved maiden needn't speak to God or
spend two weeks washing her face: she simply reads *Cosmopolitan*, her
monthly guide to girlish guerrilla raids on that dumb but elusive enemy
known as "men." This fifty-cent field manual for the frantic has turned
bachelor bagging into the newest military science.

The leader of the greatest manhunt since Stanley found Livingston is
Helen Gurley Brown, author of those estrogenic inspirations *Sex and
the Single Girl* and *Sex and the Office Girl*.

There are twenty million single girls in America today and she's their
Commander-in-Chief, the frilly MacArthur who will lead them out of
the shame of spinsterhood. Each of these tarnished Snow Whites is
roused by the thought that Helen *herself* has done it: a little girl from
Little Rock, she sallied forth with only an iron will and detachable bust
and bagged a big executive. This tender idyl then moved her to start
publishing her tactics for trapping the enemy, tactics so brilliant and
bold that they already have given tens of thousands of girls the courage
to start bad marriages.

Helen's grand strategy for an orbit to the alter consists of three steps:

(1) Camouflage.

(2) Selecting the best combat zone.

(3) Going into battle.

In *Sex and the Single Girl*, Helen boasted that the most fetching parts of her came from drugstores; and thus was born the cult of the prefabricated siren, the erotic erector set who didn't need anything innate to catch a man. She didn't even have to be pubescent, for every single girl from Christine Jorgensen to Little Orphan Annie could reassemble herself irresistibly by just adding all the luscious parts that silly old nature forgot.

"Are you a beautiful phony?" asked Helen in an early *Cosmopolitan.* "I certainly *hope* you are. They're always telling you to be the most natural girl in the world . . . well, they just ought to *see* you in your natural state! Pale . . . lashless . . . bustless . . . and occasionally, after a grinding day at the typewriter, almost *fingernail*-less!"

And then Helen describes the revised ideal woman: not a rag, a bone, and a hank of hair, but a wig, new nose, and a foam *derrière.* Should the sweetheart of Sigma Chi have a false bottom? Is a removable rump only for spies? Helen's answer is one to stir the heart of each incomplete nymph: "The beautiful phony can look scrumptious in a nylon elastic net girdle with padding of foam rubber."

There's a picture of this armor in which the girl seems to be wearing a knapsack that has slipped a great distance down her back, a kind of low-slung field pack for hunting the biggest game of all—and just as handy for playing hockey.

This issue of *Cosmopolitan* also recommends wigs, false eyelashes, nose jobs, tinted contact lenses, beauty spots, false fingernails, false toenails, and padded bras. Helen doesn't say how long it takes to shed all this gear when the beautiful phony finally lures Mr. Right into a pitch black bedroom, where he can make love to the real her while wildly picturing all the stores she came from. Let us hope she can molt in a hurry; or perhaps the most enchanting pieces of paraphernalia can be removed by *him*, especially if he's an engineer.

> *The girl that I marry will have to be*
> *Disassembled conveniently.*

In other issues, Helen has run separate stories on bust building, a subject close to her heart. She is all for breasts, one on each side, and both pointing towards the preacher; but you don't have to grow your own. A BEAUTIFUL BOSOM . . . YOURS! is the title of a piece that goes on to say:

> You see a lovely girl with beautiful cleavage . . . the deep-dish
> kind that was never created by pushing anything together, up-
> ward, or out . . . *God* gave it to her. And you wish you were she.

The poor flat working girl then learns that she can *help* the Big Boob-Maker Upstairs with silicone shots and taxidermic surgery. And if she can't afford a doctor, she can still land her dreamboat with a savage assortment of padded bras. Yes, girls, beauty need no longer be just in the eye of the beholder: it can now be in his *hand*; but by the time he drops it on the floor, he'll have fallen for the real you, wherever that may be. Of course, he'll never discard your fake teeth, which you'll have added for just a thousand bucks after reading TEETH-CAPPING, ANYONE?, a piece in the same issue as the lyrical LITTLE NOTHING UNDER-THINGS THAT MAKE YOUR FIGURE REALLY SOMETHING. The latter says, "It's all due to ingenious design and fool-the-eye construction . . . your slimmed down thighs, flat tummy, and firmed up (but oh so pliant!) *derrière*."

Helen is quite fussy about reshaping the bust to *just* the right size, for another piece is called BOSOM REDUCTION, which tells all the topheavy how a surgeon can shave off the excess. What Helen seems to be implying is that the ideal single girl should have adjustable mammaries to fit the current style. Perhaps the next step is the use of helium controlled by an oh so pliant little valve.

Once the huntress has faked her entire body, she is ready to add that luscious intangible, sensuosity. This isn't for sale with all the other gear: she has to cook it up in that unadorned wasteland between her false lashes and her wig.

"Believing in white—that's thinking sensuously," says a story called HOW SENSOUS SHOULD A WORKING GIRL BE? "It takes very special moments and places. To me it happens mostly in the tub and sometimes lying in bed, wrapped in the cuddliest of all cashmere sweaters."

What kind of girl wears sweaters to bed? One whose landlord has turned off the heat? No, an *animal*, the girl that Rona Jaffe describes in THE ANIMAL GETS ALL THE PELTS. "Are you a *nice* girl?" says Rona. "Or are you that sensuous animal who gets all the man?" She then reveals that just lying around in sweaters and bathtubs isn't enough: "An animal will take the dinner dishes out of the living room (men hate garbage), but won't wash them when he'd rather talk."

And so now the beautiful phony knows one of the greatest secrets of all: there can come infatuation from minor sanitation.

What kind of talk should she make while the dishes are a-molderin' in the sink? Why, spontaneous talk that she has rehearsed for days. "Remember," says Rona, "that anything can be learned with practice, even spontaneity."

Now that the huntress is armed, sensuous, and full of polished spontaneity, she is set to zero in on the right zone for battle. America is chock full of bachelors, from J. Edgar Hoover to H. Rap Brown, so she must carefully pick the type that she wants to pursue. Luckily, Helen and her writers have already done a job of scouting that would awe Von Clausewitz: they have studied the whole country as if it were a giant game preserve, and similar reconnaissance has come from overseas. For example, it was one of Helen's scouts who revealed that there are 556,878 men in Houston, Texas, although this sum isn't broken down to show how many of them are in hospitals, rest homes, and prisons. Nevertheless, this scout gaily reports:

> If I were a girl leaving home for the first time, I'd pack my bags and head for Houston.Why? Because it's the *manliest* city in the world. Houston's oil companies are famous for their rugged, handsome men. But men of every shape and type have also been migrating to the shipping lines, the chemical plants. . . .

The huntress who wants a man with cleaner hands can go to the Midwest, where Lois Mandel reports that the Chicago game preserve is overflowing with virile goodies:

> Imagine a tall, dark 29-year-old lawyer living all alone in a two-story apartment above Chicago's Saks Fifth Avenue. Imagine a handsome TV newsman of 25, all by himself in a Near North Side coach house with only a Great Dane for company.
>
> They're here in all sizes, shapes, and forms—from brainy young atomic scientists at the Argonne National Laboratory to the bachelor fullback star of the Chicago Bears.
>
> But how do you meet them?
>
> You'll try the job route, naturally.

The lawyer works at 1 North LaSalle Street (where you'll also run into stockbrokers, market analysts, and public accountants).

The newsman is with ABC-TV. The fullback? He's a challenge, but you can apply for a job as girl Friday to team owner George Halas.

Does a girl really have to join the Chicago Bears? Or must she take all that radiation at the Argonne lab? No, she need only read the issue of *Cosmopolitan* with THE POOR GIRL'S GUIDE TO AMERICA'S RICH YOUNG MEN, which Helen introduces with the kind of breathless prose that triggers dreams of old shoes and rice:

> If you're really serious about the husband-hunting business, this guide is for you. It gives the background on some of the richest, liveliest bachelors in America . . . tells where they live, where they vacation, where they dine, what they like. Knowledge is power!

These stirring words ran in STEP INTO MY PARLOR, the page leading each issue on which Helen promotes all the latest premarital ploys, the page where this cooing Knute Rockne reminds her girls that they have the guts and the glands to crash through to the altar. Helen's teen-age prose style, a kind of souped-up semi-literacy in which parentheses, elipses, and exclamation points gaily riot, also pervades all the titles and coming attractions:

> WIN HIM IN A SINGLE NIGHT WITH THESE POW-ZONK DATE DRESS-ES . . . THE DUDE RANCH VACATION (Go West and get in on all that fun) . . . I LIVE WITH A BACHELOR (it would almost seem easier to live with a *rattlesnake!*) . . . An outspoken primer you've never seen anything like before . . . Italian men *do* make you feel like a sleek pussycat . . . You'll never read anything like *this* article, I promise! . . . and much much more! . . *Do* have a wicked August!

Helen wisely realizes that not every girl is so shallow that all she wants is to marry a millionaire, and so *Cosmopolitan* has also run a story called THE TEN MOST WANTED MEN (BY THE FBI). It's an offbeat guide to men who are not *uninterested* in money but have *other* qualities as well, men like Chester C. Collins, under whose picture is written:

One morning in 1956, Chester broke into his girl's apartment in Winter Haven, Florida, and attacked her with a razor-sharp hatchet. Later he escaped from prison and hasn't been seen since. His girl is reported quite worried. Chester loves poetry, dream reading, crooked card games, and firing guns in public.

In other words, he's perfect for one of Rona Jaffe's animals. And Helen could show her the most *scrumptious* outfits for kibitzing at a crooked card game or taking a stroll with her guy into a gun battle.

The Ten Most Wanted list is no anomaly in *Cosmopolitan*, for Gael Greene advises the girls to MARY THE MAN NOT QUITE UP TO YOU. "Even if he's rough around the edges," she says, "or he's not the smartest man in the world . . . or he's shy while you're scintillating—don't scorn him!"

Her story implies that the girls should feel free to aim pretty low, for any man who's not quite up to the users of Helen's ploys may well be a certified moron. These ploys, such as putting a live beetle in your bag at the beach and then screaming so a man can run and save you, will soon be discussed in part three of Helen's battle plan.

Needless to say, Helen doesn't feel that you should go hunting just *any* old jackass, even though single girls do outnumber bachelors by 4,961,000. For example, in WHAT KIND OF MAN MAKES THE BEST LOVER? we learn about "the lunatic fringe":

> Designers, copywriters, and men in advertising and publishing represent a mixed bag of opportunities. Most of them fall into the ivy-league-blazer Irish-coffee set; they read all the latest book reviews and do everything that's In. They always look boyish and prefer golf and skiing to women. But they know it's smart to talk sexy and their Bunny club memberships are natural offshoots of their college smoker days. They couldn't make a pass at a sophisticated woman if their lives depended on it.

The sophisticated woman is, of course, one who moves not just to Houston but right into the Manned Space Center, whose false rump is lined with silk, and whose beach bag holds, not just beetles, but eels and iguanas.

The single girl who doesn't care for Houston or famous fugitives still has hope: she can emigrate. MEN IN TAHITI tells her that all she needs to bag a friendly native is a bright cotton shift: but the piece doesn't add that when he makes her shed the shift *and* the two deceptive coconuts underneath, her own mini-mammaries could mean paradise lost. She'll do better by keeping her shirt on in Europe, a zone well dissected in TRAVEL BROADENS YOUR MALE HORIZONS. Or she can seek the ultimate challenge, revealed in ON SAFARI: MEN DON'T DO ALL THE HUNTING:

> You meet a hunter in town and he's gauche. But go with him into the bush and suddenly he's the man you turn to for everything. After all, your life is in his bronzed and capable hands.

If you're over forty and a bit plain, you might have to nudge romance by standing downwind from a rhino, but you *can* make him notice you. And it's still better than going after Chester Collins or an ivy-league editor.

Now that the beautiful phony knows the kind of man she wants (rich, virile, and backward), and now that she knows the place where she wants to fight for him (everywhere from Bel Air to gorilla country), she is ready to go for the kill. *Cosmopolitan* is richest in stories about the moment of truth, stories like THE MAN-TRAP APARTMENT, HOW TO GET HIM TO MARRY YOU—A REVOLUTIONARY NEW METHOD, BATTLE PLAN AGAINST THE OTHER WOMEN, SEDUCTIVE COOKERY, and SOME FAR OUT TIPS FOR MEETING AND MATING THEM.

For example, HOW GIRLS REALLY GET HUSBANDS—IT WORKS! tells the inspiring tale of Erica, who looked like a dog but had the guts of a wolf and the mind of a fox in her frantic quest of the glamorous Teddy.

> And then that fateful New Year's Eve. Erica didn't have a date with Teddy. He was taking Hildy to a party. But he felt so sick that afternoon that he called Hildy to cancel the date. It was one of those 24-hour intestinal things, but he was convinced he was dying. He also called Erica . . . just to say a plaintive adieu. She arrived at his apartment twenty minutes later in her sexiest stretch pants and a devastating pullover.
>
> There Teddy was, thinking how he should dictate a will, when she burst in smelling of Joy (about seven dollars' worth) and loaded with bundles. She took temperatures, pulses, applied compresses, made the bed with him still in it, and fed him rice pudding, tea, and cinnamon toast. By morning he was saved. Feeling strangely weak and never more vulnerable, the big eight-letter word

escaped his lips . . . "marriage." It wasn't exactly a question, but she said Yes . . . as if it was. Then she got out a calendar and said "When?"

Yes, Helen's girls know how to make the most of a fever. In fact, the story of Erica, that angel with stretch pants and pudding, has probably sent thousands of secretaries in search of malaria cases with bank accounts.

Another heroine of HOW GIRLS REALLY GET HUSBANDS also learned that the way to a man's heart is through disease. Maria's prey was healthy, so instead of becoming the nurse, she became the patient. The big break she needed was her leg, which cracked just below the knee. At last, she had the chance to let Karl see her in the pink ruffled bed jacket that she'd never been able to wear to cocktail parties.

But perhaps the most thrilling case of all is Suzanne, whose marital monomania makes Captain Ahab seem like a Sunday fisherman. "I'm practically an evangelist on the subject of getting your man," she says. "I captured Jack and I want other girls to know how it can be done. And I was thirty-nine, a little too plump, with slightly buck teeth."

How did Suzanne lure Jack from his jet-set crowd? By instant orthodontia? By breaking her spine and wearing lacy traction? No: she simply spent three hundred bucks on cosmetics, dieting, exercise, and a sable wrap, and then another five thousand on casually sprinkling her apartment with the pre-Columbian art that Jack loved. But still he didn't succumb. If only he didn't keep seeing those teeth. Should she try walking backwards? Or putting the sable over her face? No, she subtly followed him to parties with three escorts: one good friend, one co-worker, and one husband of a friend. At last, he proposed, probably because he feared that the next event would be the Coast Guard band playing his college songs under his window.

"In meeting men as in making money," says one of Helen's scouts, "one must be single-minded. And till recently, I had left no stone unturned. I had looked for men everywhere, from the Central Park Zoo's cafeteria to my psychiatrist's waiting room."

Of course, the clever girl doesn't *have* to prowl the zoos and mental wards: she can stay home and build a man-trap apartment, of which Helen says:

> Be wily . . . be smart . . . be romantic . . . turn your living
> room into an amatory ambush (He'll never know!) . . . with twen-
> ty secret traps specially designed to snare him !

The cozy quicksand, shown in a two-page layout, includes such
seductive decor as:

> One (almost erotic) drawing on the wall—spotlighted . . . some
> intimate, silken piece of lingerie "accidentally" left in the living
> room . . . perfumed light bulbs whose heat releases the fra-
> grance . . . sensuous textures—like velvet pillows . . . rheostat con-
> trol switch to turn lights down, down, *down* . . . glasses so big that
> *he* can hold the glass in one hand but *you* have to (vulnerably)
> hold it in *two* . . . and a plaything—like a kaleidoscope.

But suppose the gentleman stubs his toe on your padded bra, the one
you left so accidentally on the bearskin rug? Or suppose he ignores *you*
and instead falls for the scented light bulbs? Will their perfume compete with yours? And how can you hold that drink in two hands
and still control the rheostat? With your *toes*? No, *they'll* be playing
with the kaleidoscope. Helen's engineers clearly need more time at the
drawing board.

If a girl doesn't want to build this romantic booby trap, she can make
her kill at the beach, which Helen calls "the biggest bed in the world . . .
comfortable and warm and a great mating ground." In HOW TO MAKE
GOOD AT THE BEACH we learn not just the fear-of-your-own-beetle ploy
but some equally splendid tactics from Pamela Rothon, the beauty
editor. "Pamela has learned," says Helen, "that American boys at the
beach or anywhere else are so anxiety-ridden that you feel like a nanny
listening to their problems. But she's not above telling you how to
capture one! Like a good beauty editor, she wears false eyelashes and
even perfume to bed!"

And so Pamela tells all her seaside nannies to appear at the beach in
sexy sunglasses, iced cologne, and a false hairpiece with a saucy red
ribbon. Of course, if nanny forgets to remove the hairpiece before
swimming, her dreamboat will see one girl enter the water and another
emerge, but the change might just enchant him. And if it doesn't,
Pamela suggests something even more dramatic:

Take a bottle of champagne (we're serious!) out of that beach bag and chances are you won't be alone for long. That POP! attracts men instantly, especially if you hit one with a cork.

Helen's battle plan for the war on bachelors has finally included the use of a real cannon. The only reason she doesn't suggest a larger millimeter is that there obviously has to be something left to capture—although one of her lieutenants *has* been doing impressive research on the use of a carbine for shooting oil workers in the foot.

If you would rather use champagne for a less violent attack on Mr. Right, you can stay home and follow the recipes in SEDUCTIVE COOKERY; and if those don't make him forget his mother, you can HI-FI YOUR WAY INTO HIS HEART. If he happens to be tone deaf you can MOTORCYCLE YOUR WAY INTO HIS HEART. Needless to say, the gal who gets her guy by joining Hell's Angels will find that her false behind is not only fetching but utilitarian. The motorcycle attack is a happy solution for the girl who has failed to find her man at a ski lodge, peace march, or requiem mass, the girl who has finally decided that it's time to put a saucy red bow on her helmet and wreck her kidneys for romance.

If she doesn't happen to have a motorcycle, she can still attack on foot with one of these tactics from SOME FAR OUT TIPS FOR MEETING AND MATING THEM:

> —Go up to one and tell him you're a writer doing a story about how to meet a man in the city.
>
> —Walk up to a man you don't know and, from the back, put your hands over his eyes and shout, "Guess who?" When he gives up, let him look at you and say, "Omygod, I'm so embarrassed, I thought you were someone else."

There is no record of how many girls who played these games have been arrested for prostitution.

Amazingly, in a military manual that seems to hold every conceivable tactic for trapping men, from hunting at the zoo to setting up a casino (POKER WITH THE BOYS . . . AT YOUR PLACE), from raiding analyst's offices to raiding smart saloons (THE DATING BAR—YES, IT'S O.K. TO PICK UP MEN), there's a bad omission: Helen has overlooked one great mother lode of bachelors. Had she seen it, she might now be telling her girls:

I've just discovered the *dreamiest* new place to find men . . . at any U.S. Army induction center! And if you go into the right room, you'll find them all *nude,* so you'd better be looking your powiest!

Now . . . how can you tell the single ones from the waste matter? Well, that's the peachiest part of it! They're almost *all* single at those induction centers! Some of them may be half your age, but we can't *all* wait around for Cary Grant and Justice Douglas, now *can* we?

So just forget about the men at beaches, bullfights, fairs, funerals, duck blinds, embassies, and first communions. Go pick off Prince Charming at an induction physical—and watch love bloom when the first thing he does is leave you for two years.

Well, *you're* going to put those two years to good use . . . rebuilding your nose, erasing freckles, reinforcing hair, adjusting ears, exchanging teeth, shedding old skin, and putting new life in your *derrière.* You just don't *need* any of those old parts that you started with. Be the female impersonator you were *meant* to be!

Now when you walk into the induction center to trap your true love, keep your chest held high—with the scrumptious new bra called the Darling Dirigible. No more padding for *you* . . . each cup is firm, fetching inner tube that inflates to the *real you* by bicycle pump or mouth. Silicone shots, goodbye!

Now your big question is . . . should you let *him* inflate you? And I say of *course! Poo* on old Billy Graham! *He* doesn't know how it feels to have to massage your own back!

By the way, this bewitching bra can *also* be used as a life preserver at the beach so you won't drown while looking for men beyond the three mile limit.

*Must* you remain true to your GI while he's away? Must you take off your false lashes, false nails, false chest, false hair, false behind, and false teeth, and just walk the streets as the neuter stick you really are? Well, I'll answer that *next* month, along with a *really* kooky new way to his heart . . . surprise him on his birthday with a bronzed set of his kidney stones!

*T HERE can be all kinds of honeymoons, but most people only have one of them. And if you're young enough, you can have a very special honeymoon: one with majestic bathrooms but without liquor, getting a start, at no extra effort, on your first Green Stamp collection.*

# Honeymoonsville: The Case of the Lost Honeymoon Generation

## *by Joel Lieber*

In Paradise Valley, by the shores of Lake Tranquillity, love keeps the grassy hillocks of the Poconos green, although the pockets of the purveyors of honeymoon hideaways are a richer, riper green. But love is blind, and, relying on that blindness, the Pocono honeymoon resorts have carved out of the forests a mythical land of romantic Pennsylvania make-believe, Americana-derived and Americana-directed, a design of carefully planned absurdities that initiates newly-weds into the fantasy of their lives.

The Poconos (from an Indian word meaning "stream between mountains") are the first connubial grounds for between forty thousand and fifty thousand young Americans every year. Developed as the center of America's honeymoon industry just after World War II, the Poconos form the northeast corner of Pennsylvania, between the Blue Mountains on the south and Moosic Mountains on the north, fifteen hundred square miles of lakes, tumbling streams, waterfalls, quiet meadows, and deep woods.

Having heard about the bizarre doings in the Pocono honeymooneries, my wife and I set out as bogus newly-weds (we'd been married four years) to see what we could see.

The dozen honeymooneries themselves, half of which are honor-bound to refuse would-be guests who are not newly-weds, share much common ground. However, each has its particular theme: one advocates wholesomeness and teetotalism; another stresses piped-in music and spiritual counsel; another lavish, Pompeiian bathrooms; another riflery; and another gives Green Stamps as incentive.

Honeymooning—a substantial, recession-proof business—nets its Pocono operators upward of $5 million a year. So specialized is this resort trade that it often becomes difficult to see the difference between sentimentality and sharp business acumen in these lush, green hills. Elaborate catering to the needs of honeymooners brings in young couples from throughout the northeast, and at any resort one sees car licenses from as far away as Virginia and Illinois.

To the brides and grooms, the fact that they may spend as much as $300 a week, possibly $400, appears of little concern. Honeymooners, according to the resident merchants of the self-designated "Honeymoon Mecca of the World," are the freest spenders of all vacationers. Although the vast majority of Pocono honeymoon patrons have not gone beyond a high school education, and are usually in a tight economic bracket, they have little in common with their predecessors a generation ago who had to borrow $2 for a marriage license.

Honeymooning knows no economic barrier. The honeymoon is the thing, and no one ever hears any complaints about money. As one young man, commenting on his $300 a week bill, said: "So what if it's expensive? It's our only honeymoon. It's a fling. We'll never be here again."

Birchwood, outside East Stroudsburg, is a spread of fifty identical honeymoon bungalows, each with a TV antenna aimed at heaven, and each with an American eagle on the front door.

The bungalows are arranged around a little lake where side-by-side couples are usually meandering in paddle boats. The resort is owned by Carol and Wally Hoffman, whose social director, Ed Coover, daily presides over a full program of recreational activities for the guests. Ed, a short, wiry man who rarely smiles, makes his headquarters in the main house, a converted barn that doubles as a curio shop. A rich, sweet odor pervades the shop.

"What you're smelling is the candles," Ed noted, pointing to a workbench drippy with wax and stalwart with tall, red candles. Next to it stood a deep tub, the center of the odor. "The couples make their own candles by dipping them. They have to dip them around the mold, holding the wick, and they dip them around twenty-seven times."

The explanation seemed self-evident, and Ed turned away.

"Why do they do that?" I asked.

"Oh, you know, it's for their anniversary. They burn the candles they made on their honeymoon for their first anniversary. Maybe they have dinner by the light of the candle." Candlemaking, he concluded, is a standard activity with a large following at Birchwood.

Ed picked up one candle and showed it off admiringly. "They do all the work by themselves. Look at how well this couple's doing. But," he paused, picking up another, an inferior specimen, "just look at *that*. This couple hasn't been doing very much work on their candle at all."

Birchwood's social director scoots around the grounds in an electric-powered go-cart which usually serves as a baggage-carting machine. Parking just opposite the lake, Ed showed off the interior of one of the cottages with the spread-winged American eagle about the entrance. Beyond the door was a double-room unit decorated in a vigorously patriotic Early American motif. Each such cottage contains its complement of Boston rockers, flowered, canopied beds, and rich-heritage wallpaper.

Separating the bedroom and tiny living room is a room-divider, in the middle of which, on a swivel, sits a television set. Ed whirled the TV set. "The newly-weds can watch it either on the sofa or in bed," he said.

The bathroom, equipped with a coffee-maker and departing from the Colonial design to Futuristic American, amply revealed that someone had indeed kept the honeymooner in mind when designing this room: the toilet itself was discreetly enclosed within swinging doors.

After a look at a handsome indoor swimming pool and a game room full of ping-pong and billiard tables, we went to the bowling alley—four spanking new alleys. I asked Ed if honeymooners really used this sporting facility. "Do they use it?" he asked, astonished. "Do they ever! Here, look." He flipped through a stack of score sheets behind the counter. "That's just from this morning."

Going through the door into a great room under heavy construction, smelling richly of fresh lumber and sawdust, Ed announced that this would be the gymnasium and roller-skating rink. It was here that Ed expounded his Philosophy of Honeymooning—the Theory of Maximum Participation.

"At Birchwood, we feature activities that the honeymooners can *participate* in. We don't have shows where they just sit around and are entertained. They got their whole life to be entertained. Here, they participate. By that, I mean bowling, square dancing, outings, all the other sports. No hypnosis shows or anything like that."

It's the rare bird, Ed explained, who doesn't participate, although each week's crowd brings a couple or two who keep to themselves. "Generally, we get maximum participation at activities—one hundred per cent attendance. Yesterday, for example, we had a hobo lunch, and out of all the couples here only one couple didn't go along." He paused, and the expression on his face suggested that it might be the same pair as the delinquent candlemakers.

"Last night we had an old-fashioned swimming party. We gave the boys old-time trunks and the girls those bloomer suits. I greased up a log and put a silver dollar in the middle of it and whoever could walk got a prize. Silly stuff like that, but everyone loves it."

"Are there activities like that every night, or is there a bar?"

"No alcohol served here," Ed snapped.

When I asked why, Ed revealed that alcohol was a sore spot at Birchwood. "Serving alcohol attracts a lower type of crowd," he said.

"On the other hand, we don't force our non-alcoholic ideas on anyone. Not serving alcohol is an asset. People come here because of it. Occasionally though, like last week, we have an incident."

"What happened?"

"An airline captain wanted to bring a bottle into his room and he asked us for ice. We wouldn't give it to him because it's not our policy. He became indignant. So we refunded his two hundred fifty dollars and that was that."

He clarified this determined discipline by volunteering, "It's not just a matter of dollars and cents. With us, it's a matter of faith, of conviction."

"Oh, are you—Quaker? Mormon?" I tried.

"No, we're Baptists."

"What about dancing? Is there a band, or a juke box?" I asked, only to be told that the Birchwood outlook on honeymooning takes a fairly dim view of dancing. There is never a band, and no juke boxes are allowed on the grounds.

"But after all," I said, "your guests *are* on their honeymoon, aren't they?"

"Absolutely. Exclusive honeymoon trade. Occasionally we'll get some young marrieds."

"And no dancing?"

"No *social* dancing. Social dancing and alcohol go hand in hand. You can't have one without the other. Same kind of people go in for both. But once a week we have square dancing, and as I say, everybody comes out for that."

Back in the cart, zipping toward the main house, Ed hailed a group of four couples. "Hey, who won the game?" he called out.

"We did!" they all shouted back in enthusiastic unison.

Ed tossed me a sidelong glance, full of professional satisfaction.

At the desk, I turned through a Birchwood brochure, noting the prices at between forty and fifty dollars a day. The man who is the guardian of honeymoon morals, who takes the honeymoon so seriously, turned to me and said, "I've got to run along now. Got to give out the trophies to yesterday's winners."

In shepherding Birchwood's honeymoon flock, Ed has many daily chores, and uppermost among them (supervising the candlemaking, filling out "Official Birchwood Honeymooner" certificates, etc.) is the tallying and tabulating of score sheets from the many different sporting activities. All winners receive trophies, and trophies are given out at least once a day.

In his office, beneath the mountain of trophies awaiting award-winning honeymooners, Ed cradled an armful of the trophies and motioned toward a stack of forms on the desk. He said that he studied the questionnaires to help him decide how best to pair off couples at the dining room table. They are also useful in helping him organize the right kind of activities for a given honeymoon group.

"See, this is what I mean," Ed said. "See on this one here where it says 'what did you hear about Birchwood that interested you?'"

The guest had written "activities, no liquor, freindliness (sic)."

"And that's just a random answer, right off the top of the pile," Ed noted, giving me another pleased look.

We left this clean and upright connubial atmosphere, having been duly convinced that a young couple here could have the kind of honeymoon of which their parents would wholeheartedly approve.

We checked in at Strickland's, the Mount Pocono resort just a mile past the turn-off sign to a chapel called Our Lady of the Poconos. From what I could see, Strickland's seemed to have more billboards along the surrounding roads than any other resort: looming up at prominent points along Routes 196 and 611 are big, brown signs exhorting "Strickland's—For Newlyweds and Young Marrieds." At any rate, as undercover honeymooners, we would now be able to launch an investigation from the inside, as two who have really been there.

The registration desk at this rambling honeymoon resort faces a slate which informs the just-arrived that breakfast, conveniently enough, is scheduled from 9:30 a.m. to 1:30 p.m. (Contrary to expectation, bells began to clatter loudly over the loudspeaker system promptly at 9:00 the following morning.) The list of events also showed that a hypnotist performance was scheduled that night at 8:30. Mindful of how the mentalist's role in *The 39 Steps* provided the key to puzzle, I became a bit anxious: a *hypnotist*.

Upon reviewing the posted notices, according to management sources, the bride and groom waiting at the registration desk may still feel "kind of jumpy." To cope with the ill-at-ease factor, a grandfather clock is strategically positioned alongside the desk. A huge, elaborate mechanism, the clock reputedly has a way of giving nervous, checking-in honeymooners something neutral to talk about.

Accommodations at Strickland's range from the least expensive quarters in the main house to medium-priced ($39-a-day) Mansionette bungalows in a wooded, sylvan glen to brightly colored, Mother Hubbard-looking honeymoon villas ($46 a day) which are further back in the woods. The bungalows, which are attached dwellings and by no means soundproof, are modestly furnished with no particular decor in mind. The outer room contains two chairs, a big fireplace, and the inevitable television set.

Ours was an attached dwelling and our half of it was called The Pines. The bellboy, upon carrying in our bags and being tipped, bid us a pleasantry and departed.

Inside the cottage something seemed terribly wrong. It was the piped-in music, coming from a speaker on the wall, playing, in tinkling strings, "My Wild Irish Rose."

"Turn that thing off," my wife cried, and then added, "We *can* turn it off, can't we?"

We could indeed, and I hit the switch. But "My Wild Irish Rose" lingered on, being quickly followed by "Cuddle Up a Little Closer." Silenced in our room, the music tinkled on outside. We pulled the venetian blinds, and there, in a tree above, sitting next to a squirrel, was another loudspeaker box.

The Strickland's management places special emphasis on little things —like the necessity for the clock—and the music was no exception. A guiding editorial hand selected the tunes, which, although they came out tinkling and stringy, were not the nameless, anonymous background tunes of ordinary Muzak. Over a fifteen minute period we heard "Baby Face," "Side by Side," and "I Love You a Bushel and a Peck."

Another gesture that Strickland's directs to its unique clientele sits on the dresser in the bedroom next to the Gideon's Bible. Here the bride and groom may find a booklet provided with the magagement's best wishes, entitled *Some Thoughts and Prayers For a Happy, Lasting Marriage*. Underneath the title appears the words "The couple that prays together, stays together." The brochure lists sermons and devotions written especially for the management by the clergymen of local churches. Several faiths are represented, and its message reminds newcomers of the utilitarian nature of the devotions and suggests that they get into the swing of saying the prayers.

In his *Meditation for Newly-Weds* the pastor of the Methodist Church, Mt. Pocono, asks: "Why did you marry? It was because you found it was not good to be alone. Your loneliness was not a result of being separated from other people. You had friends and relatives. Rather, your loneliness was a sense of being incomplete in yourself. You did not marry because you wanted only to talk to each other and to do things with each other. You married because you wanted to become a part of each other. Marriage is more than a partnership; it is a merger. . . ."

Spiritual advice of a slightly different nature is dispensed under *A Prayer For the Newly Married* by the Rabbi of Temple Israel in East Stroudsburg. "May we ever remember that the home is the foundation of civilization; that happiness does not depend on the mere acquisition of material things; and that it cannot exist where selfishness abounds. Grant, therefore, O God, that our new home be based on justice, illuminated by truth, warmed by love, filled with idealism, surrounded by friendship, safeguarded by a faithful spirit of devotion and service, and protected by Thee, O God of our fathers."

The Monsignor of St. Mary of the Mount, Mt. Pocono, whose message covers an entire page of text, begins with, "It is a great pleasure to welcome you to the Poconos at the beginning of your married life." He tells the brides and grooms that "your vocation will not always be such a carefree vacation" and that love is best measured by the capacity for sacrifice. "Sacrifice means giving something up. You must now give up your own selfish pleasures whether that be in emotions, food, drink, or entertainment. What you will receive is well worth the sacrifice."

A schedule of masses and special devotions for newly-weds follows, together with an invitation to attend, as well as a word about preparing for the career of marriage. "To help you have as much marital happiness as possible, I am recommending to you a correspondence course from the University of Ottawa. It consists of ten (10) excellent and practical chapters, which you take in your home. I cannot praise this course enough. You may obtain a free application after the special Newlywed devotions. Yes, this devotion is brief but beautiful."

Strickland's painstaking indulgence of honeymooners—running the wide gamut from conversation pieces to atmospheric melodies and spiritual advice—has its own built-in opposition. The prepared mood is frequently and audibly shattered by an official p.a. system voice, barking, "Marilyn Brown—telephone" and "Mr. Strickland—main office please."

Yet, further helping the brides and grooms get their minds off each other are a spate of outdoor sports, a commodity by no means underestimated here. A tour of the grounds reveals an archery range (deserted), an indoor swimming pool (unused), and a ping-pong table (unengaged) in the recreation room. Only the shuffleboard court, located next to a wishing well and in front of a Valentined "I Love You" sign, draws a steady following.

That the recreational facilities at the resort are frequently without players is "reasonable," according to a member of the hotel staff. "What the hell—at least we have to provide them. And some weeks we do get groups here that just go from one sport activity to the next all day long." A couple of verteran hoteliers in the area immodestly account for the heavy load of honeymooning activities by reasoning that the newly-weds must be grateful to them for the opportunity of meeting other young couples who have their newly married state uppermost on their minds. "The variety of activities helps bring couples together more," said one experienced operator.

Picture-taking is easily the most popular activity at Strickland"s. The hotel's photographers really get around., lining up shot after shot for a "Memory Book" photo album. Some couples even devote an entire honeymoon day to posing for pictures. Every few days, proof sheets and finished products appear in the lounge outside the dining room and on the ping-pong table in the recreation room—followed by a scramble for placing orders. Favorite poses consist of bride and groom lying across the bed grinning at the lens; a symbolic shot of two hands clasped across the bed; two heads peaking out from behind the shower curtain; the bride, *derrière* in slacks unbecomingly thrust toward the camera, being carried over the threshold, and a couple seated on either side of the colossal red valentine under the "I Love You" sign.

Dinner at Strickland's is a dress-up affair, and a casual visitor might suspect that the dining room is the scene of a high school prom. The boys are a uniform eighteen and nineteen; the girls tend toward seventeen and eighteen. I told myself I was supposed to know that Americans got married young: it was an academic statistic. But these people—were they truly classifiable as newly-weds? They were more like honest-to-goodness *teen-agers*. What brought this home even more forcefully was the fact that almost all of these $40- and $50-a-day honeymoon kids were drinking milk with their dinners.

Strickland's prides itself on the excellence of its baked goods and pastries, the latter frequently reordered two and three times by the honeymooners. Because for many of the newly-weds it is their first experience as hotel guests, the management places a card on each table reminding them, "Tipping is an old American custom."

During dinner, the social director, known simply as Chase, makes a regular appearance. He is a sixtyish, roly-poly man with a white goatee. He announces the upcoming activities, which, typically, may consist of a hayride at ten after the evening hypnosis act and the next afternoon's ride on the Camelback ski lift, three thousand feet high. He speaks to his young charges with whimsical, good-natured indulgence, mannered in a strangely dry, machine-gun-fast pitchman's voice that he appears to be restraining: the impression is that although he has said the same thing to a hundred groups before this present audience, he still must be civil and register some enthusiasm.

"So bring your cameras because it's so beautiful up there on the lift that on a clear day you can see all the way to the Catskills." On the subject of the hayride, he counsels, "Bring a sweater, but don't take a blanket. We'll provide them. And if you can't keep warm with the hay, a blanket, and each other, well, the hell with it: you better get a divorce."

After his departure, on a recent evening, the boys jumped up from their tables and rushed out to sign up for the hayride. But apparently there were only two trucks going, accommodating a total of twenty-four newly-weds. A few minutes after they all dashed out, several grooms slowly filtered back—too late to make the hayride list—and were met by their brides in the dining room with disapproving looks.

During dessert (lemon meringue pie), Chase continually made the same odd loudspeaker announcements that echoed frivolously through the dining room: "Poker game in five minutes, you guys. Five minutes to poker time." Since nobody paid much attention to these intrusions, I assumed it was some kind of running joke. But after dinner I saw a group off in the corner of the lounge playing poker. The social director, it seemed, was already sowing the seeds of taking that night off with the boys to play poker, indoctrinating the brides at the outset into doing without their menfolk. If Birchwood's social director knew about his colleague's playful little trick, I'm certain he'd disapprove.

For the hypnotist act, the brides and grooms dressed down out of suits and dresses into sport shirts, sweaters, and slacks, mainly because

Chase had sternly instructed them that the hayride activity would begin five minutes after the end of the show, leaving them no time to go back and change. As they filed into the recreation hall, the boys in jacket sweaters and the girls in yellow and pink slacks, the idea was even more vivid that this was a high school outing and not a honeymoon resort.

Chase, making coy and patronizing faces, gave out a few trophies to award-winning honeymooners, who in turn posed with their cups as the ever-present photographer captured the moment. Then he brought on the hypnotist, a tall, suave gentleman in a tuxedo and white tie. Discreet, diplomatic, giving off a no-nonsense, confidence-inspiring aura, he delivered a short lecture on the medical uses of hypnosis. He assured the brides and grooms that under hypnosis they would not do or reveal anything which might be embarrassing to them in a fully conscious state. Then he launched a performance which caused mouths to drop and eyes to pop in disbelief. Simply by telling the brides and grooms to concentrate on his eyes while he counted backward from ten, he proceeded to put half the audience into a trance. He seemed to have no trouble with such receptive minds.

The hypnotist brought up onto the stage Florence, Pat, Chuck, Pam, Janet, and Judy. He informed the remainder of the audience that many among them were under hypnosis right then but didn't know it. Then, for about an hour, he performed—or rather he suggested, while Florence, Pat, Chuck and company did the performing. He asked Florence's husband to pose a tough question for his wife, who wore the smiling, eyes-closed expression of the mesmerized. Florence's husband asked his semiconscious wife what she thought about his losing money at the poker game a little while ago. Eyes closed, the faint smile smirking, she shot back: "I hate you for it." The hypnotist quickly explained this was the normal, starkly truthful answer that one achieves with hypnosis, and he took the occasion to add a few more words about the value of his art in dentistry and psychiatry.

Then he got Florence to fly in a plane, convinced Chuck he was driving his car, and similarly arranged Pat's psyche so that he smoked a straw and thought it was a cigarette. He found that Pat was a good subject, and, upon giving him a real cigarette, advised him that as hard as he might try, he would be unable to flick his ashes into the ashtray in front of him. Pat continually missed the ashtray by a generous distance and a disturbed frown crept over his face.

As Pat grew frustrated over the ashtray, Pam kept jumping up because she was convinced her seat was too hot (whenever the hypnotist snapped his fingers), and Janet laughed to tears over a nonexistent TV show that the hypnotist suggested was hysterically funny. But it was from Judy that he elicited the most striking performance: he convinced her that she was at her seventh birthday party (eyes shut and a dreamy little-girl look of contentment), and when he asked her to write her name, she did so in the exact penmanship you would expect of a child that age. Everyone who saw the signature oo-ed and ah-ed.

The parallel was less with *The 39 Steps* than I had imagined. The really sinister note lay in the way the hypnotist acted out what the management had been doing to the newly-weds since they arrived: sending them into flights of fantasy, controlling their activities, rushing them off into strange pursuits, and every now and then restoring them to consciousness. Who knows but that the planners of the act are shrewder, more demonic than I give them credit: maybe they stage the hypnosis show as their own personal joke.

Despite—yet more likely because of—the hypnotist's fanciful manipulation of their minds, the brides and grooms loved the act. Only one young man appeared a little upset. As the hypnotist was about to awaken one of his dazed helpers, he remarked: "And when I awaken her, she will feel as refreshed as if she had an eight-hour sleep."

Her husband, seated behind me, exclaimed, "Uh-oh!"

Donning dark glasses, and hoping we looked as irrepressibly youthful as possible, we first stopped in to canvas several other honeymooneries before spending a night at another place, the one that looks like a left-over set from *The Fall of the Roman Empire*.

Paradise Valley Lodge, in the village of Memorytown, pastoral in soft green descending gently to a fairy-tale lake, houses a gift shop overflowing with native ware: Colonial kitchen bric-a-bracs; bowls of wax fruit; frosty bells, and hundreds of twelve- to eighteen-inch scented candles, all colors and shapes, giving off a thick essence of lemon and geranium. A small room comprises the shop's dazzling green house, abundant with splashy-colored flowers, all of which, upon inspection proved artificial. Distlefinks are everywhere displayed—the gaily painted hex signs with which the superstitious Pennsylvania Dutchmen coat their barns. At all hours of the day, the shop is crowded with both honeymooners and tourists sightseeing in the area.

Not far from Promised Land State Park, Paradise Valley Lodge abounds in valentines: they are decorated on the honeymoon cottages, on the many signposts, and when I saw the pillory with heart-shaped openings for head and feet, I knew for sure what was the favorite album pose at Paradise Valley.

Down the slope toward the lake there stands a red railway caboose, where, morning and afternoon, brides and grooms cavort like little children on its ladders. Photos taken by the bride of the groom standing atop the caboose and looking down are also a favorite here.

The fairy-tale motif is further carried through on the waggish copy that characterizes the trail markers. One signpost states: "This is Happiness Lane on the Shore of Memory Lake." Entering and leaving Paradise Valley, you pass a tall, crossed sign, the X-kind usually found at a railway junction, that reads: "Caution—Newlyweds Crossing."

Merry Hill, on a high knoll commanding a dramatically peaceful scene of gentle, green mountains, seems a departure from the prevailing trend. It doesn't go in for the cornball affectations found elsewhere. The only apparent vestige of local stylings is a modest wishing well on a hill overlooking the lake. Merry Hill's most expensive honeymoon cabins are sleek and tasteful $17,000 renderings of graceful Japanese and Scandinavian designs, partially inspired by the lodge's owner, Vickie Young, whose own home on the grounds, with its paneling and delicate wooden stairways, is a monument to Japanese architecture in the Poconos.

A few miles from Cresco, Merry Hill maintains a more moderate price scale than some of its $50-a-day competition. The handsome Scando-Japanese cabins are $31, and, according to the management, "sometimes a group of young folks come up and one couple takes the expensive place and the others take cheaper cabins. They split the price and meet in the expensive cabin at night to have parties."

One disquieting note here is that riflery constitutes the leading honeymoon sport, and the stillness of the surrounding woods has a way of abruptly exploding in a crescendo of fire. A maintenance man spotted the explosions for us, his ear picking out the distinctions between the .22's and .44 pistols, as well as between the .375 Magnum and a supersized elephant gun that once splattered a deer all over a honeymoon cabin. I told him that the steady bark of gunfire made it sound like the young lovers were under siege. He laughed and said: "Maybe it's because we serve alcohol here and the ones that don't are trying to shoot us out of this neck of the woods." (Strickland's also observed the no-alcohol-for-honeymooners pact—as do three other local honeymooners that are similarly fruit-punch oriented: the extreme youth of the clientele makes a liquor license impractical.)

Merry Hill's office manager, commenting on the local anti-alcohol policies, said that the position didn't make much sense since the bar at Merry Hill is a solid, money-making proposition. She suggested that liquor license concerns and moral viewpoints were really not the reasons for the teetotaling point of view. "There's a story going round that the people who sold Strickland's to its present owners stipulated in the contract of sale that no liquor would ever be sold on the premises. I can't tell you about some of the other places. The stories are too involved," she noted cryptically.

Was there any other reason why the competition didn't serve alcohol to honeymooners?

"Sure," she said. "They're all crazy."

Dave Artzt, owner of Pocmont Lodge in Bushkill (next to Bushkill Falls, "the Niagara of the Poconos"), was once an Olympic track star who became scandalously disqualifed one day when, in the midst of competition, the officials discovered he was married. He is reluctant to say just how much this incident influenced his introduction into the honeymoon market. Today, in addition to Pocmont, he owns a couple of travel agencies and a cosmetics-distribution firm.

Fiftyish, barrel-chested, and cigar-smoking, identifying himself as the only Jewish honeymoon purveyor in the Poconos, Dave is probably the leading authority on the subject of anti-Semitism in the honeymoon circuit. He relates that he has "been cursed up and down the Poconos for years"—not just for being a Jew and taking Jews, but for providing alcohol, orchestras, and big-name entertainment for his guests. Dave also brags that he is disliked for offering give-aways to honeymooners when they register: $25 worth of Revlon cosmetics and cologne for the girls, Pinaud after-shave lotion for the boys, and other sundries. He gives away many things and provides all kinds of free entertainment, defying the honeymoonery's tradition of making guests pay for all extra activities, including those hayrides and at one place even the towels the guests take to the swimming pool.

Dave's clientele is also a bit older than the norm, mostly college-educated, too. He upset the honeymoon equilibrium again when he opened his doors to Negro guests, an act of hospitality that, he claimed, just about threw the other matrimonial havens into a state of hysteria. (One travel agent who sent a Negro couple to another honeymoon resort has never been able to book a couple to that resort again: to him, the resort is always "fully booked.")

"I have one rule about Negro guests," Dave said. "I will never seat a Negro couple with another Negro couple. The tables are always mixed."

The Negro's emergence into the honeymoon field, which only occurred, according to Dave, within the last two years, is indicative of the burgeoning Negro middle class. "Look," he pointed out, "before, even though the doors were closed to them around here, they still couldn't afford it. Now the Negro *can* afford a honeymoon."

Pocmont is also proud of its somewhat mysterious tradition of not having locks on the honeymoon cottage doors. Dave's latest gambit is a $25,000 contract he signed with S&H Green Stamps, making him sole distributor of the trading stamps in all the Pocono honeymooneries. Certain that Green Stamps will prove "a tremendous incentive" for drawing newly-weds, Dave said his clients are now heading home with twenty-six hundred and fifty stamps after a $265-a-week honeymoon stint at Pocmont.

Pocono Gardens calls itself America's most unique honeymoon estate. There is more than just wishful thinking in their boast. A rambling, garden-decked lover's nest, with overtones of a Marienbad without its beautiful people, Pocono Gardens is Romanesque design gone amuck.

Stone vases, statues, and Doric columns are garishly arranged throughout the grounds in a style reminiscent of an amusement park—or a
Fellini dream sequence. Its swimming pool, entered under a lofty
archway, is guarded by two head-high, regal stone lions who, according
to one legend, are supposed to bellow when a virgin passes between
them.

But above all, the Rossis, owners of Pocono Gardens, have paid
particular homage to the bathrooms in their deluxe Roman Forum
suites. It is here that the claim for the country's most unique honeymoon estate receives its fullest support. A brochure on these suites,
which is mostly devoted to aspects of their bathrooms, further reveals
this pre-eminence. To the management, the bathrooms are the *pièce
de resistance*, the most conspicuous symbol of their effort to arouse the
Roman in their honeymooners.

About twenty by twenty feet, the honeymoon bathrooms, embel-
lished with pink-tiled walls, are Romanized by virtue of "Pompeiian"
stone benches, a tall stone vase, and a sunken, oval bathtub. Next to the
deep, double-size bathtub is a wall-to-wall mirror which makes the
huge room (equal in size to the bedroom) seem even larger. For cloudy
honeymoon days, a sun lamp is provided, conveniently located above a
chaise lounge. The double-sink vanity table features a marble-
patterned pink formica design, while up two steps on the bathtub
platform stands a tall pink column above which protrudes the shower
head. Atop this column, surveying the entire bathroom, rests a stone
cupid who wears a dazed, open-mouthed expression, as if of disbelief.

"If you've ever yearned to feel like Cleopatra, you will here . . .
especially now that you have a Caesar to call your own!" So states a
Pocono Gardens brochure in a confidential aside to the young brides.
Another brochure reminds the young men that "the Romans were a
virile people."

The owner's profess the belief that the way to a man's heart is
through a romantic Roman bathroom. A prospectus tells the brides that
the bathroom is "designed to make you the most glamorous bride that
ever bewitched an unsuspecting new husband."

"Dreams of ancient luxury" are supposed to "dance" through her
head in these $49-a-day Roman bathroom suites. She is further coun-
seled: "Accustomed though they were to the utmost in luxury, the most

pampered aristocrats of ancient Rome would have gasped in delight at the unbelievable splendor of these lavish Roman baths. Now you are the spoiled favorite as you step into the soothing calm of translucent blue water. . . ."

One travel agent, who had been sending honeymooners here for several years, finally came up to inspect the premises and was stunned when he confronted the bathrooms. He now refers to Pocono Gardens as the resort with "the sexy plumbing" where "Groucho, Harpo, and Chico should have made a 'Marx Brothers on Their Honeymoon' epic."

But Pocono Gardens is not alone in spotlighting its bathroom virtues; all the honeymoon resorts concentrate heavily on their elegant bathrooms, supporting a *Life* Magazine spread on America's bathroom-directed culture which stated that Americans have nearly fifty million bathrooms, more than the rest of the world put together. Every honeymoon resort brochure I saw devotes a dramatic amount of art and copy to the bathrooms. One resort, with a more flamboyant product than most, lavishly spotlights its heart-shaped, jumbo-size bathtubs.

Pocmont's brochure, for example, demonstrates how bathroom adjectives are indicative of the price fluctuations. During the high season, June 29 to September 13, the $56 plan offers a bathroom that is super-enlarged, ceramic-tiled, twin-sinked, sun-lamped, air-conditioned, step-down-Roman-sunken-tubbed. In the copy for the $48 plan, one finds "a tastefully decorated, cozy bathroom," for $42, a "lovely bathroom," and way down the list, for $34, "complete bath and shower across from the room."

Pocono Gardens' Roman motif continues into the bedroom, whose most prominent feature is a gargantuan, six-foot-wide bed. ("King size? No king ever dreamed such magnificence. No queen ever sank into such luxury.") The bed itself is flanked by marble columns of the pink formica pattern found in the bathroom. Promotional pamphlets hail the bedroom as "a retreat worthy of the most fastidious honeymooners."

Most newly-weds here aren't the least distressed by this overpowering, decidedly burlesque appeal. The general effect of the Roman suite is to give the honeymooning couple a feeling of opulent indulgence and to make them feel larger than life. Pocono Gardens' accommodations for fifty couples are solidly booked almost year-round and it is frequently difficult for a bride and groom to receive space for anything less than a week—a sure sign that the public is pleased.

That the merchandisers of Pocono honeymoons amply understand their clientele is evidenced by a costly color brochure put out by Honeymoon Haven. The resort could have used professional, glamorous models for their pamphlet—but they deliberately chose not to. Instead, its cover pictures a young, ordinary-looking couple gazing into each other's eyes in front of a fireplace. The boy's skin is vaguely blemished; the girl is pasty-skinned with bleached blond hair that didn't come out right. Theirs are the faces of average people—Everyman and Everywoman—real people.

Although Pocono Gardens puts out a daily newspaper, printed on pink paper and called "Honeymoon Gossip," which reminds guests that "shorts and hair curlers are not permitted in the dining room," dinner often reveals a couple of brides in pin-curls. Indulging themselves in the dream world of a once-orgiastic civilization, the majority of the girls wear slacks to dinner, while the boys usually wear sport shirts and sweaters.

The age level is on a par with most other local establishments, roughly eighteen- and nineteen-year-olds. Further information about the resort's honeymooners is conveyed on a certificate posted near the office, inscribed "The Midnight Club," on which are listed the honeymooners who had stayed up past midnight. During a recent week the names were: Mascis, McColgan, DiSanto, Errico, Smith, Maddalone, Otero, and Ponzio.

Ed, the social director who formed the post-midnight honeymoon club, generally moves from table to table, kibitzing with his guests in the dining room. Not married, he is an extrovertish, glib young man in his mid-twenties.

"Hey," he hailed us. "I'm Ed, the social director. You folks going to be with us for the week?"

"No, just for the day, through tomorrow afternoon," I replied.

"Oh—" Ed broke off, immediately giving us the once-over. "Well, are you coming to the magic show tonight?"

"You bet," I responded.

"Swell," he laughed. "See ya . . ."

The waiters in the Pocono Gardens dining room contribute to the relaxed atmosphere by frequently sitting down at the tables of the guests and making small-talk with them. The waiters, who do not wear togas, are young enough so that, out of their steward uniforms, they could pass for honeymooning grooms themselves.

Our waiter, Bob, approached our table just as Ed left. Not yet acquainted with the resort's informality, we had on suit and tie and dress and heels—unconventional dining room attire that immediately marked us as newcomers.

"Hi," Bob called out from halfway across the dining room. "You miss the sign or something?"

My wife flushed, embarrassed at being in the wrong costume, and wondering why we didn't see the sign that would have told her how to dress.

"What sign?" I asked.

"Hey," Bob laughed, turning to the other tables. "How 'bout that. Whaddya think? They didn't see the sign."

Laughter greeted his announcement.

"I mean you missed lunch. You must have passed the sign and kept going. It's the *biggest* sign in the Poconos," he roared.

The laughter swelled.

"Oh," I said, catching on, "You mean the big red and white sign on the highway that says 'Pocono Gardens.' Sure, we saw *that* sign."

"Well, *that's* the sign," Bob said, hefting a trayload of dishes. Shaking his head, chuckling still, he went back to the kitchen.

Conversations among groups of honeymooners at Pocono Gardens are generally as wholesome as the activities offered to them. The only subject scrupulously avoided is honeymooning *per se*. "Put your arm around me. Peck me on the cheek, for heaven's sake," my wife cautioned, lest we be spotted for phony honeymooners. But I saw no evidence of passion at the honeymooneries, nothing that suggested these newly-wed teen-agers were doing anything less wholesome than engaging in a clean-cut, well-coordinated, perfectly surrealistic program of activities planned by a good summer camp.

But what exactly *do* the honeymooners talk about? In the main lounge at Pocono Gardens, where there is always a couple sitting around watching television, one evening's small talk among the grooms focused on cars, how much to tip, the temperature of the water in the pool, and what a wiseguy Ed the social director was. Of the boys in this particular group, one worked in the General Motors plant in Tarrytown; another, Frank, at a service station near Hartford; another at the Sylvania factory in Williamsport, Pa.; and another was a rookie policeman in New York.

While the boys joked about Ed, their brides discussed fashion and domestic subjects: whether to wear their hair up or down, and who ever had any experience cooking. One of the girls was a telephone operator in Camden; another was a secretary in a Staten Island insurance office; a third worked in a lingerie shop in Binghamton, N.Y. Sue, the Camden girl, noted that her best friend came here on her honeymoon and loved it. Apart from her friend's recommendation, she said she had first heard about Pocono Gardens from reading the ads in the bride's magazines.

The Staten Island secretary concurred. Her face pale under a heavy layer of white make-up, she said she knew about the honeymoon resorts because they all had regular advertisements in the bride's magazines. And since there are so many of them, she and her husband, two months before they were married, had come up to scout around the honeymoon places and see which they preferred. As soon as they saw Pocono Gardens, they both agreed immediately. "It's the greatest," she said. "The Roman stuff is so cute."

The bespectacled Binghamton girl said that she always read the bride's magazines because they had so much in them on setting the table, buying a trousseau, sending out thank-you cards, getting along with your in-laws, and things like that. She said she had been reading the bride's magazines for the last six months. "But it's funny," she said with a plaintive look. "All of a sudden I guess I won't be reading them anymore." Her friends laughed.

A young bride named Sandy, thin and looking scarcely sixteen, who was later to serve the magician as a helper with many of his tricks, laughed over the fact that her husband didn't have a job. "I'm not worried. When we get back, he'll get something. I'm going to be at home, though, a real housewife, while he's out looking for a job. I mean, my mother never worked."

On that particular evening, in the recreation room next to the lounge,

Ed the social director brought out The Great Schankweiler, the magician. According to Ed's introduction, The Great Schankweiler lived six miles away, across from the bowling alley. Sporting a wide-mouthed grin, The Great Schankweiler looked like a lanky Fernandel. He received a generous round of applause and catcalls from his audience.

Appearing a bit sensitive by the reference to his home, The Great Schankweiler (while a girl named Dolores—who said she was from the Bronx—held a rope that he cut with a giant scissors) related that he really came from Inwood. "That's in Manhattan, above the George Washington Bridge," he noted, as he showed how the rope miraculously became a single strand after all his snipping.

"Anybody out there know where Inwood is?" he asked.

Nobody did.

Presiding over a tableful of odd-shaped boxes, eggs, red and yellow scarves, black wands, and decks of giant cards, the magician by turns mystified and delighted his audience. Although his routine ranged over some fairly standard now-you-see-it-now-you-don't material, he progressed professionally from card choosing and scarf gambits through eggs in tophats. His most successful trick, judging from the laughter accompanying it, concerned calling Sandy up to face her husband and turn an eggbeater at him. The eggbeater was supposed to represent a divining rod through which she would be able to read her husband's mind as he wrote down various numbers in collaboration with the magician. Sandy, churning the eggbeater pointed at her husband, squealed excitedly every time the right number came up.

In another trick, The Great Schankweiler passed around five envelopes and asked five brides and grooms to place a small object in each, something about the size of a coin or a matchstick. He knew the five whom he had given the envelopes, but did not know who put what object in which envelope. He then set about returning the objects to their rightful owners. Correct on each one, he returned the last of the five small objects to Sandy. She had enclosed her wedding ring.

The Great Schankweilers's magic act ended promptly at 9:30. Within a few minutes, everyone disappeared from the room—except the one couple remaining behind to play the pinball machines. A new couple, he in a suit and she in tall spikes and a gold-flecked cocktail dress, came in at ten, both casting disappointed glances over the empty recreation room where the young Caesar in jeans out-pinballed his Cleopatra in pink slacks.

The next morning I took my Pocono Gardens receipt, with the word *paid* rubber-stamped inside a heart, and I left.

That something is terribly out of whack with all this was emphasized recently by one jaded New York travel agent who specializes in booking honeymoon trips: "I've never quite understood this compulsion to stay at an exclusively honeymooning hotel. Why is it so necessary for them to be with their own kind and have all these social programs? It's like some kind of group therapy."

He went on: "For every twenty couples I send to these resorts, I send four or five divorce cases to Mexico each week. Many of them are my former honeymoon clients. I mean, they're just kids and they don't know any better. If they knew better, they wouldn't stand for what goes on at these places. But the owners of a few of those honeymoon resorts must be millionaires. They do a fantastic business. They treat these kids like kings and queens, but they make monkeys out of them at the same time. Sometimes I think these honeymoon places are a dangerous institution."

Ultimately, the question remains: what are the Pocono honeymoon factories? Are they just a vaudeville joke in vulgar taste? Or are they the real American love story?

*So you're worried about the day you'll reach the last stop and how you don't want financing your finish to be a burden. But look, grin a little, decomposition can be fun. A cemetery is for the living, too. You can even take photographs and sunbathe.*

# The Fun Cemetery

## by Ralph Schoenstein

Some of Freud's disciples may be a bit strange, but the old man knew what he was talking about. For example, he said that we all have a death wish, a longing I confirmed a few years ago when I discovered the most colorful part of the American security blanket. One day while reading a newspaper, I saw an attractive full-page ad. Seated on a white filigreed bench were two pretty young women, who seemed to be enjoying a garden party. Nearby on a flowery lane, two smiling boys strolled with their father, who was pointing to some happy sight. At first, I thought the ad was for picnic baskets or lawn seed; and then I saw the print below: all these people were enjoying a cemetery.

Jessica Mitford may have told you about morticians, but I suspect you haven't met the cemetery salesmen who've followed such ads into my home. They haven't come for me because I'm thirty pounds under-weight but because they want to make me happy, for this is the age of the fun cemetery. Not only is death sweet, but tomb-hopping is a treat. The old graveyard has more than a new look: it has good times for *all* the family. Not only can Dad enjoy a stroll with the boys, but there's even a place for lovers: another ad says, "Cheerful Long Island Cemetery Appeals to Young Couples." And this romantic spot isn't even as gay as most of the new bone heaps, for the modern cemetery isn't a cemetery at all: it's a resort.

"Young Families Choose Pinelawn Because It Doesn't *Look* Like a

Cemetery," says another ad. It's heartening to see that interment has become a sentimental favorite of smart young marrieds who know how to enjoy a brighter tomorrow today. In spite of the triumph of geriatrics, teen-age couples with *joie de vivre* have been flocking to Pinelawn to get more out of life. They never mistake it for a cemetery. To some, it's a game preserve; to others, a national park. Still others see it as a friendly roadside mausoleum, a Howard Johnson's of the Great Beyond. "Every detail of Pinelawn," says the ad, "gives people an entirely new feeling about cemeteries." To be honest, which of us really cared for his old one? But now, when a young couple ends a day of frolicking at Pinelawn, the boy can tell the girl with a brave smile and hope in his heart, "You know, darling, I have an entirely new feeling about cemeteries. I *like* them."

After reading more than a dozen such ads, I wrote to some of the cemeteries to see how I could get in on the fun. These eternal resorts were so full of pleasure that I just had to look into them, even though my blood pressure was normal. By return mail, I received pamphlets, maps, and blotters from six sporty graveyards, each of which was eager to plant me, each of which was trying to prove that *it* was the smartest place to decompose. In one of the pamphlets, a smiling father is reading to his smiling son and daughter while nearby their mother smiles, too. Why are they all so tickled? Because on the table are papers labeled LIFE INSURANCE, LAST WILL AND TESTAMENT OF GEORGE SMITH, and CEMETERY DEED. I can't imagine what Dad is grinning about, but Mom and the kids know the insurance is fully paid and they know what's in that will. In fact, wouldn't you like to come stair-climbing with us, Dad?

"This cemetery is for the living!" cries Mount Ararat.

"We are the Garden Cemetery," answers Woodlawn. "We have lots to suit every taste and need." When you see the dazzling flora in Woodlawn's brochure, you feel that this place would rather plant roses than people.

But Pinelawn is even further from death. "Pinelawn Memorial Park is designed for the living," says its ad. "Visits there are pleasant." Pleasant? They're delightful. During one of my recent gambols at Pinelawn (I often weekend there if the weather holds), I realized that this fun cemetery is *entirely* designed for the living. I saw only three graves, charming relics of an earlier time. The number of graves is so carefully restricted because most of Pinelawn is devoted to "priceless works of art and magnificent formal gardens—just like a private estate." This is why I look forward to the time when I can weekend there forever: I've always wanted to be buried under a Venus de Milo in someone's home instead of in a field that's cluttered with the dead.

"The appearance of our park is so pleasing," says Beth Israel Memorial Park, whose ad shows two pretty girls at a lawn party. "Each section looks like a private garden. Beautiful trees and flower beds are on every side." This is the horticultural view of eternity. Americans no longer die: they go to botanical gardens; and at Woodlawn, they have a choice of plant. A map that Woodlawn sent me divides this ghostly garden into more than forty species of vegetation, including butternut, honeysuckle, juniper, sycamore, magnolia, hyacinth, and sassafras. Judy says she's dying for primrose, but I won't go unless I get syringa. My mother would love to join us, but she can't; she's allergic.

Once the modern cemetery has convinced you that it has nothing to do with death, it goes on to lure you with more specific attractions and rewards. Says Pinelawn: "The use of bronze memorial tablets set level with the lawn, instead of competing headstones, is exactly what younger people want." How true! Just last night, I passed a junior high school where younger people were staging a big pep rally. When I saw them leaping through a bonfire, I knew they were moved by a great cause. Some carried posters saying NO COMPETING HEADSTONES! DON'T MAKE DEATH THE OLYMPICS! Soon they began to chant:

> *Listen to our angry chorus:*
> *No competing headstones for us!*
> *We got the brains, we got the brawn*
> *To lay bronze tablets on the lawn!*

Beth Israel Memorial Park also pushes bronze, while Mount Ararat entices you with a choice of flat bronze or raised marble; but it reminds you that the bronze gives you "a saving that may equal the cost of a plot for four." In other words, why be foolish enough to put Dad under some silly angel when you could add Mom and the twins to him under a

hunk of bronze. Moreover, the angel would spoil Dad's "unobstructed
view of multicolored flower beds, meditation retreats, and velvety
lawns."

Besides the stylish use of bronze, there are many other features that
make the modern fun cemetery so appealing. For example, Pinelawn
has its own station on the Long Island Rail Road, the one station where
more people always get off than on. Thus Pinelawn is the only cemetery
in America that's a local stop as well as the last one. However, since the
Long Island often is, fittingly enough, late when it reaches Pinelawn,
many commuters prefer to use car pools.

At first, my sepulchral education came only from ads, brochures, and
picnics at Pinelawn; but then I was assaulted by the salesmen with the
world's hardest job: to make death attractive, to convince you that you
don't have to take it with you because things will be delightful when
you get there. They are not only a cheerful breed, they are strangely
optimistic. Soon after I'd sent for my brochures, I got a telephone call
from a man at Beth Israel. He called himself a "memorial counselor,"
which sounded as though he were an undertaker at a boys' camp.

"First of all," he said breezily, "I want you to know right away that
we're *not* a cemetery." In one encouraging line, he had dissociated
himself from the dead. Then he spoke the words I had grown to love:
"We're a memorial park. Naturally, our program costs a little more . . ."

"But it's worth the extra pennies," I said, glad to learn that Beth
Israel had all the class of Chock full o' Nuts.

"Absolutely," he said. "You see, since we're a memorial park, we have
flat bronze markers, not upright stones."

"Oh, *several* places can give me *that*," I said, throwing him off stride
with my new knowledge.

"But—well, are you also aware that our groundskeepers can cut, seed,
and lime ten thousand graves a day?"

"Wow! That's *liming*, all right—and seeding, too. Yes, I *do* want my
neighbors to be trim."

"Right. You don't want your cemetery to look like a graveyard!"

"You mean your *memorial park*."

"Of course. And you know, we're the *only* park where people can
take pictures."

Funereal photography was surely a unique attraction; but I saw no reason why it shouldn't be part of a family outing at the park—if, of course, it's kept in good taste.

"We are known among other cemeteries as the elite," said the counselor. "Discriminating people are going for our way of protection— and this is the time to get it; prices keep going up, you know."

"Well," I said, feeling my pulse, "I'll have to think this over awhile. Let me call you in a few weeks."

"I think I'd better call *you*, Mr. Schoenstein. The last thing a young man does on his own is buy cemetery property. He must have either of two motivations: death or a memorial counselor."

The following day, a motivation from Pinelawn offered me even better attractions. This man didn't say whether he was a counselor or even a junior counselor, but he was so anxious to bury me that he came to my home. As I hid in the shower, Judy told him I was out and expressed surprise at such a visit since I'd only sent for a brochure.

"I thought it was a rush order," he said.

Judy assured him we all felt fine and told him to return in a few days, for she knew I was still shaken from my talk with the memorial counselor. In fact, I'd started drinking cheap sacramental wine, the only sensible thing to do after hearing a cemetery salesman.

Moments after Pinelawn's man had left, the phone rang.

"Mr. Schoenstein," said a bright voice, "this is Mr. Hardin, of Mount Ararat. You wrote for our booklet and I was wondering how you learned about us. Was it from a friend or from our landscape ad?"

I dropped the phone and followed it to the floor. "*Listen*," I cried, "I can do *nine* pushups! One . . . two . . . three . . . four . . . five . . . six . . . seven . . . eight—and . . . *nine!* You see, I just wrote 'cause I'm in-vestigating—I mean, I'm not really ready to—look, could I call you back in a few months?"

"How about our having a little talk here at the office?"

"No, I'd rather call you back—say sometime around the middle of next year."

"Mr. Schoenstein, I think it would be better if I called *you* next week."

"But I'm only *thirty!*"

"Of course—and you probably have many years left; but we find that young people keep postponing the selection of a plot. And we understand why: it *is* a big investment; but it's one you have to make sooner or later. We'd like to help you make it sooner." He was delicately hinting at something his brochure had said more bluntly: REMEMBER— YOU'RE NOT IMMORTAL.

True to his word, he called back the next week and insisted on a meeting.

"Mr. Harding," I said, "I didn't tell you this, but my whole family is at Union Fields, so I think I'll stick with them. Grandma always wanted us to spend more time together."

"I see," he said coldly. "I can respect that. Of course, you realize that prices there are quite high since there's such little space left. Now let me just give you our prices as compared to Union Fields, and then you can see if you're still anxious to go there. I can give you two graves for only . . ."

After he'd explained the various ways he could plant me wholesale, I told him to stay in his own memorial park, which was a polite way of saying drop dead.

"All right, then," he said. "Good luck."

To be wished good luck by a cemetery salesman is to receive a decidedly mixed blessing.

Meanwhile, two days after his first visit, the man from Pinelawn returned. "I know all about Pinelawn," I said, trying to shorten his pitch. "I often sunbathe there. You're a memorial park, not a stone cemetery, and you even have your own railroad station."

"Yes," he said with a smile, "*everyone* knows that; but there are several other features that I think you'd like to hear about. For example, we're forty feet above sea level."

"Oh, then there's no problem with tides."

"None whatsoever. Moreover, all our grave care is by automation. One man with a power mower can handle so many more graves than a gardener mowing by hand. Mr. Schoenstein, with our various gardens and our European marble statuary, we're the most beautiful park in America." He opened a small map. "Now this is Heritage Garden, our loveliest and most exclusive section. In here, we have our most beautiful plantings. Also, the graves are larger than average, so you can walk completely around them, something you can't usually do with graves. As you see, all these plots radiate from the Pool of Herons."

"Well," I said, "how much would—oh, say two poolside graves be?"

"Two graves near the center of Heritage Garden would be fifteen hundred dollars. As you see, the choice locations are against the walls. These go first because they afford more privacy. Of course, just as most people don't own Cadillacs, most people at Pinelawn aren't in Heritage Garden; it's just for a discriminating few." He put down the small map and opened a huge one. "Most people are quite happy to be in the rest of our park, which you see is almost as lovely. This is our main Garden of Sanctuary. The plantings aren't as lush and you can't walk completely around the graves, but the prices are modest and you enjoy almost the same advantages: there's wall space available and there are several benches and Japanese cherry trees."

For five minutes, he talked of the most permanent low-cost housing, of why I should turn to dust at popular prices. "To be perfectly frank," he finally said, pointing to a corner of the map, "in this area, where two graves are four hundred dollars, you don't get our most elegant plantings. However—and this is something that only *we* have—no matter *where* your plot is, a driveway takes you right to the grave. A woman can step from her car, throw a stone, and hit her family plot."

He was so proud of this feature that I didn't have the heart to tell him that we could never take advantage of it because Judy couldn't hit a mausoleum at ten feet; she has no control of her fastball in cemeteries. But I did have the heart to launch a general counterattack: "Well, I appreciate your frankness and I'm going to be just as frank with you: I like what I see at Woodlawn."

"Oh, Woodlawn is fine," he said, "if you happen to like stone cemeteries. Some distinguished names are there. It has—well, snob appeal; you know, sort of a keeping up with the Joneses. Of course, we have several big names, too, but we don't advertise."

I showed him a page in my Woodlawn brochure. "I don't mean to flaunt your competition, but—"

"Oh," he said with a laugh, "there's room for all of us."

"But this place does give a feeling of quiet class. I like the crowd. See, it says, 'For the elite.' I think it may be more important to be with a group you like and have five thousand graves limed a day than to be with an unsociable group and lime ten thousand."

"Of course. But—"

"And their prices also vary according to location. Since it's a New York cemetery, I imagine the East Side is smarter than the West." He rose and went for his coat. "In fact, Woodlawn even has a different flower for each section. I wonder if the prices also vary according to scent."

"I wouldn't know. You see, I—"

"Of course, there *is* no subway on the grounds. You've got them there with your railroad station."

"Mr. Schoenstein, suppose we talk again in a few days."

As he walked to the elevator, I fired a parting shot: "All right, but I think you should know that I'm also quite interested in Rosedale."

"Oh, no," he called back, "don't get something in Jersey. You don't know how much red tape there is when you take a body across a state line." And then he was gone, while I wondered how much red tape *is* there when you take a body across a state line? Perhaps I should call the Mafia and find out.

At all the parks I've explored, prices vary not only by location but also by elevation. That is, you can have two interments in a single grave: one at seven feet and the other at five. No park would tell me which is more stylish, the upper or the lower; but no matter which you want, you must book yourself in advance, as if you were sailing on the *Queen Elizabeth.*

You may feel that the exact location of your corpse doesn't really matter, just as long as it's out of the house; but in America today, the street where you lie is the mark of your ultimate status. In one pamphlet, two smiling old sweethearts are pointing to a spot on a map being held by their friendly cemetery salesman. "This is just what we want!" says the husband. And you can tell that he and his girl have spent their lives dreaming of being put in that special hole, that final security for senior citizens. Junior citizens in the pamphlet have the same dream, for it tells us beneath the picture of a young couple, "By selecting long before need, there is ample opportunity to get the best of many preferred locations, to make sure that resting places will be just where you want them—not 'stuck in some corner.' "

This pamphlet also discusses the financing of your finish, a matter on which the salesmen are poetic. "Because fate makes no appointments," it says, "select a location now and 'take your time' on our Convenient

Payment Plan. Your family is protected from the moment you make a small down payment. It's like 'money in the bank.' " True, but it's the kind of vault that's hard to open.

The Beth Israel salesman told me that the moment you put some money down, you can drop dead. But the Pinelawn man said that you can feel free to die only when a whole grave is paid for. You can't be buried on margin, he explained, because once you're settled there, eviction is a sticky business. "But we do have an extended-time payment plan," he said, "with no interest or carrying charges."

Judy feels we should enroll in Pinelawn's die now–pay later plan because it would give us gorgeous gardens, noncompetitive headstones, priceless works of art, flood insurance, high-speed seeding, graveside strolling, and a railroad station. The Pinelawn package is surely inviting, but I'd like us to die for Beth Israel. Of all the parks with their gay enticements, this one has the most inspired bonus: the Bible Gardens of Israel, a sprawling outdoor museum with such displays as "the miracle of the splitting of the Red Sea, the discovery of the infant Moses in an authentic bulrush pond, authentic Bible plants, a twelve-ton Holy Land boulder with a sculpture of Moses receiving the Ten Commandments, episodes from the lives of the early Kings of Israel, authentic Cedars of Lebanon, ore from King Solomon's mines, and the well of Rebecca." All these wonders are bounded by such streets as Jordan Avenue, Emanuel Drive, Spinoza Place, Goshen Walk, Hope Lane, and Farm Road. One of these streets takes you past The Burning Bush to the Divine Oath to the Patriarchs, engraved on the biggest block of marble ever carved out of the Holy Land.

Beth Israel calls all this "an atmosphere in which children visit willingly and often." Of course. Kids will always go to Disneyland.

*YOU have listened to the insurance agent and you have provided for your loved ones in the event you meet accidental death, dismemberment, or some form of medical catastrophe. Now that you are covered, why don't you find security in the thought that you are worth more dead than alive?*

# Hands Up! They've Got You Covered

*by Chris Welles*

Perhaps tonight is your night for a visit from a Protector, the man who has the answer to all your worries in his Slimline attaché case. He, and his counterparts (Blue-Chip Agent, MONY Man), are fanning out about the city tonight and every night, dapper Johnny Appleseeds stepping into living rooms and kitchens to bestow, through careful direction of a little family drama, the American Dream of blissful freedom from financial care. Their good works are responsible for that monument of capitalistic achievement, the life insurance industry, which has some three quarters of a trillion dollars worth of "protection" in force. By the end of each day, another $300 million worth is added.

He is standing there in your doorway in his dark suit and white shirt, with his hat in his hand, smiling, eager to come in and give you coverage and provide your loved ones with a Family Security Check-up, to "help you lay the groundwork for a lifetime of financial security" so you can be "certain everything comes out right."

You didn't want to talk to him at first, of course. You're often badgered by insurance salesmen. Even though he quickly mentioned he was your sister's brother-in-law's friend when he called you at the office, you told him you already had plenty of insurance.

"I realize you've been buying a lot of policies to keep pace with your growing family responsibilities," he replied. "But let me tell you what happened when I was out for a long drive with my family last Sunday after church. I noticed that I hadn't heard a sound for a long time from the back seat where my wife and two sons were riding. I looked back and they were all fast asleep. *They were asleep*, while *I* was steering the car along the highway at sixty miles an hour. My family—and your family, too—have great confidence that their Daddy will bring them safely home and keep them out of trouble.

"This little incident gave me an insight into my responsibility for those who confidently 'leave it to Daddy.' Listen, I *know* you want the right thing for your family. Let's make sure their confidence in you is not misplaced. How about tomorrow evening around eight at your home?"

His comments about responsibility hit you rather hard. The times are tough, what with your associates climbing all over you on the job, your wife snatching at the reins of family decision-making when you're too tired to care, your kids snickering at your over-thirty obtuseness. But though everyone may carp, you get some solace knowing *you supply the bread*—that's your little area of unassailable expertise and authority— and you figure you just better find out whether it's in good shape.

And besides, you had to admit, he was, as he made clear to you, an Expert, backed by an "electronic computer programmed to come up with the optimum level of security for your family." He may even have had the National Quality Award. He may have been a Chartered Life Underwriter or a member of the renowned Million Dollar Round Table.

(*He didn't tell you, of course, that most likely he has been selling life insurance only a few weeks—indeed, according to one estimate, some 90 per cent of all new insurance salesmen quit within ninety days. Insurance companies hire salesmen in droves—they'll take virtually anyone who can read. The companies know selling insurance is extremely frustrating, often demeaning, and usually very low paying— expecially when one is earning only straight commission right from the start. But before the new man quits, the companies figure he will at least be able to sign up a fair number of his relatives and friends, who*

*are naturally much easier to sell. These new policies more than com-*
*pensate for the expense of the new man's brief training, which usually*
*consists much more of the psychology of the sell than of the nature of*
*life insurance itself. One of the first things the novice learns is that it is*
*usually a good thing to meet with you at home where your defenses*
*are down and where your wife can "help" you make a decision.*)

He is casual and smooth when he walks in, willing to talk about
anything but life insurance. He admires your tasteful choice of furniture, your wife's well-appointed kitchen. "You mean that lovely water
color was done by a mere seven-year-old?" He sits back and lets you
talk proudly about your childrens' undeniable precocity.

Then, after a while, when the coversation hits a lull, he remarks, "You
know, that reminds me of a friend of mine, George Collins. George
asked me just the other day, 'Frank, how do people these days, with the
cost of living and other financial factors as high as they are, find a way
to save the money they need for later on?' And, you know, it *is* a
problem, don't you think so?" It certainly is, you agree.

"Now let's just take you for example," he says. "Let's look at your
situation in the later years and see what would happen if [a long meaningful pause] *your time is cut short.*" You certainly want the children
to be able to continue living in the house they love, he says. Certainly, you say. And you'd like them to get the best education, he goes
on. Of course, you nod. And naturally you would want your wife to
maintain her same standard of living. He looks briefly at your wife, who
glances at you and smiles.

"Of course," he says, "nobody can expect *any* father to provide for
all of this *all by himself*—in the event that he is no longer on the scene."
Oh, of course, you quickly agree. *Nobody* could expect that. You begin
to feel a kind of growling, deep down in the intestines someplace.

He nods. After eliciting a bit of information on your salary, your
mortgage and present insurance program, and so forth, he spends a
couple of minutes figuring away on a piece of graph paper. You feel
like you were back in college, waiting around for the professor to post
the mid-term grades up on the bulletin board.

Finally he looks up, his face showing just a trace of concern. Your
wife looks first at him, then at you. You lean forward. "Well, I mean

you've made a fine start on a realistic insurance program and I want to commend you. You're obviously a breadwinner who cares deeply about his family. However there *are* a few things you should know. The figures here show that, with your present insurance, if you were suddenly not in the picture tomorrow, things could be a little rough for mom and the kids. For instance, she would have only a third of your present income to live on and even that would run out once your children reached college. That says nothing about your children's expenses in college, and you know how high they're getting to be. And, I might add, that income at retirement is going to be mighty, mighty small."

"My goodness, dear," your wife says helpfully. "I never realized our situation was so bad." She is frowning. For an instant, you see her on a shabby street corner, wrapping a moth-eaten shawl a little tighter around her neck to keep out the driving snow, her wizened outstretched hand holding a tin can of pencils.

"What would you think if I had a plan," the salesman says, his voice building like the last movement of a Mahler symphony, "that could solve these problems and satisfy all your other future financial needs, that would not only protect your family if you were not here but would build up a nice nest egg for the golden years of retirement?" That would be a heck of a good thing, you say much too fast.

(*He doesn't tell you, of course, that it is virtually impossible for you to buy enough insurance to compensate fully for your disappearance from this life, to pay all your debts, support your family in the style to which they have become accustomed, finance college educations, and take care of you and/or your wife in old age. You'd almost be bankrupt after the first premiums. But playing on your feelings of inadequacy, the salesman will squeeze as much of a premium out of you as he thinks you will go along with. In other words, it is the premium, not the protection, that is adjusted to fit your salary.*)

"Well," he says smiling, the kettle drums rolling, "I think I've got just the plan for you. It will substantially increase the income your wife would receive until the children are all eighteen, and also add a lot to the money you and your wife will receive after retirement." He reels off some figures, then asks, "Do you think you could put aside just $25 a week to accomplish all these things? Certainly you could do that. Now let's see, when did you last visit a doctor? You were born in 1937, weren't you?"

He begins taking some more papers out of his attaché case and spreading them on the table. Your wife has her eyes closed and her lips are moving as if she were updating her estimate of how much she would get if you were not in attendance tomorrow.

You realize that not only have you given implied consent to additional insurance but you've virtually committed yourself to a premium. Signing is only seconds away.

"Now hold it a moment," you demand. "Just what is this plan you're talking about." The salesman smiles paternally.

(*He doesn't mention, of course, that all of his training emphasizes this basic principle: stress not what insurance is but what it does. Trying to explain it only interferes with selling it. Indeed, often the salesman himself will be unsure of many of the intricacies.*)

"What we're talking about," the salesman says matter-of-factly, "is a standard StraightWholeOrdinaryPaid-UpPermanentParticipatoryLife-AnnuityEndowmentRetirement-IncomePermanentCashSurrenderValue ExecutiveSpecial-Type plan."

Oh I see, you say. Well, maybe I don't see, you say. What does participatory mean? "That of course involves," he answers, "the DividendAdditionContingency-LaybackProvision with the GuaranteedInsurabilityDividend-OptionRiderMinimumDepositExtraSpecialAutomaticConversion-DoubleIndemnity privilege. It's one of our newest programs."

Oh. Your wife is making impatient clicking sounds with her tongue. "Now dear, we don't want to waste this nice man's time, do we?" she offers. Both your wife and the salesman are looking at you a little as though you were the last person in third grade to catch on to long division.

But you persist. Why can't I just buy some straight life insurance protection without trying to build up a lot of cash, you ask. Wouldn't that be a lot cheaper? "That's a good, perceptive question and I'm glad

you asked it," the salesman replies. "But I'm afraid that you're missing the point. If you think about it for a moment, you will agree, I'm
sure, that you really *need* the total security package." His voice lingers
long and lovingly over the last three words, squeezing out their full
quota of overtones. "You need the rock, solid foundation of growing
cash reserves so that you may enjoy the rich harvest of those comfortable, safe, guaranteed savings in your Golden Years. You don't want
to miss out on all that, do you? Of course you don't."

*(He doesn't tell you, of course, that the trick of combining a straight
insurance policy with a savings or investment plan—as is done in most
individual policies—results in an almost scandalous waste of money to
most policyholders. Premiums, for a number of ingenious hidden ac-
tuarial reasons, are grossly high and while your so-called nest egg
accumulates at a miserably slow rate unprotected from inflation, the
insurance company meanwhile invests that money itself at two, three,
or more times that rate. The tables are tilted against you in other ways:
if you die before retirement, your widow never gets the benefit of all
those nest-egg provisions. She simply receives the face value of the
policy. Take a $10,000 policy with a cash value of $4,000. She receives
$10,000 all right, but that's $4,000 of your money and only $6,000 from
the insurance company. And if in an emergency you want to withdraw
your cash, you actually have to borrow it from the insurance company
at about 5 per cent interest. The result of this perfidious overcharging
and finagling is that insurance companies have been able to pile up im-
mense amounts of money, including some $45 billion that they will
never have to pay out at any time under any circumstances.*

*If the salesman really had your welfare in mind, he would advise you
to buy a simple "term" policy—straight protection and nothing more for
one third or one fourth the cost. A term policy gives most young
families maximum protection, at the lowest cost, when they need it
most. The difference between the premiums for the term policy and the
high-priced alternative can then be invested on your own at a much
higher interest. Not only will the nest egg build up much faster, but
you can get at it without paying interest. The salesman won't tell you
any of these things because, not unexpectedly, his commission is several
times greater for the nest-egg policy than for the term policy.)*

Despite the salesman's frequent reassurances, you still have nagging suspicions. I see what you're driving at, you say, but I'd still like to think it over for a while. There are more clicking noises from your wife.

"Now *honestly*, John," she says, "I *don't* think you should be so rude to the man. He's only trying to help you."

"I can well understand your hesitation," the salesman says sympathetically. "This is a big decision for you. But, just for a moment, forget I'm an insurance agent and regard me as an old friend who's had plenty of experience hitting the bumps down through the years. Now just think for a moment. If your wife should have to be rushed to the hospital for an emergency operation, you wouldn't want to hold things up while you inquired about surgeon's fees, would you?"

Um, of course not, you say.

"*Of course not*," he echos triumphantly. "Well . . . how long do you think you can put off making preparations for the day when you're no longer around the house? How long can your wife and children afford to be without this protection? What would happen if you should [unleashing the zinger at last] WRAP YOUR CAR AROUND A TREE TOMORROW? OR EVEN TONIGHT? WHAT THEN?" He sits back in his chair, folding his arms in front of him.

"You really have to think what could happen, John," your wife contributes.

They both stare at you. You feel that while you're getting upset about a bothersome mosquito, the Viet Cong are massing to overrun your outpost. You sigh and relax your shoulders.

"Now, let's get some of the bookkeeping details out of the way," the salesman says smoothly. "When did you say the last time was that you saw a doctor?"

You submit to the questions. Then after your form is filled out, the salesman, jabbing for your increasingly soft underbelly, declares, "And now that we have you all taken care of, don't you think we ought to start thinking about your wife?"

My wife?

"Certainly. Now if something happened to her, God forbid, it would take not just one but several full-time employees to do all the work she does for you and the kids around the house." Your wife unsuccessfully tries to supress a modest smile "Don't you think you should have some insurance for her, too? I mean, we have to think about her contribution to the family, too, don't we? Don't you think I'm right?" The salesman starts writing again.

*(He doesn't explain, of course, that the wages of these replacement employees would probably be far less than the cost of feeding, clothing, doctoring, and entertaining your wife, and that premiums on your wife's policy would do much more good adding to your own.)*

"And what about your children?" he inquires mercilessly. "A policy taken out now will help pay college costs—the quality education your two young boys deserve—and give them a good solid start in life when they're twenty-one."

*(He doesn't point out that in addition to all the disadvantages of letting the insurance company do your saving for you, even straight protection insurance on children is pointless. A child's death actually lessens the parents' financial burden—if he dies he can't go to college. Premium money in an outside savings account will give children a much better start in life.)*

You nod resignedly about this, too. Quickly, after the salesman has extracted a prepayment check, a signature, and your agreement on a doctor's appointment, he is gone into the night. But unless you're curious enough in the interim to read some unbiased analyses of life insurance by organizations like Consumers Union, all your doubts will have vanished by the time the salesman delivers the policy a week or so later.

You'll believe, your arm comfortably over wife's shoulder, that you've defeated the ravages of death, the bleakness of old age, the financial uncertainties of these perilous times. And most important, you've fulfilled your responsibilities as a father, husband, and breadwinner. It's a good feeling, knowing you've entrusted your family's security to an Expert.

*So you've got some vacation time saved up
and you'd like to check out the desert, maybe do
a little gambling in those exciting, revolving, os-
cillating, shrieking, clattering, yahooing casinos
you've heard so much about.*

# Las Vegas (What?)

*by Tom Wolfe*

Hernia, hernia, hernia, hernia, hernia, hernia, hernia, hernia, hernia, hernia, hernia, hernia, hernia, HERNia; hernia HERNia, hernia hernia hernia hernia, HERNia, HERNia, HERNia, hernia hernia, hernia, hernia, hernia, hernia, hernia, eight is the point, the point is eight; hernia, hernia, HERNia, hernia, hernia, hernia, hernia, all right, hernia, hernia, hernia, hernia, hernia, hard eight, hernia, hernia, hernia, HERNia, her- nia, hernia, hernia, HERNia, hernia, hernia, hernia, HERNia, hernia, hernia, hernia, hernia.

"What is all this *hernia hernia* stuff?"

This was Raymond talking to the wavy-haired fellow with the stick, the dealer, at the craps table about 3:45 Sunday morning. The stickman had no idea what this big wiseacre was talking about, but he resented the tone. He gave Raymond that patient arch of the eyebrows known as a Red Hook brush-off, which is supposed to convey some such thought as, I am a very tough but cool guy, as you can tell by the way I carry my eyeballs low in the pouches, and if this wasn't such a high-class joint we would take wiseacres like you out back and beat you into jellied madrilene.

At this point, however, Raymond was immune to subtle looks.

The stickman tried to get the game going again, but every time he would start up his singsong, by easing the words out through the nose, which seems to be the style among craps dealers in Las Vegas—"All right, a new shooter . . . eight is the point, the point is eight" and so

118

on—Raymond would start droning along with him in exactly the same tone of voice, "Hernia, hernia, hernia; hernia HERNia, HERNia, hernia; hernia, hernia, hernia."

Everybody at the craps table was staring in consternation to think that anybody would try to needle a tough, hip, elite *soldat* like a Las Vegas craps dealer. The gold-lamé odalisques of Los Angeles were staring. The Western sports, fifty-eight-year-old men who wear Texas string ties, were staring. The old babes at the slot machines, holding Dixie Cups full of nickels, were staring at the craps tables, but cranking away the whole time.

Raymond, who is thirty-four years old and works as an engineer in Phoenix, is big but not terrifying. He has the sort of thatchwork hair that grows so low all along the forehead there is no logical place to part it, but he tries anyway He has a huge, prognathous jaw, but it is as smooth, soft, and round as a melon, so that Raymond's total effect is that of an Episcopal divinity student.

The guards were wonderful. They were dressed in cowboy uniforms like Bruce Cabot in *Sundown* and they wore sheriff's stars.

"Mister, is there something we can do for you?"

"The expression is 'Sir,'" said Raymond. "You said 'Mister.' The expression is 'Sir.' How's your old Cosa Nostra?"

Amazingly, the casino guards were easing Raymond out peaceably, without putting a hand on him. I had never seen the fellow before, but possibly because I had been following his progress for the last five minutes, he turned to me and said, "Hey, do you have a car? This wild stuff is starting again."

The gist of it was that he had left his car somewhere and he wanted to ride up the Strip to the Stardust, one of the big hotel-casinos. I am describing this big goof Raymond not because he is a typical Las Vegas tourist, although he has some typical symptoms, but because he is a good example of the marvelous impact Las Vegas has on the senses. Raymond's senses were at a high pitch of excitation, the only trouble being that he was going off his nut. He had been up since Thursday afternoon, and it was now about 3:45 a.m. Sunday. He had an envelope full of pep pills—amphetamine—in his left coat pocket and an envelope full of Equanils—meprobamate—in his right pocket, or were the Equanils in the left and the pep pills in the right? He could tell by looking, but he wasn't going to look anymore. He didn't care to see how many were left.

He had been rolling up and down the incredible electric-sign gauntlet of Las Vegas' Strip, U.S. Route 91, where the neon and the par lamps—bubbling, spiraling, rocketing, and exploding in sunbursts ten stories high out in the middle of the desert—celebrate one-story casinos. He had been gambling and drinking and eating now and again at the buffet tables the casinos keep heaped with food day and night, but mostly hopping himself up with good old amphetamine, cooling himself down with meprobamate, then hooking down more alcohol, until now, after sixty hours, he was slipping into the symptoms of toxic schizophrenia.

He was also enjoying what the prophets of hallucinogen call "consciousness expansion." The man was psychedelic. He was beginning to isolate the components of Las Vegas' unique bombardment of the senses. He was quite right about this *hernia hernia* stuff. Every casino in Las Vegas is, among the other things, a room full of craps tables with dealers who keep up a running singsong that sounds as though they are saying "hernia, hernia, hernia, hernia, hernia" and so on. There they are day and night, easing a running commentary through their nostrils. What they have to say contains next to no useful instruction. Its underlying message is, we are the initiates, riding the crest of chance. That the accumulated sound comes out "hernia" is merely an unfortunate phonetic coincidence. Actually, it is part of something rare and rather grand: a combination of baroque stimuli that brings to mind the bronze gongs, no larger than a blue plate, that Louis XIV, his ruff collars larded with the lint of the foul Old City of Byzantium, personally hunted out in the bazaars of Asia Minor to provide exotic acoustics for his new palace outside Paris.

The sounds of the craps dealer will be in, let's say, the middle register. In the lower register will be the sound of the old babes at the slot machines. Men play the slots too, of course, but one of the indelible images of Las Vegas is that of the old babes at the row upon row of slot machines. There they are at six o'clock Sunday morning no less than at three o'clock Tuesday afternoon. Some of them pack their old hummocky shanks into Capri pants, but many of them just put on the old print dress, the same one day after day, and the old hob-heeled shoes, looking like they might be going out to buy eggs in Tupelo, Mississippi. They have a Dixie Cup full of nickels or dimes in the left hand and an Iron Boy work glove on the right hand to keep the calluses from getting sore. Every time they pull the handle, the machine makes a sound much like the sound a cash register makes before the bell rings, then the slot pictures start clattering up from left to right, the oranges, lemons, plums, cherries, bells, bars, buckaroos—the figure of a cowboy riding a bucking bronco. The whole sound keeps churning up over and over again in eccentric series all over the place, like one of those random-sound radio symphonies by John Cage. You can hear it at any hour of the day or night all over Las Vegas. You can walk down Fremont Street at dawn and hear it without even walking in a door, that and the spins of the wheels of fortune, a boring and not very popular sort of simplified roulette, as the tabs flap to a stop. As an overtone, or at times simply as a loud sound, comes the babble of the casino crowds, with an occasional shriek from the craps tables, or, anywhere from 4 p.m. to 6 a.m., the sound of brass instruments or electrified string instruments from the cocktail-lounge shows

The crowd and band sounds are not very extraordinary, of course. But Las Vegas' Muzak is. Muzak pervades Las Vegas from the time you walk into the airport from landing to the last time you leave the casinos. It is piped out to the swimming pool. It is in the drugstores. It is as if there were a communal fear that someone, somewhere in Las Vegas, was going to be left with a totally vacant minute on his hands.

Las Vegas has succeeded in wiring an entire city with this electronic stimulation, day and night, out in the middle of the desert. In the automobile I rented, the radio could not be turned off, no matter which dial you went after. I drove for days in a happy burble of Action Checkpoint News, "Monkey No. 9," "Donna, Donna, the Prima Donna," and picking-and-singing jingles for the Frontier Bank and the Fremont Hotel.

One can see the magnitude of the achievement. Las Vegas takes what in other American towns is but a quixotic inflammation of the senses for some poor salary mule in the brief interval between the flagstone rambler and the automatic elevator downtown and magnifies it, foliates it, embellishes it into an institution.

For example, Las Vegas is the only town in the world whose skyline

is made up neither of buildings, like New York, nor of trees, like
Wilbraham, Massachusetts, but signs. One can look at Las Vegas from a
mile away on Route 91 and see no buildings, no trees, only signs. But
such signs! They tower. They revolve, they oscillate, they soar in shapes
before which the existing vocabulary of art history is helpless. I can
only attempt to supply names—Boomerang Modern, Palette Curvilinear, Flash Gordon Ming-Alert Spiral, McDonald's Hamburger Parabola, Ming Casino Elliptical, Miami Beach Kidney. Las Vegas' sign
makers work so far out beyond the frontiers of conventional studio art
they they have no names themselves for the forms they create.
Vaughan Cannon, one of those tall, blond Westerners, the builders of
places like Las Vegas and Los Angeles, whose eyes seem to have been
bleached by the sun, is in the back shop of the Young Electric Sign
Company out on East Charleston Boulevard with Herman Boernge,
one of his designers, looking at the model they have prepared for the
Lucky Strike Casino sign, and Cannon points to where the sign's two
great curving faces meet to form a narrow vertical face and says:

"Well, here we are again—what do we call that?"

"I don't know," said Boernge. "It's sort of a nose effect. Call it a nose."

Okay, a nose, but it rises sixteen stories high above a two-story
building. In Las Vegas no farseeing entrepreneur buys a sign to fit a
building he owns. He rebuilds the building to support the biggest sign
he can get up the money for and, if necessary, changes the name. The
Lucky Strike Casino today is the Lucky Casino, which fits better when
recorded in sixteen stories of flaming peach and incandescent yellow in
the middle of the Mojave Desert. In the Young Electric Sign Co. era
signs have become the architecture of Las Vegas, and the most whimsi-
al, Yale-seminar-frenzied devices of the two late geniuses of Baroque
Modern, Frank Lloyd Wright and Eero Saarinen, seem rather stuffy
business, like a jest at a faculty meeting, compared to it. Men like
Boernge, Kermit Wayne, Ben Mitchem and Jack Larsen, formerly an
artist for Walt Disney, are the designer-sculptor geniuses of Las Vegas,
but their motifs have been carried faithfully throughout the town by
lesser men, for gasoline stations, motels, funeral parlors, churches,
public buildings, flophouses, and sauna baths.

Then there is a stimulus that is both visual and sexual—the Las Vegas
buttocks décolletage. This is a form of sexually provocative dress seen

more and more in the United States, but avoided like Broadway message-embroidered ("Kiss Me, I'm Cold") underwear in the fashion pages, so that the euphemisms have not been established and I have no choice but clinical terms. To achieve buttocks décolletage a woman wears bikini-style shorts that cut across the round fatty masses of the buttocks rather than cupping them from below, so that the outer-lower edges of these fatty masses, or "cheeks," are exposed. I am in the cocktail lounge of the Hacienda Hotel, talking to managing director Dick Taylor about the great success his place has had in attracting family and tour groups, and all around me the waitresses are bobbing on their high heels, bare legs, and décolletage-bare backsides, set off by pelvis-length lingerie of an uncertain denomination. I stare, but I am new here. At the White Cross Rexall drugstore on the Strip a pregnant brunette walks in off the street wearing black shorts with buttocks décolletage aft and illusion-of-cloth nylon lingerie hanging fore, and not even the old mom's-pie pensioners up near the door are staring. They just crank away at the slot machines. On the streets of Las Vegas, not only the show girls, of which the town has about two hundred fifty, bona fide, in residence, but girls of every sort, including, especially, Las Vegas' little high-school buds, who adorn what locals seeking roots in the sand call "our city of churches and schools," have taken up the chic of wearing buttocks décolletage step-ins under flesh-tight slacks, with the outline of the undergarment showing through fashionably. Others go them one better. They achieve the effect of having been dipped once, briefly, in Helanca stretch nylon. More and more they look like those wonderful old girls out of Flash Gordon who were wrapped just once over in Baghdad pantaloons of clear polyethylene with only Flash Gordon between them and the insane red-eyed assaults of the minions of Ming. It is as if all the hip young suburban gals of America named Lana, Deborah, and Sandra, who gather wherever the arc lights shine and the studs steady their coiffures in the plate-glass reflection, have convened in Las Vegas with their bouffant hair above and anatomically stretch-pant-swathed little bottoms below, here on the new American frontier. But exactly!

None of it would have been possible, however, without one of those historic combinations of nature and art that creates an epoch. In this case, the Mojave Desert plus the father of Las Vegas, the late Benjamin "Bugsy" Siegel.

Bugsy was an inspired man. Back in 1944 the city fathers of Las Vegas, their Protestant rectitude alloyed only by the giddy prospect of gambling revenues, were considering the sort of ordinance that would have preserved the town with a kind of Colonial Williamsburg dinkiness in the motif of the Wild West. All new buildings would have to have at least the façade of the sort of place where piano players used to wear garters on their sleeves in Virginia City around 1880. In Las Vegas in 1944, it should be noted, there was nothing more stimulating in the entire town than a Fremont Street bar where the composer of "Deep in the Heart of Texas" held forth and the regulars downed fifteen-cent beer.

Bugsy pulled into Las Vegas in 1945 with several million dollars that, after his assassination, was traced back in the general direction of gangster-financiers. Siegel put up a hotel-casino such as Las Vegas had never seen and called it the Flamingo—all Miami Modern, and the hell with piano players with garters and whatever that was all about. Everybody drove out Route 91 just to gape. Such shapes! Boomerang Modern supports, Palette Curvilinear bars, Hot Shoppe Cantilever roofs and a scalloped swimming pool. Such colors! All the new electrochemical pastels of the Florida littoral: tangerine, broiling magenta, livid pink, incarnadine, fuchsia demure, Congo ruby, methyl green, viridine, aquamarine, phenosafranine, incandescent orange, scarlet-fever purple, cyanic blue, tessellated bronze, hospital-fruit-basket orange. And such signs! Two cylinders rose at either end of the Flamingo—eight stories high and covered from top to bottom with neon rings in the shape of bubbles that fizzed all eight stories up into the desert sky all night long like an illuminated whisky-soda tumbler filled to the brim with pink champagne.

The business history of the Flamingo, on the other hand, was not such a smashing success. For one thing, the gambling operation was losing money at a rate that rather gloriously refuted all the recorded odds of the gaming science. Siegel's backers apparently suspected that he was playing both ends against the middle in collusion with professional gamblers who hung out at the Flamingo as though they had liens on it. What with one thing and another, someone decided by the night of

June 20, 1947, that Benny Siegel, lord of the Flamingo, had had it. He was shot to death in Los Angeles.

Yet Siegel's aesthetic, psychological, and cultural insights, like Cézanne's, Freud's, and Max Weber's, could not die. The Siegel and the Siegel aesthetic were already sweeping Las Vegas like gold fever. And there were builders of the West equal to the opportunity. All over Las Vegas the incredible electric pastels were repeated. Overnight the Baroque Modern forms made Las Vegas one of the few architecturally unified cities of the world—the style was Late American Rich—and without the bother and bad humor of a city council ordinance. No enterprise was too small, too pedestrian, or too solemn for The Look. The Supersonic Carwash, the Mercury Jetaway, Gas Vegas Village and Terrible Herbst gasoline stations, the Par-a-Dice Motel, the Palm Mortuary, the Orbit Inn, the Desert Moon, the Blue Onion Drive-In— on it went, like Wildwood, New Jersey, entering Heaven.

The atmosphere of the six-mile-long Strip of hotel-casinos grips even those segments of the population who rarely go near it. Barely twenty-five hundred feet off the Strip, over by the Convention Center, stands Landmark Towers, a shaft thirty stories high, full of apartments, supporting a huge circular structure shaped like a space observation platform, which was to have contained the restaurant and casino. Somewhere along the way Landmark Towers went bankrupt, probably at that point in the last of the many crises when the construction workers *still* insisted on spending half the day flat on their bellies with their heads, tongues, and eyeballs hanging over the edge of the tower, looking down into the swimming pool of the Playboy Apartments below, which has a "nudes only" section for show girls whose work calls for a tan all over.

Elsewhere, Las Vegas' beautiful little high-school buds in their buttocks-décolletage stretch pants are back on the foam-rubber upholstery of luxury broughams peeling off the entire chic ensemble long enough to establish the highest venereal disease rate among high-school students anywhere north of the yaws-rotting shanty jungles of the Eighth Parallel. The Negroes who have done much of the construction work in Las Vegas' sixteen-year boom are off in their ghetto on the west side of town, and some of them are smoking marijuana, eating peyote buttons, and taking horse (heroin), which they get from Tijuana, I mean it's simple, baby, right through the mails, and old Raymond, the Phoenix engineer, does not have the high life to himself.

I am on the third floor of the Clark County Courthouse talking to Sheriff Captain Ray Gubser, another of these strong, pale-eyed Western-builder types, who is obligingly explaining to me law enforcement on the Strip, where the problem is not so much the drunks, crooks, or roughhousers, but these nuts on pills who don't want to ever go to bed, and they have hallucinations and try to bring down the casinos like Samson. The county has two padded cells for them. They cool down after three or four days and they turn out to be somebody's earnest breadwinner back in Denver or Minneapolis loaded with the right credentials and pouring soul and apologies all over the county cops before pulling out of never-never land for good by plane. Captain Gubser is telling me about the life and eccentric times in Las Vegas, but I am distracted. The captain's office has windows out on the corridor. Coming down the corridor is a covey of girls, skipping and screaming, giggling along, their heads exploding in platinum-and-neon-yellow bouffants or beehives or raspberry-silk scarves, their eyes appliquéd in black like mail-order decals, their breasts aimed up under their jerseys at the angle of anti-aircraft automatic weapons, and, as they swing around the corner toward the elevator, their glutei maximi are bobbing up and down with their pumps in the inevitable buttocks décolletage pressed out against black, beige, and incarnadine stretch pants. This is part of the latest shipment of show girls to Las Vegas, seventy in all, for the "Lido de Paris" revue at the Stardust, to be entitled *Bravo!*, replacing the old show, entitled *Voilà*. The girls are in the county courthouse getting their working papers and fifteen days from now these little glutei maximi and ack-ack breasts with stars pasted on the tips will be swinging out over the slack jaws and cocked-up noses of patrons sitting at stageside at the Stardust. I am still listening to Gubser, but somehow it is a courthouse where mere words are beaten back like old atonal Arturo Toscanini trying to sing along with the NBC Symphony. There he would be, flapping his little toy arms like Tony Galento shadowboxing with fate, bawling away in the face of union musicians who drowned him without a bubble. I sat in on three trials

in the courthouse, and it was wonderful, because the courtrooms are all
blond-wood modern and look like sets for TV panel discussions on
marriage and the teen-ager. What the judge has to say is no less formal
and no more fatuous than what judges say everywhere; but inside of
forty seconds it is all meaningless because the atmosphere is precisely
like a news broadcast over Las Vegas' finest radio station, KORK. The
newscast, as it is called, begins with a series of electronic wheeps out on
that far edge of sound where only quadruplets can hear. A voice then
announces that this is Action Checkpoint News. "The news—all the
news—flows first through Action Checkpoint!—then reaches You! at the
speed of Sound!" More electronic wheeps, beeps and lulus, and then an
item: "Cuban Premier Fidel Castro nearly drowned yesterday." Urp!
Whep! Lulu! No news a KORK announcer has ever brought to Las
Vegas at the speed of sound, or could possibly bring, short of word of
the annihilation of Los Angeles, could conceivably compete within the
brain with the giddiness of this electronic jollification.

The wheeps, beeps, freeps, electronic lulus, Boomerang Modern and
Flash Gordon sunbursts soar on through the night over the billowing
hernia-hernia sounds and the old babes at the slots—until it is 7:30 a.m.
and I am watching five men at a green-topped card table playing
poker. They are sliding their Bee-brand cards into their hands and
squinting at the pips with a set to the lips like Conrad Veidt in a tunic
collar studying a code message from SS headquarters. Big Sid Wyman,
the old Big-Time gambler from St. Louis, is there, with his eyes looking
like two poached eggs engraved with a road map of West Virginia after
all night at the poker table. Sixty-year-old Chicago Tommy Hargan is
there with his topknot of white hair pulled back over his little pink
skull and a mountain of chips in front of his old caved-in sternum.
Sixty-two-year-old Dallas Maxie Welch is there, fat and phlegmatic as
an Indian Ocean potentate. Two Los Angeles biggies are there exhaling
smoke from candela-green cigars into the gloom. It looks like the
perfect vignette of every Big Time back room, "athletic club," snooker
house, and floating poker game in the history of the guys-and-dolls
*lumpenbourgeoisie*. But what is all this? Off to the side, at a rostrum,
sits a flawless little creature with bouffant hair and Stridex-pure skin
who looks like she is polished each morning with a rotary buffer. Before

her on the rostrum is a globe of coffee on a hot coil. Her sole job is to
keep the poker players warmed up with coffee. Meantime, numberless
uniformed lackeys are cocked and aimed about the dogs to bring the
five Big Timers whatever else they might desire—cigarettes, drinks,
napkins, eyeglass-cleaning tissues, plug-in telephones. All around the
poker table, at a respectful distance of ten feet, is a fence with the most
delicate golden pickets. Upon it, even at this narcoleptic hour, lean
men and women in their best clothes watching the combat of the titans.
The scene is the charmed circle of the casino of the Dunes Hotel. As
everyone knows, or believes, these fabulous men are playing for table
stakes of fifteen or twenty thousand dollars One hundred dollars rides
on a chip. Mandibles gape at the progress of the battle. And now Sid
Wyman, who is also a vice-president of the Dunes, is at a small
escritoire just inside the golden fence signing a stack of vouchers for
such sums as $4500, all printed in the heavy Mondrianesque digits of a
Burroughs business check-making machine. It is as if America's guys-
and-dolls gamblers have somehow been tapped upon the shoulders,
knighted, initiated into a new aristocracy.

Las Vegas has become, just as Bugsy Siegel dreamed, the American
Monte Carlo—without any of the inevitable upper-class baggage of
the Riviera casinos. At Monte Carlo there is still the plush mustiness of
the nineteenth-century noble lions—of Baron Bleichroden, a big winner
at roulette who always said, "My dear friends, it is so easy on Black."
Of Lord Jersey, who won seventeen maximum bets in a row—on black,
as a matter of fact—nodded to the croupier, and said, "Much obliged,
old sport, old sport," took his winnings to England, retired to the
country, and never gambled again in his life. Or of the old Duc de Dinc
who said he could win only in the high-toned Club Privé, and who won
very heavily one night, saw two Englishmen gaping at his good fortune,
threw them every mille-franc note he had in his hands, and said, "Here,
Englishmen without money are altogether odious." Thousands of Euro-
peans from the lower orders now have the money to go to the Riviera,
but they remain under the century-old status pall of the aristocracy. At
Monte Carlo there are still Wrong Forks, Deficient Accents, Poor
Tailoring, Gauche Displays, Nouveau Richness, Cultural Aridity—
concepts unknown in Las Vegas. For the grand debut of Monte Carlo

as a resort in 1879 the architect Charles Garnier designed an opera house for the Place du Casino; and Sarah Bernhardt read a symbolic poem. For the debut of Las Vegas as a resort in 1946 Bugsy Siegel hired Abbott and Costello, and there, in a way, you have it all.

I am in the office of Major A. Riddle—Major is his name—the president of the Dunes Hotel. He combs his hair straight back and wears a heavy gold band on his little finger with a diamond sunk into it. As everywhere else in Las Vegas, someone has turned on the air conditioning to the point where it will be remembered, all right, as Las Vegas-style air conditioning. Riddle has an appointment to see a doctor at 4:30 about a crimp in his neck. His secretary, Maude McBride, has her head down and is rubbing the back of her neck. Lee Fisher, the P.R. man, and I are turning ours from time to time to keep the pivots from freezing up. Riddle is telling me about "the French war" and moving his neck gingerly. The Stardust bought and imported a version of the Lido de Paris spectacular, and the sight of all those sequined giblets pooning around on flamingo legs inflamed the tourist. The Tropicana fought back with the Folies Bergère, the New Frontier installed "Paree Ooh La La," the Hacienda reached for the puppets "Les Poupees de Paris," and the Silver Slipper called in Lili St. Cyr, the stripper, which was going French after a fashion. So the Dunes has bought up the third and last of the great Paris girlie shows, the Casino de Paris. Lee Fisher says, "And we're going to do things they *can't* top. In this town you've got to move ahead in quantum jumps."

Quantum? But exactly! The beauty of the Dunes' Casino de Paris show is that it will be beyond art, beyond dance, beyond spectacle, even beyond the titillations of the winking crotch. The Casino de Paris will be a behemoth piece of American calculus, like Project Mercury.

"This show alone will cost us two and a half million a year to operate and one and a half million to produce," Major A. Riddle is saying. "The costumes alone will be fantastic. There'll be more than five hundred costumes and—well, they'll be fantastic.

"And this machine—by the time we get through expanding the stage, this machine will cost us $250,000."

"Machine?"

"Yes. Sean Kenny is doing the staging. The whole set moves electron-ically right in front of your eyes. He used to work with this fellow Lloyd Wright."

"Frank Lloyd Wright?"

"Yes. Kenny did the staging for *Blitz*. Did you see it? Fantastic. Well, it's all done electronically. They built this machine for us in Glasgow, Scotland, and it's being shipped here right now. It moves all over the place and creates smoke and special effects. We'll have everything. You can stage a bombardment with it. You'll think the whole theater is blowing up.

"You'll have to program it. They had to use the same mechanism that's in the Skybolt Missile to build it. It's called a 'Celson' or some-thing like that. That's how complicated this thing is. They have to have the same thing as the Skybolt Missile."

As Riddle speaks, one gets a wonderful picture of sex riding the crest of the future. Whole tableaux of bare-bottomed Cosmonaughties will be hurtling around the Casino de Paris Room of the Dunes Hotel at fantastic speed in elliptical orbits, a flash of the sequined giblets here, a blur of the black-rimmed decal eyes there, a wink of the crotch here and there, until, with one vast Project Climax for our times, Sean Kenny, who used to work with this fellow Frank Lloyd Wright, presses the red button and the whole yahooing harem, shrieking ooh-la-la amid the din, exits in a mushroom cloud.

The allure is most irresistible, not to the young, but the old. No one in Las Vegas will admit it—it is not the modern, glamorous notion—but Las Vegas is a resort for old people. In those last years, before the tissue deteriorates and the wires of the cerebral cortex hang in the skull like a clump of dried seaweed, they are seeking liberation.

At eight o'clock Sunday morning it is another almost boringly sunny day in the desert, and Clara and Abby, both about sixty, and their husbands, Earl, sixty-three, and Ernest, sixty-four, come squinting out of the Mint Casino onto Fremont Street

"I don't know what's wrong with me," Abby says. "Those last three drinks, I couldn't even feel them. It was just like drinking fizz. You know what I mean?"

"Hey," says Ernest, "how about that place back 'ere? We ain't been back 'ere. Come on."

The others are standing there on the corner, squinting and looking doubtful. Abby and Clara have both entered old babehood. They have that fleshy, humped-over shape across the back of the shoulders. Their torsos are hunched up into fat little loaves supported by bony, atrophied leg stems sticking up into their hummocky hips. Their hair has been fried and dyed into improbable designs.

"You know what I mean? After a while it just gives me gas," says Abby. "I don't even feel it."

"Did you see me over there?" says Earl. "I was just going along, nice and easy, not too much, just riding along real nice. You know? And then, boy, I don't know what happened to me. First thing I know I'm laying down fifty dollars. . . ."

Abby lets out a great belch. Clara giggles.

"Gives me gas," Abby says mechanically.

"Hey, how about that place back 'ere?" says Ernest.

". . . Just nice and easy as you please . . ."

". . . Get me all fizzed up . . ."

"Aw, come on . . ."

And there at eight o'clock Sunday morning stand four old parties from Albuquerque, New Mexico, up all night, squinting at the sun, belching from a surfeit of tall drinks at eight o'clock Sunday morning, and—marvelous!—there is no one around to snigger at what an old babe with decaying haunches looks like in Capri pants with her heels jacked up on decorated wedgies.

"Where do we *come* from?" Clara said to me, speaking for the first time since I approached them on Fremont Street. "He wants to know where we come from. I think it's past your bedtime, sweets."

"Climb the stairs and go to bed," said Abby.

Laughter all around.

"Climb the stairs" was Abby's finest line. At present there are almost no stairs to climb in Las Vegas. Avalon homes are soon to go up, advertising "Two-Story Homes!" as though this were an incredibly lavish and exotic concept. As I talked to Clara, Abby, Earl, and Ernest, it came out that "climb the stairs" was a phrase they brought along to

Albuquerque with them from Marshalltown, Iowa, those many years
ago, along with a lot of Protestant taboos against drinking, lusting,
gambling, staying out late, getting up late, loafing, idling, lollygagging
around the streets, and wearing Capri pants—all designed to deny a
person short-term pleasures so he will center his energies on bigger,
long-term goals.

"We was in 'ere"—the Mint—"a couple of hours ago, and that old boy
was playing the guitar, you know. 'Walk right in, set right down,' and I
kept hearing an old song I haven't heard for twenty years. It has this
little boy and his folks keep telling him it's late and he has to go to bed
He keeps saying, 'Don't make me go to bed and I'll be good.' Am I
*good,* Earl? Am I *good?*"

The liberated cortex in all its glory is none other than the old babes at
the slot machines. Some of them are tourists whose husbands said, *Here
is fifty bucks, go play the slot machines,* while they themselves went off
to more complex pleasures. But most of these old babes are part of the
permanent landscape of Las Vegas. In they go to the Golden Nugget or
the Mint, with their Social Security check or their pension check from
the Ohio telephone company, cash it at the casino cashier's, pull out the
Dixie Cup and the Iron Boy work glove, disappear down a row of slots
and get on with it. I remember particularly talking to another Abby—a
widow, sixty-two years old, built short and up from the bottom like a
fire hydrant. After living alone for twelve years in Canton, Ohio, she
had moved out to Las Vegas to live with her daughter and her husband, who worked for the Army.

"They were wonderful about it," she said, "Perfect hypocrites. She
kept saying, you know, 'Mother, we'd be delighted to have you, only we
don't think you'll *like* it. It's practically a *frontier* town,' she says. 'It's so
*garish,*' she says. So I said, I told her, 'Well, if you'd rather I didn't
come . . .' 'Oh, no!' she says. I wish I could have heard what her husband
was saying. He calls me 'Mother.' '*Mother,*' he says. Well, once I was
here, they figured, well, I *might* make a good baby-sitter and dishwash-
er and duster and mopper. The children are nasty little things. So one
day I was in town for something or other and I just played a slot
machine. It's fun—I can't describe it to you. I suppose I lose. I lose a
little. And *they* have fits about it. 'For God's sake, Grandmother,' and so
forth They always say '*Grand*mother' when I am supposed to 'act my

age' or crawl through a crack in the floor. Well, I'll tell you, the slot machines are a *whole lot* better than sitting in that little house all day. They kind of get you; I can't explain it."

The childlike megalomania of gambling is, of course, from the same cloth as the megalomania of the town. And, as the children of the liberated cortex, the old guys and babes are running up and down the Strip around the clock like everybody else. It is not by chance that much of the entertainment in Las Vegas, especially the second-stringers who perform in the cocktail lounges, will recall for an aging man what was glamorous twenty-five years ago when he had neither the money nor the freedom of spirit to indulge himself in it. In the big theater–dining room at the Desert Inn, The Painted Desert Room, Eddie Fisher's act is on and he is saying cozily to a florid guy at a table right next to the stage, "Manny, you know you shouldn'a sat this close—you know you're in for it now, Manny, baby," while Manny beams with fright. But in the cocktail lounge, where the idea is chiefly just to keep the razzle-dazzle going, there is Hugh Farr, one of the stars of another era in the West, composer of two of the five Western songs the Library of Congress has taped for posterity, "Cool Water" and "Tumbling Tumbleweed," when he played the violin for the Sons of the Pioneers. And now around the eyes he looks like an aging Chinese savant, but he is wearing a white tuxedo and powder-blue leather boots and playing his sad old Western violin with an electric cord plugged in it for a group called the Country Gentlemen. And there is Ben Blue, looking like a waxwork exhibit of vaudeville, doffing his straw skimmer to reveal the sculptural qualities of his skull. And down at the Flamingo cocktail lounge—Ella Fitzgerald is in the main room—there is Harry James, looking old and pudgy in one of those toy Italian-style show-biz suits. And the Ink Spots are at the New Frontier, and Louis Prima is at the Sahara, and the old parties are seeing it all, roaring through the dawn into the next day, until the sun seems like a par lamp fading in and out. The casinos, the bars, the liquor stores are open every minute of every day, like a sempiternal wading pool for the childhood ego. ". . . Don't make me go to bed . . ."

Finally the casualties start piling up. I am in the manager's office of a hotel on the Strip. A man and his wife, each about sixty, are in there raging. Someone got into their room and stole $70 from her purse, and they want the hotel to make it up to them. The man pops up and down from a chair and ricochets back and forth across the room, flailing his great pig's-knuckle elbows about.

"What kind of security you call that? Walk right in the god-dern room and just help themselves. And where do you think I found your security man? Back around the corner reading a god-dern detective magazine!"

He had scored a point there, but he was wearing a striped polo shirt with a hip Hollywood solid-color collar, and she had on Capri pants, and hooked across their wrinkly old faces they both had rimless wraparound French sunglasses of the sort young-punk heroes in *nouvelle vague* movies wear, and it was impossible to give any earnest contemplation to a word they said. They seemed to have the great shiny pop-eyes of a praying mantis.

"Listen, Mister," she is saying, "I don't care about the seventy bucks. I'd lose seventy bucks at your craps table and I wouldn't think nothing of it. I'd play seventy bucks just like that, and it wouldn't mean nothing. I wouldn't regret it. But when they can just walk in—and you don't give a damn—for Christ's sake!"

They are both zeroing in on the manager with their great insect corneas. The manager is a cool number in a white-on-white shirt and silver tie.

"This happened three days ago. Why didn't you tell us about it then?"

"Well, I was gonna be a nice guy about it. Seventy dollars," he said, as if it would be difficult for the brain to grasp a sum much smaller. "But then I found your man back there reading a god-dern detective magazine. *True Detectives* it was. Had a picture on the front of some floozie with one leg up on a chair and her garter showing. Looked like a god-derned athlete's-foot ad. Boy, I went into a slow burn. But when I am burned up, I am *burned up!* You get me, Mister? There he was, reading the god-derned *True Detectives*."

"Any decent hotel would have insurance," she says.

The manager says, "I don't know a hotel in the world that offers insurance against theft."

"Hold on, Mister," he says, "are you calling my wife a liar? You just get smart, and I'm gonna pop you one! I'll pop you one right now if you call my wife a liar."

At this point the manager lowers his head to one side and looks up at the old guy from under his eyebrows with a version of the Red Hook brush-off, and the old guy begins to cool off.

But others are beyond cooling off. Hornette Reilly, a buttery hipped whore from New York City, is lying in bed with a bald-headed guy from some place who has skin like oatmeal. He is asleep or passed out or something. Hornette is relating all this to the doctor over the Princess telephone by the bed.

"Look," she says, "I'm breaking up. I can't tell you how much I've drunk. About a bottle of brandy since four o'clock, I'm not kidding. I'm in bed with a guy. Right this minute. I'm talking on the telephone to you and this slob is lying here like an animal. He's all fat and his skin looks like oatmeal—what's happening to me? I'm going to take some more pills. I'm not kidding, I'm breaking up. I'm going to kill myself. You've got to put me in Rose de Lima. I'm breaking up, and I don't even know what's happening to me."

"So naturally you want to go to Rose de Lima."

"Well, yeah."

"You can come by the office, but I'm not sending you to Rose de Lima."

"Doctor, I'm not kidding."

"I don't doubt that you're sick, old girl, but I'm not sending you to Rose de Lima to sober up."

The girls do not want to go to the County Hospital. They want to go to Rose de Lima, where the psychiatric cases receive milieu therapy. The patients dress in street clothes, socialize and play games with the staff, eat well and relax in the sun, all paid for by the State. One of the folk heroines of the Las Vegas floozies, apparently, is the call girl who last year was spending Monday through Friday at Rose de Lima and "turning out," as they call it, Saturdays and Sundays, on the Strip, to the tune of $200 to $300 a weekend. She looks upon herself not as a whore, or even a call girl, but as a lady of assignation. When some guy comes to the Strip and unveils the little art-nouveau curves in his psyche and

calls for two girls to perform arts upon one another, this one consents to
be the passive member of the team only. A Rose de Lima girl, she
draws the line.

At the County Hospital the psychiatric ward is latched, bolted, wired
up, and jammed with patients who are edging along the walls in the
inner hall, the only place they have to take a walk other than the
courtyard.

A big brunette with the remnants of a beehive hairdo and decal eyes
and an obvious pregnancy is the liveliest of the lot. She is making eyes
at everyone who walks in. She also nods gaily toward vacant places
along the wall.

"Mrs. — is refusing medication," a nurse tells one of the psychiatrists. "She won't even open her mouth."

Presently the woman, in a white hospital tunic, is led up the hall. She
looks about fifty, but she has extraordinary lines on her face.

"Welcome home," says Dr. —.

"This is not my home," she says.

"Well, as I told you before, it has to be for the time being."

"Listen, you didn't analyze me."

"Oh, yes. Two psychiatrists examined you—all over again."

"You mean that time in jail."

"Exactly."

"You can't tell anything from that. I was excited. I had been out on
the Strip, and then all that stupid—"

Three fourths of the 640 patients who clustered into the ward last
year were casualties of the Strip or the Strip milieu of Las Vegas, the
psychiatrist tells me. He is a bright and energetic man in a shawl-
collared black silk suit with brass buttons.

"I'm not even her doctor," he says. "I don't know her case. There's
nothing I can do for her."

Here, securely out of sight in this little warren, are all those who have
taken the loop-the-loop and could not stand the centripety. Some, like
Raymond, who has been rocketing for days on pills and liquor, who has
gone without sleep to the point of anoxia, might pull out of the toxic
reaction in two or three days—or eight or ten. Others have conflicts to
add to the chemical wackiness. A man who has thrown all his cash to
the flabby homunculus who sits at every craps table stuffing the take

down an almost hidden chute so in won't pile up in front of the customers' eyes; a man who has sold the family car for next to nothing at a car lot advertising "Cash for your car—*right now*" and then thrown that to the homunculus, too, but also still has the family waiting guilt-lessly, guilelessly back home; well, he has troubles.

". . . After I came here and began doing personal studies," the doctor is saying, "I recognized extreme aggressiveness continually. It's not merely what Las Vegas can do to a person, it's the type of person it attracts. Gambling is a very aggressive pastime, and Las Vegas attracts aggressive people. They have an amazing capacity to louse up a normal situation."

The girl, probably a looker in more favorable moments, is pressed face into the wall, cutting glances at the doctor. The nurse tells her something and she puts her face in her hands, convulsing but not making a sound. She retreats to her room, and then the sounds come shrieking out. The doctor rushes back. Other patients are sticking their heads out of their rooms along the hall.

"The young girl?" a quiet guy says to a nurse. "The young girl," he says to somebody in the room.

But the big brunette just keeps rolling her decal eyes.

Out in the courtyard—all bar sand—the light is a kind of light-bulb twilight. An old babe is rocking herself back and forth on a straight chair and putting one hand out in front from time to time and pulling it in toward her bosom.

It seems clear enough to me. "A slot machine?" I say to the nurse, but she says there is no telling.

". . . And yet the same aggressive types are necessary to build a frontier town, and Las Vegas is a frontier town, certainly by any psychological standard," Dr. — is saying. "They'll undertake anything and they'll accomplish it. The building here has been incredible. They don't seem to care what they're up against, so they do it."

I got out to the parking lot in back of the County Hospital and it doesn't take a second; as soon as I turn on the motor I'm swinging again with Action Checkpoint News, "Monkey No. 9," "Donna, Donna, the Prima Donna," and friendly picking and swinging for the Fremont Hotel and Frontier Federal. Me and my big white car are sailing down the Strip and the Boomerang Modern, Palette Curvilinear, Flash Gor-

don Ming-Alert Spiral, McDonald's Hamburger Parabola, Ming Casino
Elliptical, and Miami Beach Kidney sunbursts are exploding in the
Young Electric Sign Company's Grand Gallery for all the sun kings. At
the airport there was that bad interval between the rental-car stall and
the terminal entrance, but once through the automatic door the
Muzak came bubbling up with "Song of India." On the upper level
around the ramps the slots were cranking away. They are placed like
"traps," a word Las Vegas picked up from golf. And an old guy is
walking up the ramp, just off the plane from Denver, with a huge
plastic bag of clothes slung over the left shoulder and a two-suiter
suitcase in his right hand. He has to put the suitcase down on the floor
and jostle the plastic bag all up around his neck to keep it from falling,
but he manages to dig into his pocket for a couple of coins and get
going on the slot machines. All seems right, but walking out to my plane
I sense that something is missing. Then I recall sitting in the cocktail
lounge of the Dunes at 3 p.m. with Jack Heskett, district manager of
the Federal Sign and Signal Corporation, and Marty Steinman, the
sales manager, and Ted Blaney, a designer. They are telling me about
the sign they are building for the Dunes to put up at the airport. It will
be five thousand square feet of free-standing sign, done in flaming-lake
red on burning-desert gold. The d—the D—alone in the word Dunes,
written in Cyrillic modern, will be practically two stories high. An inset
plexiglas display, the largest revolving, trivision plexiglas sign in the
world, will turn and show first the Dunes, with its twenty-two-story
addition, then the seahorse swimming pool, then the new golf course.
The scimitar curves of the sign will soar to a huge roaring diamond at
the very top. "You'll be able to see it from an airplane fifteen miles
away," says Jack Heskett. "Fifty miles," says Lee Fisher. And it will be
sixty-five feet up in the air—because the thing was, somebody was out
at the airport and they noticed there was only one display to be topped.
That was that shaft about sixty feet high with the lit-up globe and the
beacon lights, which is to say, the control tower. Hell, you can only see
that forty miles away. But exactly!

H AVING *set your career spinning, searched out a mate, and married, you suddenly find yourself mismated. Divorce? There are so many ways, and one of them—Reno-style—requires relatively few lies. Just a six-week investment in purposeful residence.*

# Reno: The Great Divide

### by Herbert Gold

Women are purposeful in Reno. The lovely blonde critter strolling the lobby of the Hotel Mapes, with a mole on her cheek accented by make-up as if she were Alice Faye miraculously preserved, did not come all the way to Reno in order to stake out uranium claims. She did not pack her kit bag to examine the pelicans and fossils of Pyramid Lake, where, during more idyllic days, Arthur Miller and Marilyn Monroe quietly strolled and waited for legal technicalities to be arranged. Nor is she a cultural anthropologist studying the Paiute Indians or the sheepherding Basques who gather at the Santa Fe Hotel in downtown Reno to eat and drink in French, Spanish, and Basque. She may sample all these incidental lures, but primarily she has come to Reno for one of two purposes: either to gamble (and also to find a man) or to shed a man (and also to gamble). When she pauses in her slow amble across the lobby, straightening her stocking—she bends, and *harken!* —we have time to examine her third finger, left hand.

We find the circle of the abandoned wedding ring, sunburned a bright red. She is a member of the Six Week Club. She is a joyous Jill, with her tanned face hit by a vision of the good life, her rump constricted by her new magenta Western pants and poutingly pressing for freedom. She wears heavy Indian jewelry and the stunned, goofy look of imminent divorce. She is in the molting phase, resentful but

139

cute, ready for fun and making with rotating eyes. There are lots of
women. They are waiting and bored, waiting and anxious, waiting and
numerous.

Perhaps she is even one of the ladies who follow the apocryphal
tradition of dropping her wedding band into the Truckee River near
the Washoe County Courthouse, but more likely, our friend in the
lobby of the Mapes has pawned her slender gold band in order to
increase her capital at the gaming tables. Reno visitors are idealists—
and practical; people of action—and people who wait. They have come
to Reno after much deep thought, quiet analysis, and broken crockery.
Now they busy themselves with making the most of their decision.

Helping them in this task is a permanent cadre composed of several
types of specialized workers, including lawyers, gamblers, and a local
brand of cowboy who is not often home, home on the range. There are
other classical Reno types, including the obedient judges (trained to
say "Granted" without hesitation), landladies, and ranch proprietors
(trained to bear witness to the continous residence of the plaintiffs in
divorce actions)—laborers all in the vineyard of marital afterthought.

Reno, "The Biggest Little City in the World," has constituted itself
the Great American Divide—a man from his money, a wife from her
husband. Lady Luck and Legal Liberty. There is also sex. In Reno, this
is slightly more complicated than buying a drink in a saloon, but if you
wait about five minutes, and smile, or scowl, or do something, *anything*,
someone will surely come along.

A few years ago, they closed the Stockade, Reno's alley of legalized
prostitution, but that was not a very lively place anyway. It was
guarded by a policeman and the girls behaved as dully as minor
bureaucrats. You transacted your business without shilly-shallying and
then skedaddled, making room for the next in line—a little like getting a
haircut or paying a parking ticket. Other towns in Nevada still exercise
local option on the matter of commercial sack-play, and in Reno many
fine citizens fought the passing of the Stockade. They felt that this was
a step away from the right to free assembly guaranteed by the Consti-
tution. It also put their "innercent dotters" in terrible danger from
desert rats and those crazed tourists from San Francisco and the East. It

abolished a reliable money-making and tax-paying business. But what with a steady influx of divorce-seekers, plus the legion of cooperative ladies who patrol the lobbies of the hotels, the passing of the old Stockade deprived only the most boorishly impatient and the most stubborn admirers of Nevada frontier tradition.

In all fairness to Reno's hospitality, it must be insisted that divorce, gambling, drinking, and sex do not provide a complete summary of its services to the visitor. There is also marriage. Five times as many marriages as divorces are performed along the banks of the Truckee. Of course, these marriages have a tendency to return to Reno a few years later in the form of divorces; but still, the Park Wedding Chapel, festooned in neon ("Ring Bell for Service at Any Hour"), is the scene of a rapid marital drone and congratulation. The children of such marriages turn out to be complex creatures, often with curiously interrelated parents. ("My previous stepfather's brother was the uncle of my present stepfather's second wife . . . ")

"We're not backward," declared one proud Reno cosmopolite. "We've got our Beats, too, and it's doing a production of *Guys and Dolls*." The cast meets after rehearsals at *The in,* spelled with a lower-case (or hungry) "i," where a little group discusses Samuel Beckett and Sam Cooke, Kafka and Sinatra. Reno is perhaps the unhippest and zippiest town in all the fifty states. The women, clicked silly by the keno tabulator, puffy from grief and alcohol, play *femme fatale* in the gambling clubs, with shades jutting out over their sunglasses. This is the promissory land where the oppressed are liberated and the hopeful stream by on South Virginia Street. The chippies compete with the divorcettes in all the clubs, casinos, and hotel lobbies.

Our lady of the Mapes is called a divorcette in Reno. She is a prospective divorcee. She is still legally bound to a man hereinafter referred to as Defendant. Defendant has a job some place and sends her money. She is a Permanent Resident, which is not to be confused with an Old Inhabitant. A Permanent Resident is someone in the final convulsions of marriage who plans to stay for six weeks and a day, and can prove it with witnesses. (Appropriately enough, Reno was named after a General Reno, killed in the Civil War back East, who never once set foot in Nevada. The founding fathers were looking for a convenient short name and drew the General's out of a Stetson. A practical, unsentimental people.)

Mrs. Permanent Resident may pass her six weeks weeping her eyes out, or she may spend her time in a patio discussing philosophy with other Permanent Residents. ("Beneath that rough exterior, girls, beats the heart of a wife-beater.") Or she may hit the slots or the tables or the bars, or she may shyly peek around for a cowboy or a fresh future Defendant. Itchily she seeks to revenge herself on the flunkout back home in Chicago or New York. She is the made-to-order prey for the opportunities, con men, and brutal rancheros who hang around Reno. She blinks her eyes into cool desert space as they park the Hertz car off one of the roads winding into the vacant hills. Sliding across the seat, she murmurs, "Oh, Mr. What's-Your-Name, he was so mean to me." Bright desert stars wink above them.

"Call me Slim," says the wrangler, and takes a firm hold. A new groom sweeps clean.

The specialized Reno cowboy is a local representative of one of the most curious professions in contemporary America. He is known in all the great centers; his granddaddy, the gigolo, wore evening attire and a silken mustache; his unacknowledged ancestor was the simpering Greek Ganymede. Now, in New York and other urban centers, he may occupy himself with tennis or modeling or claim to be an actor while he waits to be chosen by some joy-hunting, moneyed lady. In Reno he manifests himself as a dude cowboy, based on a ranch, watching the air terminal, scouting in the better bars and gambling clubs.

Slim is a subtle, part-male creature who probably has not wrangled a four-legged cow since Reno last housed a WCTU convention. He is a shill of love, faking high stakes of passion for a small profit, just as a gambling shill pretends to gamble in order to make the house look sharp and busy. A skinny chap in chaps and a duckass haircut, he keeps busy holding hands with the blue-haired, fifty-year-old lady in the TV room of the Holiday Motel; the Trap has gleaming white teeth and the Victim has a subscription to *The Wall Street Journal*; they will make beautiful moolah together, he hopes.

Like other professional dude cowhands, Slim dwells in a series of six-week liaisons, looking always for the Big Strike—the woman who will either take him home in order to goad Defendant or perhaps will move her bank account to sunny, tax-free Nevada. When he uses rodeo language, he is thinking of stock on the wobbly high heel. A "re-run" is a cow that has been tuckered out by much use and is "generally easier to wrestle and tie." "Snuffy" describes stock that is wild, ready to go. A "twister" is himself—a cow twister, suffering from scaly elbows and nocturnal premonitions.

In sad fact, he is not a happy wrangler. He sits with his aging broad, his water-slicked hair growing low down his neck, his creased, tended tan, his bland, pleased, angry, hurt, princely, bored clasp of lips; he turns his ankle anxiously in its fancy-worked Western boot. It is costly after all, making out this way. Hard to give up joy in sex and work; its hard to give up being human. "But what is man," his neurotic ankle seems to ask, quoting Scripture in its dismay of soul, "that thou art mindful of him?"

"Nothing doing," answers the silence between his ears, the creak of his leather.

Cool, professional, a freckled desert hipster, he is tired and wants to go to bed, but there is no mama to cradle him, only this rich bitch whose particular mattress needs he tries to predict as they watch the "Tonight" show together. Well, maybe he is neither man nor woman, but our bored buckaroo with his corseted prey is in business, and doing pretty well.

There are fine hotels in Reno—the Riverside, the Mapes—and the usual glorious motels with swimming pools and round-the-clock boozing. There are also the guest "ranches" (a horse or two) or houses that cater to economical divorcettes. "Bonny Bode Inn—Divorcees Welcome" hints the newspaper advertisement; "Join the Happy Crowd at Harmony House" another chimes in winsomely; "Liberty Rooms—Free Coffee At Any Hour—Make Your Stay a Memorable One."

The proprietors of these permanent residences for permanent six-week residents also serve as cheer-mongers to the sad, introducers for the solitary, and witnesses in court to swear that the plaintiff was really here for six weeks. (Efforts to shorten the time of legal residence are met by the practical objection that Reno needs the money spent here in ransom after matrimonial jags; conversely, greedy ideas about lengthening the stay are met by prudent commercial warnings of the threat from sordid, rapid Alabama and immoral, speedy Mexico.)

Life in these guest houses generally follows a simple, healthful routine. The marital convalescents share place at table, space in the laundry room, and stories about the rat, jackal, hoot owl, dog, porcupine, hyena, or stercoricolous beetle in Washington, D.C., or San Francisco, Dallas, Bangor, or wherever. Nevada law in its majesty almost always agrees that the One Back Home is some sort of jungle beastie; those in Reno, men and women, are wronged angels. Many a joyous conversation in a Guest House patio concerns ways to settle his/her hash, which badly needs settling. For current news of what he/she is up to you can always get word from detective agencies or crystal ball snoops who do a thriving business:

PHYCHIC RUTH—*Card Reader and Counselor 17th Successful Year in Reno.* $3.00. "Phychic" is probably a combination word, meaning fidgety and fishy, and it characterizes the stories to which poor, long-suffering, three-dollar Ruth has had to lend an ear. "My husband, listen, he used to . . ." "That wife of mine, by God, I wanted to . . ."

Some, of course, have untraceable spouses who, for all they know, might be working for the Post Office; she lies dead in a schoolteacher's closet in Tulsa; he is producing a movie entitled *Teenagers at the SEATO Conference;* Phychic Ruth cannot see him clear. He has disappeared from the ken of mortal and gypsy, and will be symbolically reached only by that final invocation published in a legal advertisement:

> The State of Nevada sends you greetings! Not having cohabited with the plaintiff. . . .

And he'll never know what was said about him before the Reno judge. The judge probably won't know, either. He has heard too many stories that all have the same ending. He turns off the hearing aid and pores over his copy of *Poker—A Gentleman's Pastime.*

The garrulous camaraderie of the boarding house gives wounds a chance to heal under the gentle urging of that famous law—misery loves company of the opposite sex. One should always describe one's trouble to those who cannot check for accuracy; sympathy begets sympathy in return; and listen, pal, it sure is good to get away after what I been through. "I know, I know, and how about making a tour of the clubs?"

There are plenty of shaky stomachs and trembling lower lips, plenty of secret tears in narrow beds, but there is also the lovely resilient chick who comments, "I learned a greal deal from my marriage. I don't regret anything. I learned how to give big parties and how to keep the maid from stealing."

Most things that you do furtively in other places you can do without shame in Reno. This is to Reno's credit; honesty is one of the good policies. The popular acceptance of gambling is indicated by a recent debate in the City Council. Should the city get out of the slot machine business at Municipal Airport? Of course. Why? Declared the mayor: "We don't want to compete with private enterprise."

The private enterprise includes Harold's Club (in addition to The Nevada, The Golden, Harrah's Club, and other secondary institutions), a giant seven-floor department store of luck, with blackjack, craps, roulette, and eight hundred slot machines grinding up money twenty-four hours a day. The customers pull, wait, and stare like the distraught heroes of horror movies who look at their monster and say, "I think it's trying to tell us something." (It is trying to tell them: "The grind is against you, buddy—bell, cherry, and orange.") Some slots are "humanized," being built into gorgeous female bodies, with the coins, when you hit, emerging from a dismally appropriate place.

"We build slot machines," stated one manufacturer, "but we don't build machines to force people to play." Nevertheless, the mechanism seems to be built into most of us. Jean-Paul Sartre once committed a famous remark: "Hell is other people." This is an easy epigram, since any definition of hell with such an outrageous and dogmatic format will take us by surprise and sound briefly, pretentiously true. For example: hell is oneself; hell is nobody. But those hip-to-hip rows of cattle before the slot machines, blind to anything but the rolling fruit, suggest some particular dramatic sense to the French philosopher's remark. Hell is other people playing slot machines.

This repetitive, ritualistic, manual game recalls fantasies in which the child defies logic—he is all-powerful; he controls his fate simply by force of will. (Dylan Thomas made fun of this primitive dream when he wrote about a rocky transatlantic flight, "Only my iron will will keep the great bird aloft.") The gambler's iron will commands a jackpot

when he wants it—*right now*—and refuses to admit failure until he
wakes from his dreams of omnipotence to find his pockets empty.
Perhaps—while we are walking on these psychological waters—there is
another factor at work: in his heart of hearts the gambler wants to lose,
a stubborn guilty child asking to be punished for trying to stand outside
the laws of chance.

One of the saddest, most instructive sights in the world is that of a
gambling creep shuffling out of a room on South Virginia Street and
over to the Western Union office on Center Street, there to mouth his
stub of pencil and try to transform himself into a poet with a new way
of saying SEND MONEY QUICK. Going from club to club you see the
System Players, clutching their notebooks, grinning hard, with harassed
eyes and chewed lips, sure that next time the laws of statistics, which
they have invented, will take hold. Next time.

The Smith family, owners of Harold's Club, are respected leaders of
community life in Reno. They endow concerts and the Harold's Club
Scholarships at the University of Nevada (one condition: the Scholar
must not cross the threshold of Harold's Club during his college
enrollment). Legalized gambling is an important industry. The high
desert skies are clear of industrial smoke; the fume and fuss of gambling leave little mark on the Nevada landscape.

Reno and environs display a distinct physical charm and diversity of
terrain. Besides the gambling/divorcing Reno, there is also the typical
Western town in which people live much as they do in a thousand
similar places, blessed by lovely homes and mortgages, spacious lawns
and chickweed, happy youngsters thronging to school, church, and
dragstrip. This ignored Reno boasts magnificent surrounding mountains, the snow-fed Truckee making green the center of the city, skiing
in winter and healthful dry desert air in summer—plus the University of
Nevada, "finest institution of learning in the state." (It is also the only
institution of higher learning in the state.)

But it is not for these advantages in culture and climate that Reno is
so much better known than, say, Ottumwa, Iowa, or Bellingham,
Washington, both towns of comparable size. Reno is a rambunctious,
brawling Mickey Rooney among cities. The workaday Reno grudgingly
harbors its wild, permissive twin, without which, of course, any

renowned Reno at all would be impossible. The two Renos are joined by common elements of the picturesque and the bizarre: the traditional rodeo, the splendors of desert sage and mountain pine, the romantic outcroppings of silver-bearing rock in nearby, antique Virginia City, where ragtime is the rule, the hot mineral springs for swimming, the general morality of No Speed Limit in Nevada.

The true churchly, cultural Reno, of which some old residents defensively prattle, also has some basis in fact, once you leave Virginia Street (the major casinos), Commercial Row (pawn shops, Indian bars, prodding policemen), and Lake Street (Chinese and Negro gambling clubs —Reno is covertly Jim Crow). But it's hard to keep the wistful visitor in church once he has found the Mint Club, where Rosemarie has been Held Over by Popular Demand—and by popular demand she holds it over the drinkers at the bar on which she prances. The place of the great rose window of the cathedral of Notre Dame is taken by the grandiose outdoor mural of an Indian massacre which is the entrance to Harold's Club, the dominating structure in town.

Over this cathedral of chance shines a beacon; within it the multitude throngs. The slot machines whir, the process servers knock, the courts do their work. A woman sniffles, a woman laughs, a dude moves in. Someone asks for change of a paper twenty in silver dollars. A spur jangles. Six weeks begin for someone; six weeks are over for another.

T HOU *Shalt Not Be Fat is the eleventh com-*
*mandment. Fat people just don't make it: they*
*don't get dates, they don't fit their clothes, they*
*are embarrassed at the beach, they eat chocolate*
*ice cream every day, and they look silly jogging.*
*Still, if worrying about your appearance all the*
*time gets to be a bore, remember that there are*
*many ways to lose those 314 pounds.*

# An Evening with Sherri

*by Vivian Yudkin*

Sherri Haimes is Leader of the Faithful at the Arlington Jewish Community Center every night of the week except Tuesdays (and she
works days). The Faithful are the Northern Virginia Weight Watchers
Group. They use a rented hall at the Center at eight in the evening
every week night except Tuesday—different Weight Watchers on different evenings, but any evening is representative.

To become a Weight Watcher is a whole secret other *thing.* One
Weight Watcher can spot another Weight Watcher in a restaurant even
if they have never laid eyes on each other in their lives. There are
certain tell-tale signs instantly recognizable to the initiated only. One
heard about it from an aunt in Boston who after *twenty-five years of*
*trying to lose* found her true self at Weight Watchers. Another heard it
from a cousin in Philly whose own mother proudly admits she can't
recognize her daughter now.

There's this *hive* near the door of the room upstairs at the Community Center. A distraught man with sweat-plastered hair cries out, "Upstairs?" and a dozen women soothingly tell him there is something the
matter with the air conditioning in the usual downstairs room. A voice
with the twang and penetration of a buzzsaw proclaims, "I *gotta* do it
all my life! It runs in the family."

That's the voice of Sherri the Leader and she comes on strong. She comes on like a nine-thousand-watt light bulb. The ladies in the registration line-up at the door ($3 registration fee gets you in, $2 a week for the next fifteen weeks pays rent on the hall, salary for Sherri and others, etc.) are already poking and prodding at her svelte size-nine chic black dress with their hopeful eyes. Ascertaining, surmising. If *she* can do it, yes, so can I!

"I dedicate my *whole life* to it," Sherri pronounces distinctly. As the distraught man sneaks into the room she pounces, "Look at how thin he is!" Mollified ecstasy irradiates his countenance.

The hundred or so fellow travelers finally get settled along rows of straight-backed chairs. They sip Diet Pepsis and study their Suggested Menus like brokers studying the market. Sherri is running up and down promising everyone she'll *begin* in a few minutes. There's a mob outside the door near the weighing machine. "Yoohoo," shouts one hefty middle-aged woman to another, "were you good this week?" The other shakes her head mournfully. "I ate a Cloret," she whispers. A slim girl in a pink Lilly pushes the weights down from 160 pounds to 100 pounds on the scale. "You're not here to *lose*," accuses the hefty middle-aged woman, "you're here to *spy*." The slim girl pushes the weights up from 100 to 130 and there is a satisfied silence.

The Weighers crowd into the room where Sherri is baptizing a group of women with Orange Blossom Cologne, a gift from a grateful Weight Watcher just returned from Florida. "It's much better *here* than there," shouts the mahogany-tanned donor. She is dressed all in white and Sherri nods as if she never expected to hear anything different.

She pushes forward glossy photographs of herself and points in disbelief at the pictured Sherri Who Used to Be and Is Now No More. "See that? See the arms? See the flab? See how I lost it all . . . gracefully?" She pats her After hips in satisfaction.

There is an awed pause and Sherri's blue-lidded black eyes start out of their sockets in hatred of the Self She Had Once Been. She goes to the front of the room and pounds a silver gavel as if she is knocking down a wall. Her smile is big and wide with room enough in it for every fat person in the whole universe. Her black dress plunges away from a tanned décolletage and fatless shoulders. Her flyaway cropped auburn head twists and turns in a halo of achievement. There she stands, a size nine as she lives and breathes!

"Look at Dolores," Sherri shrieks suddenly, clasping her hands so that the knuckles stand out mauve against the tan. "She looks terrific! Unbelievable! And she's had her hair cut!"

Everybody swivels around to view Dolores, who is an ash blonde beauty with an advanced case of pregnancy. Dolores flutters to a chair, then she stands up. "Shh," Sherri waves to the crowd. "Dolores has something to tell us." Dolores breathes heavily, fighting tears. "I *knew* I was going to eat. I asked my husband to *please* help me and he said 'Dolores, *don't eat.*' So I ate it."

There is a heavy silence. "Well," says Sherri slowly, "you see? Dolores is lovely and beautiful, but she flunked out because . . ."

"Peanut butter," whispers Dolores, and sinks down.

"Peanut butter," Sherri repeats, swallowing, then she smiles with the smile of one who is never downed. "Now look at me. You wouldn't think I was ever a *compulsive eater*, would you? Well, I was when I was pregnant. I was, I figured, 'I'm pregnant, what difference does it make anyway?' "

"I'm glad you still need me," Sherri says to the crushed Dolores. "Make sure you don't do it again."

"Oh, I won't, I won't; I'll be good, I promise," Dolores sighs in relief.

Two young plump girls in dark glasses and silver lipstick creep in and a thin man in a goatee sits silent at the back of the room. The ratio of men to women is meager, about one in twenty, and the men huddle together in one clump in the front row with the expressions of schoolboys about to be called up before the principal. The time is now a little after 8 p.m., and the show gets on the road.

Sherri cries out, "I'm a miracle come *true!*" and pauses to let this sink in. The bulk of the women in the room are in their middle years. They are dressed in shapeless cottons and their bobbed hair is iron-gray, tinted auburn or blonde. They sit with their hands in their laps, their plump shoulders bowed yet attentive, and they look as if they are quite certain some dreadful cataclysm will befall them if they goof this one last chance they have to bring themselves back into the mainstream.

"Its all in your minds." Sherri screams as if everybody in the room is stone deaf. "Look at me. I was born fat! I *made* myself into size nine! I wasn't *born* a size nine!" The eyes up and down the room go all sparkly. "All I ever dreamed of was being a size fourteen, let alone a size nine . . ." Sherri breaks off and points to the girl in the pink Lilly. "What is a civilian doing here?" she inquires. "I don't think you have enough to give us."

"I'm deceptive," murmurs the girl. "I'm 130 pounds."

"Oh, then we'll let you give us some of it," Sherri says. "Would you believe it, some of those Twiggy-type models try to sneak in here, want to go from 120 to 110. Nothing doing!" Everybody breathes more freely and closes ranks.

"I was in an ice cream parlor the other night," Sherri begins. She raises her hand at the fierce mutter of reproval: "Wait a minute! I'm *ten pounds under* and I been on maintenance for over a year! I can go inside an ice cream parlor now and tell myself a banana split won't taste good. It's all in your mind Anyway, what I want to say, there was this fat couple, *real fat*" (everyone laughs) "sitting up there behind their strawberry sundaes" (everyone groans). "Wait a minute!" Sherri wants to tell them the best part, which follows as the night the day: "I can tell you something. *They weren't happy*, they were *crying inside!*"

Pleased laughter from the audience. Sherri cries passionately with arms akimbo, "Do you know something, if a person is fat he is sick in the head! I know. *I was a pig!*" She stares around for one person to contradict her and no one is forthcoming. "I'm a lady now. Not like that time when I ate seven different types of cake at a bar mitzvah. For those of you who don't know, a bar mitzvah is where they feed you like there's no tomorrow!"

She brings up her hand and thwacks her stomach so hard it gives off a sound like a football being bounced against a stone wall. "This don't boss me no more! All my life I been bossed" (murmurs of agitation from the crowd), "my mother bossed me, my husband bossed me, my daughter bossed me, when I went horseback riding even the horse bossed me!" Her eyes gleam and her voice drops to a tone loaded with unendurable pleasure: "You know what? *I can eat cornbeef* now, if I wanta! I could even have stuffed derma if I wanta!" She looks around in wondering disbelief, and in the second row a little old lady licks her lips ecstatically and murmurs, "*Kishke, kugel!*"

"*No*," howls Sherri, and thrusts out her arms in an Al Jolson gesture. "I'll tell you something: I love you! Yes, the bigger and fatter you are, the more I love you. I'm ready to give you my *blood* if you need it. Just say you need it, that's all." There's a murmuring, humming, buzzing all through the room, and a man in navy blue bermudas, pink short-sleeved shirt and bow tie, green kneesocks and sneakers, jumps up and stands next to Sherri. She urges him like a Mama to an only son at a party. "Go on and say something to them, Max."

"I lost forty pounds in sixteen weeks," Max brings out in a rush, his face dripping with happy beads of sweat. There is a tremendous burst of applause. Smiles race from one side of the room to the other. "I'm getting hot and cold thrills," someone says, and there are further whoops of "Unbelievable!" "Wonderful!" "Terrific!"

Drunk with joy Max goes on: "I even lost four and a half more this week."

A man in the front row moans in anguish, "How does he *do* it!" as his face becomes a solid pudgy mask of misery.

"Don't worry, your time will come; everyone's different," a round-faced girl consoles him. He lapses into brooding silence as she pats his arm.

"You ate popcorn?" Sherri removes her beaming attention from Max and fastens it like a gimlet onto the hapless man in the front row. He breaks down.

"I had one *hell* of a dinner two nights ago," he confesses, "but I *dint* have 'no' breakfast and I *dint* have 'no' lunch . . ."

A woman jumps up in the center row. "Tell me this," she shrills, "why can't I have cocoa? I *love* cocoa. There's only ten calories in a table-spoon of cocoa."

"Cocoa!" everyone hisses.

Sherri silences them, stamping her feet in three-quarter time: "Let her speak, it's natural enough to love cocoa."

"I want a chocolate malted. I'm going to have a chocolate malted. What's wrong with having one tablespoon of cocoa?" the speaker de-mands resentfully.

"I'll tell you what," Sherri smiles. "You remind me of a lady who is no longer with us. *She* wanted to use her breakfast slice of bread with her lunch slice of bread. 'Can't you use a bit of psychology,' I said to her, 'and cut your lunch slice in two and make a sandwich out of your tuna fish?' But she was *determined*, and when you are that far gone there's no hope for you. 'I'm going to use my breakfast slice,' she said, and that was that!"

The cocoa lover said, bloody but unbowed, "I'm going to have cocoa; I love cocoa," but under her breath.

"When you break, you break *all the way*," Sherri said fiercely. "You go from one tablespoon of cocoa to fried chicken, to pancakes with butter and syrup, to a whole box of chocolate-chip cookies; you'll eat the whole box right down to the crumbs; you'll end up eating forty-eight chocolate cherry candies. I know! If you go out and they offer you fried chicken" (more moans and sighs from the audience), "*tear off the skin!* Right, Max?"

She turns to Max and Max nods wanly. He pulls at his Bermuda waist: "See this? Gone from a 48 to a 40 and more to go! My relatives give me shoes, coats, pants, shirts . . ."

"If any of you lose ten pounds in the next two weeks, come to my husband's store and he'll give you 10 per cent off," a woman shouts from the back row. "Don't forget to bring your weight tickets!"

There is an excited buzz of interest and Sherri shouts above the racket: "Fat! We gotta get back to fat! We don't cheat even to the tune of one raisin! If you want a drink at a party, take water and put ice in it and stand there drunk with power!"

"My husband asked about chow mein last week," cries a woman in accents which shake at such audacity.

"He ain't ready," Sherri says firmly. "You got to be ready. No use telling a fat person he's fat if he ain't ready, and *your* husband ain't ready!"

Sue comes forward to receive her graduation pin. "Sue is leaving us," Sherri says, "and I'm giving her my own graduation pin to take with her wherever she goes." Sue bursts into tears. "Oh, I cried at my graduation," Sherri compassionately says. She pins Sue and kisses her on both cheeks: "God love you!"

"I couldn't have done it without you," quavers Sue, and Sherri bestows more hugs and kisses.

"Sue's going abroad," someone says. "It's thrilling what she's done, isn't it? Lost forty pounds!"

"Keep my pin, let it be a guide to you," Sherri cries, as Sue returns to

her seat flushed with tears and triumph. "Do justice to my pin wherever
you go and wherever you are!"

And Sue says, "I promise."

After such high emotion everybody is all worn out. They lean back in
their chairs, but not for long. Sherri waves a yellow sheet of paper and
screams, "I have an announcement to make! Since March of this year
our composite weight loss has been 3,141 3/4 pounds, and our weight
gain" (she lowers her voice and eyes) "has been only twelve pounds."
There is a heavy stomping and whistling as everyone shifts and sighs
and creaks in the chairs until the whole room surges like the sea.
Radiant faces repeat the weight loss to one another and Sherri bugles:
"THIS IS MY REWARD!"

The two girls in dark glasses get up to go. "Young. You are young.
With those bodies you'll soon be wearing miniskirts," Sherri promises.
"Tell me, do you like our group better than D.C ?"

The girls nod vociferously. They have been all stirred up by Sherri's
magnificent performance, and the promise of miniskirts has gone to
their heads. "Oh, yes, oh, yes," they breathe in unison.

"God love you," Sherri calls. "Thanks for losing."

"Next week we got a fantastic meeting," Sherri says. "Alice will be
graduating. You all know Alice and what an inspiration she has been to
us. Eighty pounds she gave me! And she's promised to give more! Now
that's an achievement. She's got no patience with some of the grum-
blers, let me tell you! She *knows!*"

"I'll do better," comes a throbbing voice from the aisle.

Sherry nods and points to the girl with the pink Lilly. "You got our
manual. It's passed by the New York City Board of Obesity." The girl
nods. "Guard it, sweetheart," Sherri warns, "just guard it."

"Wait till you start with those radishes," someone leans over to the
girl in the pink Lilly. "You'll feel like Scarlett O'Hara when she was
digging for something to eat."

"I used to live by the light of the refrigerator," another woman says.
Another joins in, "I used to eat my sausages and English muffins with
jelly just like everyone else."

The first woman gives a cough and mutters, "English muffins!"

"*We* eat all the time, not like the *others.* They just have *big meals,*"
the woman who used to eat sausages says stoutly.

"You should see the painting one of my successful Weight Watchers gave to me," cries Sherri enthusiastically. "It's a painting of a *salad*! Done in oils! I got it hanging in my living room and I wouldn't give that painting away even for a piece of strawberry shortcake. So help me!"

# There's No Business Like Fat Business

## by Chris Welles

It has been a half century since Henry Ford discovered the advantages the assembly line offered to automobile production, and one would think that such a basic technique would have pretty well permeated almost all of American business. Unfortunately, there are still some primitive backwaters. One of the most notable is the medical profession, where doctors stubbornly persist in thinking in terms of the individual patient.

For dragging the doctor business, or at least part of it, into the twentieth century, we will all now rise and give a cheer for Gordon L. Green, M.D. Dr. Green is a "fat doctor" whose specialization is weight reduction through the use of diet pills. There are perhaps five thousand fat doctors in the U.S. who collect $250 million for treating five to ten million patients a year. But none has applied the principles of mass production with the brilliance of Dr. Green.

Each week, some twenty-five hundred patients—mostly women—pay $7 each to visit one of Dr. Green's 19 medical-modern wood-paneled offices conveniently located throughout Long Island and receive treatment from Dr. Green's staff of sixty-five. "I doubt," says a local doctor with another, less successful, specialty, "that there are too many fat women on Long Island who have not heard of Dr. Green."

The enticement is epitomized by Dr. Green's basic credo: "We make taking it off easy." Indeed the very phrase "taking it off," variants of which are continually enunciated in cheerfully confident tones by Dr. Green's staff, creates the anticipation that sagging flab is as easily discarded as a summer jacket on a hot day. During their first visit ($10), new patients learn from a twenty-five minute tape recording (spoken by a local disc jockey) that it is:

OK to eat as much as you want

OK to drink as much as you want ("Everyone's got to live a little," says Dr. Green)

OK to forget about exercise

OK to forget about counting calories

OK to live completely normally ("If you want a banana split, order a banana split," says Dr. Green)

OK, or almost OK, to forget about diets—you do not even have to "pay too much attention" to a booklet you are given of suggested diets.

The panacea that makes all this possible is: pills, about 40 to 45 of them a week. Obesity, says Dr. Green, is caused simply by overeating, which in turn is caused by a lot of psychological hangups which Dr. Green frankly isn't too concerned about ("Keep the mouth churning— that's their outlet for what's bothering them," says Dr. Green). To lose weight, therefore, you have to eat less. Diets are silly because "nobody pays any attention to them." So you take pills, which suppress your appetite and "count your calories for you." You just don't feel like eating as much as before. And when you start eating fewer calories than your body burns, you will start, to use one of the Doctor's most engaging phrases, "living off your own fat."

So that the maximum number of patients can flow through this system with the same low-cost efficiency and ease that soda bottles on a conveyor belt are automatically filled and capped, Dr. Green has discarded some long-cherished medical *modi operandi,* exposing them as pudgy superfluities. Samples:

*Appointments*: You need only show up during office hours.

*Bills*: You pay cash for each visit.

*Detailed examinations*: All you get is a minute or two's worth of pulse, blood pressure, and quick psychological motivation ("Twelve and a half pounds less, Mrs. Lichtenstein! That's wonderful! And how does your husband like you now?" or "You've gained, Mrs. Van Gogh. Do you see that scale? Now look, we can help but you're the one that's got to get rid of that fat").

*Prescriptions*: Dr. Green dispenses his own medicine.

*Medical ethics prohibiting advertising*: Dr. Green makes Addressograph plates for every new patient who, whether she gives up Dr. Green after the first week or not, will continue to receive periodic mailings, including Christmas cards (printed, like all his forms, booklets, and paper matter, in Dr. Green's back-office printing shop). His mailing list is about seventy-five thousand.

*The theory that, to be cured, a patient first needs to be sick*: Dr. Green is willing to collect money from practically anyone. "If their husbands want them to look like Twiggy, that's their business, not mine," says Dr. Green. "It can't hurt them. A lot of American prisoners of war came home from Japan weighing only 65 pounds, and the only thing wrong with them was their teeth—probably from lack of vitamins."

Dr. Gordon L. Green, M.D. from Loyola University, is a graying, garrulous, gravel-voiced man whose tastes run to shiny black suits and gray ties (and sometimes black turtle-necks) and whose paunch (he weighs around 210) advertises, if not the success of his methods (which he says he uses), at least a sympathy with his patients' problems. Having delegated to others responsibility for the day-to-day operation of his business, he is able to spend much of his time in his comfortable Central Park South apartment, reflecting upon the status of his corporate image.

"What would you like to drink? We serve Diet Cola here," he said meaningfully as I walked through the foyer, almost stumbling over a large scale which stands next to a rococo gilt-edged wall mirror and an electric shoe-shine machine. His apartment bristles with such electronic delights as remote-control color TV with automatic antenna rotor motors, elaborate hi-fi, several tape recorders and electric pencil sharpeners.

Stretching out on a wide, soft chair, Dr Green remarked, "When you hear a doctor talk about how he's in it for glory and the love of mankind, don't listen. Probably 995 out of a thousand medical students are in school because being a doctor is one of the best-paying professions around. And the ones who turn out to be successful are the ones who admit it and run their practices like businessmen."

I pointed out that the viability of his business had been severely

questioned by the recent hearings on the dangers of diet pills before
Michigan Senator Philip A. Hart's Subcommittee on Antitrust and
Monopoly. A number of experts testified that some diet drugs dispensed by "health hucksters" can cause mental depression, addiction,
and even death.

"We don't use digitalis or any of the drugs the Hart people complained about, and furthermore we have *never* had a lawsuit or a
hospital case," he said loudly, rising dramatically to his feet, shaking a
shiny white replica of Venus de Milo on the color TV set and rattling a
picture of his yacht Nefertiti on the wall. "We don't use anything that's
not an accepted drug. We know our business. We watch it. We don't
take chances."

There was a brief silence. "You want proof? I'll show you proof! Look
at this," he ordered, pointing to a dog-eared Xeroxed fragment. "See
what it says? 'Effective for the treatment of obesity.' Right here in the
*Journal of the American Medical Association.* That's where doctors get
their information from. What do you think of that? And look. Look at
this. 'Department of Health, Education and Welfare.' How about *that*
for a reference? Pretty good, eh? Now sure, these drugs can be abused.
But hell, you can abuse aspirin, too. And you can jump out a window
also if you want to. Right?"

Publicity from the Hart hearings has, he admits, cut his business in
half. "Only a thousand last week. That's all that came in. We've even
been thinking of closing down." But he added that he plans to retaliate
by hiring a public relations advisor and sending out an "open letter" to
the mailing list saying how his pills are "among the most useful in the
world today" and blaming all the fuss on "yellow journalism" and
people who are upset because diet doctors dispense their own pills.

But, as he said while I stepped on the scale for a quick check on the
way out, the patients will flock back to him. "People still smoke
cigarets," he added.

Life with Dr. Green's system usually involves five basic pills or
capsules a day, color-coded. They come in seventeen attractive decora-
tor hues to indicate ingredients, and are branded with Dr. Green's
initials. They are usually taken on getting up, at lunchtime, in the
afternoon, at dinnertime, and late evening. All the pills contain some

amphetamines (the highest dose is the evening when most people like to gorge themselves), which is the appetite suppressor and lasts around four hours. To balance out the amphetamines, "which can make patients a little high or nervous," some phenobarbitals are added, with highest doses around bedtime "to calm them down and help them sleep." Phenobarbitals are not included in the morning doses because "we don't want people walking around like a zombie all day."

Also in the attractive plastic pill box may be some stronger sleeping pills (Seconals) "if patients say they need them," vitamins, tranquilizers, and diuretics, which flush the body of excess fluids to make weight loss show up on the scales sooner. Mixed in, too, is some thyroid—"I don't know that it does all that much but they say it increases basal metabolism or something." Depending on the patient, six to twelve pounds will fade away the first week, fifteen to thirty the first month, and another ten to fifteen each of the following months.

Dr. Green's success is proof of the power of his pills. The problem is where to *keep* it off *without pills*. To wean patients from pills after the desired goal has been achieved, Dr. Green prescribes a smaller dose of "maintenance" pills. "Do not attempt weaning without the help of maintenance capsules," advise instructions given out to patients. "You will not succeed without them." Ultimately, in theory at least, patients learn to continue their pattern of reduced consumption without any pills.

In practice, however, a substantial number of patients, used to the Green philosophy that taking it off involves little self-denial or self-discipline, find themselves unable to cope with a pill-less existence. They experience a resurgence of appetite (the old mouth-churning psychological hangups are probably still present) and soon return to their former corpulence. They then either give up the whole idea or return more or less permanently to Dr. Green's $7-a-week regimen.

Reactions from his patients tend to vary with the amount of will power they were able to muster once they had taken off the excess weight. "Those people in Washington can say whatever they want about Doc Green," says a forty-three-year-old Riverhead mother, "but he brought me from 190 down to 115 last year, and I haven't had to go back to him since."

"It's nothing but a racket," counters a young Massapequa secretary.

"Sure, I took some weight off, but when I got fed up with the $7-a-week stuff I put it all back on, plus another ten. I'm trying Metrecal now. It's cheaper."

For his contributions to the legacy of Hippocrates, Dr. Green is well rewarded. By buying pills in lots of 100,000 direct from the manufacturer (who grinds them out at the rate of 18,000 an hour), he has reduced his cost per pill to under a penny. (He grandly tells patients he doesn't charge them for medicine.) Outside of rent, his only major expense is personnel. Because the work of examining up to a hundred patients a day is, as Dr. Green admits, monotonous (a new doctor learns all he needs to know about the business in "a couple of days"), it is sufficient to recruit the ten to twelve doctors he needs. He thus must offer them at least $35,000 a year with two-and-a-half-month vacation. Still, considering 2,500 patients at $7 a week, subtracting problem expenses and figuring in tax arrangements, Dr. Green probably nets something well into six figures.

He has periodically toyed with the idea of extending his practice into such other easily diagnosed areas as arthritis, but the cash has flowed in so abundantly from the diet business that he now asks, "What do I need it for? I'm sixty-four. I got all the money I want. Who needs the additional headaches?"

He has now settled back comfortably to enjoy his three homes (Central Park South, Huntington, and Florida), his nine cars, and an endless succession of boats (he buys one yacht, tires of it, sells it, buys another) and vacations (Caribbean, Middle East, Around the World).

But when he is directly confronted with the question of whether he's in the diet business for the cash, Dr. Green, despite his assembly-line methods and cynicism about doctors with a mission, slips abruptly into Schweitzer-land. "A patient you've made thinner is much more gratified than one whose life you've saved," he says, his voice rising. "I remember one young schoolteacher who was 235, and I brought her down to 135. One day she ran in and told me she'd gotten her first date that hadn't been fixed up by one of her girl friends. She actually grabbed me around the neck and kissed me. I get more kicks out of things like that than anything."

*IF you want to improve yourself, to make your mark as a famous writer-painter-photographer-musician-executive-salesman, you will find the woods are full of teachers. For a fee, they will mix your media. They might even mix you up. But you will be a more interesting person as a result.*

# I, a Nervous Renaissance Man

### by Marvin Kitman

A woman in a tweed pants suit came up to me at a party recently and asked, "What do you do?" I told her that I spent all my time writing magazine articles. "Man," she said, "you're really in a bag."

"Sir?" I asked politely, as she started to edge away.

After the same embarrassing thing happened several times that night, I confided in a friend who seemed to understand the scene. "What's wrong with me?"

There are some things even a friend won't tell you. But apparently this wasn't one of them. He blurted it right out: "You're not what's happening today, baby."

"If you mean I have to start letting my hair grow," I said, "forget it. That's OK for you guys with straight hair, but I'd wind up looking like Shirley Temple."

"All the beautiful people today," he continued, telling it to me the way it is, "are mixing media. Andy Warhol is a painter who's making films. Tom Wolfe is a writer who draws. Robert Rauschenberg is a painter composing electronic music. George Plimpton is a quarterback who plays triangle with the New York Philharmonic. You've got to get yourself another bag." I laughed at him.

I've lived through fads before. I missed out on the excitement of the beat generation, for example, when my mother wouldn't let me go hitch-hiking. I could sit this one out, too, until men who did one thing well came into fashion at cocktail parties again. But I read in the papers a few days later that what's happening in the arts today is the second Renaissance. The first Renaissance lasted ninety-six years. I couldn't bear the thought of being a nobody at parties that long.

When I ran into my friend, the hippie, at another party the following weekend, I explained, "I want to be what's happening. How do I get with it, man?"

"Find your thing," he advised.

"My *what*?"

"Blow your mind." he said. "Try everything and see what turns you on."

What gave me the courage to try to become a Renaissance man was a story in *Life* magazine about the discovery of the lost notebooks of Leonardo da Vinci. The master had set down his ideas and visions on the usual wide variety of subjects, including art, poetry, tanks, the nature of the human body, and bicycle chains. It reminded me of my own early notebooks.

Lost now since the 1930's and 1940's, the hard-covered "composition" notebooks from grammar school days at P.S. 186 in Brooklyn were filled with sketches of military inventions such as death rays. At ages eleven and twelve, like Leonardo, I was very much interested in anatomy, setting down my unique ideas on the subject in a series of drawings of classmates Selma and Marilyn without their clothes on. My sketches of giant hamburgers and Coke bottles, drawn as the lunch hour approached, anticipated developments in art. While others wrote down lines from Robert Louis Stevenson to memorize for poetry-appreciation class, I saw beauty in things around me. I still remember the first stanza of one of the environmental poems in my notebook:

> *Have you tried Wheaties?*
> *They're whole wheat with all of the bran.*
> *Won't you try Wheaties?*
> *For wheat is the best food of man.*
>
> *They're crispy and crunchy the whole year through.*
> *Jack Armstrong never tires of them and neither will you.*

*So just buy Wheaties,*
*The best breakfast food in the land.*

In those days, my mind had no boundaries. The only problem now
was picking out my thing.

I decided to try novel-writing first. Every writer, I had been hearing
for years, had at least one novel in him. Aware of my technical lim-
itations—I had never written fiction before—I decided to study with
the masters in my spare time. I sent in a coupon to enroll in the fiction
course at the Famous Writers School of Westport, Connecticut.

Several days later, the aptitude test, which weeded out applicants
whose talent wasn't worth developing, arrived at Kitman House in
Leonia, New Jersey. I answered the easy questions first:

Q. Name your three favorite authors.
A. Jacqueline Susann, Harold Robbins, Irving Wallace.
Q. What do you hope to achieve as a writer?
A. My goal is to write a first novel that the critics will call "prom-
   ising." I also would like to clear 1.5 mil on paperback and
   movie rights.

But I got hung up on the essay question: "Tell of an experience you
have had at some time in your life—any kind of experience you feel a
reader would be interested in." Rather than bore famous writers such as
Bruce Catton, Bennett Cerf, Rudolph Flesch, Bergen Evans, and Faith
Baldwin with anything from my dull present life, I decided to write
about the kind of experience I hoped to have once I became a Renaissance man. I copied a few paragraphs verbatim from pages 194 and
195 of my favorite literary work, *Valley of the Dolls*, giving it an original twist by writing in the first person and by changing the characters'
names from Jennifer and Tony to Selma and Marvin:

> My hands stroked her breasts. My fingers fumbled with the
> buttons on her satin robe. "Jesus . . . why do you wear robes with
> buttons?" I pulled the robe off her shoulders, down to the waist.
> I stood back, my breath coming faster.
> "Selma, no one should have boobs like that." I touched them
> lightly.

She smiled. "They're yours, Marvin."

I buried my face in them, sinking to my knees. "Oh, God, I just can't believe it. Every time I touch them, I can't believe it." My mouth was greedy. . . .

"Marvin, let's get married."

"Sure, baby, sure. . . ." I was fumbling at the rest of the buttons on her robe. It fell to the floor. She backed away. I crawled on my knees after her. She backed away again,

"Marvin, all of this"—she stroked her body—"is *not* yours . . . it's *mine!*"

I came after her. She eluded me again. She stroked her thighs, her fingers touching between her legs. "That's mine, too," she said softly. "But *we* want you, Marvin," she whispered hoarsely. "Take your clothes off. . . ."

And so forth, for two more pages.

Before I got around to mailing the test, which had been sent to me "without obligation," a member of the faculty of the Famous Writers School called and said he just happened to be in New Jersey and would be stopping by to mark my test in person. I looked forward to having an intelligent discussion with the visiting professor on technical matters such as plot, subplot, and character motivation. But he put me off with his opening words: "I just flunked a lady in Teaneck who was interested in writing only for art's sake. We're looking for students who are serious about writing for the market, people who want to earn money."

"You came to the right place," I said. "How does the Famous Writers School recommend writing a best seller—with a manual or an electric typewriter?" He said subject matter was important, too. "That's why I want to write about sex and perversion," I explained.

"Surely, as a writer," he chuckled, "you wouldn't mind getting those big beautiful checks writing about other subjects, too, would you?"

I assured him that I also wanted to write about other forms of human depravity. "You know—grass, pot, Mary Jane, Acapulco gold, acid, freak-outs, blowing your mind. I want to tell it like it really is."

Every time I discussed Proust, Stendahl, Gide, and Joyce and their influence on Burroughs, Genet, and Jackie Susann, he brought the subject back to money and how important it was for a writer to learn how to

sell his stuff. "Do you teach novelists how to invent new art forms?" I
asked. "My thing is something I call 'fictional reportage.' "

He skimmed through the "Ability to Use Words" and "Grammar"
sections of the test booklet but read somewhat slower when he reached
the essay question.

"You certainly capture the reader's interest here," he said. "You have
a way with dialogue . . . suspense builds . . . ear for language . . . terse
style . . ." Miss Susann would be pleased to learn that her work was
finally being praised at the academy level. "Frankly, this is almost
pornographic."

"You're too kind," I said modestly.

Nearing the climax of the essay, he removed his glasses to wipe the
steam off. "Holy mackerel," he said. "I know who you've been influenced by."

"Who?" I asked uneasily.

"You've been reading Mickey Spillane."

As far as I was concerned, the Famous Writers School had flunked
the test. They didn't recognize good writing when they saw it. But my
face fell anyway, when I saw my grade.

"C plus is a very good mark," the visiting professor explained,
"although not as good as B, which is superior. In all my experience, I've
heard of only one writer getting an A." That must have been Leon Uris,
I guessed. He said that I had a lot to learn about fiction but that the
school would be willing to gamble on me anyway. For only $625 I could
study the novel under a famous writer like Faith Baldwin.

Could Miss Baldwin, who hadn't written a best seller in years, teach
my anything about sex, drugs, and depravity? Could she give me the
courage to use modern words like S**T or F**K? "She's not my bag,"
I told him bluntly.

In the half hour it took to get him out of the house, the Famous
Writers School man spoke so highly of my raw talent that I decided to
start working on my first novel that night. I wrote "Chapter One" on
several pieces of paper. Everything was going according to schedule. I
had developed the biggest writer's block on my street.

While thumbing through *The Reader's Digest* in search of advice on
how to live with myself as a social failure, I came across an ad that
began: WE TEACH YOU HOW TO DRAW AND PAINT SUCCESSFULLY AT HOME.

By the time I finished reading how the Famous Artists School of Westport, Connecticut, could teach anybody with talent how to earn money in his spare time, it occurred to me that perhaps my thing was art. That's where the action was today—and the bread. Besides, a man had to use only one piece of paper to create a masterpiece, and he could erase.

A visiting professor from the Famous Artists School arrived at my house several days after the art-talent test was sent to me "without obligation." I explained that I was interested in more than just drawing, painting, or sculpting: I wanted to make a real statement with my art. He looked first at some of the statements I had made in the section of the talent test labeled "Tell Us About Yourself":

Q. Why would you like to become a good artist?
A. Make money; make the scene.
Q. Have you studied art? Where?
A. I browse in the soup and cleanser sections of the supermarket and read *Time* Magazine regularly to learn what's happening in art.
Q. Which mediums interest you most?
A. I·plan to major in human figures, but I also would like to work with auto bodies.

He said all my answers were right.

"How do I find subjects to draw for the Human Figures home-study course at Famous Artists?" I asked with some embarrassment. "Do you send the models over the state line from Connecticut?" It disturbed me to hear that I would have to find my own subjects. "Well, do you at least teach students how to get girls to take off their clothes?" That would come with experience, he explained.

Everything went smoothly on the art-talent test until the faculty member looked at my drawings for the creative portion of the exam. Question three was called "Your Sense of Form." On the page was a large pencil sketch of a nude girl. The instructions were, "Complete the outlined figure by drawing a costume on it. Use an ordinary soft pencil to clothe the figure. Be sure to retain the feeling of the human form beneath the clothes." There were three examples of how the problem might be solved—all hopelessly square, when compared with my rendering.

"I've seen ten thousand tests," the visiting professor said when he saw my creation, "but I've never seen anything like *that*." I had put a nun's coif and veil on the figure's head. Then I added a topless dress, black mesh stockings and knee-high stainless-steel boots.

"I admit that it's not fully realized," I told the professor, "but it's meant to symbolize the ecumenical mood between spiritual and secular society."

"That's what you're trying to say here?!"

"Well, sir, I wanted the figure to represent the modern church emerging, a real swinging nun. I call the genre 'pope art.'"

The master opened his black-leather portfolio and handed me a calendar published by the Hartford Mutual Insurance Company. The illustration for each month, he explained, had been done by a Famous Artists student in his spare time. "Wouldn't you rather paint like this and earn real money?"

Suspecting that this might be the art-appreciation part of the test, I put on a pair of midnight-blue sunglasses to see the calendar art better. The farm and seashore scenes still looked bilious. Then I flicked the light switch on and off to see if stroboscopic go-go lights helped. "No," I said finally. "You don't seem to understand. I want to be a *fine* artist, somebody like Andy Warhol, Jasper Johns, Claes Oldenberg, Roy Lichtenstein, or Antonio Varga."

"What is it you admire in *those* people?"

"First of all, the high prices they get for their work. But I also admire their creative approaches to capital gains, reproduction rights, the way they write off travel expenses on their income-tax forms, their investments in oil wells and art galleries. . . ."

"There is an old saying in art," he said. "Before you can paint, you must learn how to draw. You cannot put the cart before the horse. You must learn the basics. Tell me, what have you *done* in art?"

I showed him the box of Rinso from my blue period, which I had made art by adding my signature. "What do you call this?" he asked.

"Some people call it art," I said. "But I'm not completely satisfied with it."

"Good. What do you think is wrong?"

"The signature should be larger." He was frowning. "What's the matter?" I asked. "Do you doubt the authenticity of this work?"

He quickly said, "No, no. I'm sure you did it yourself "

Then I pointed to my bull's-eye, a found object from an archery range in Paramus. "That's representative of my Robert Indiana period," I explained. "And this I call *Salami Sandwich,* from my lunch period." The only thing he seemed to be enthusiastic about was a childlike painting rich in strong primary colors, entitled *Crude Oil.* "My son did that," I said coldly, steering him toward my first piece of modern sculpture, a broken-down club chair, an example of the art of destruction. "He also helped do this."

"Have you ever tried to draw people?" he asked.

*Zonk!* Another insult. I had answered the last question in the test booklet—"Make an original drawing or picture of any subject you wish in the space above"—with a portrait of Lamont Cranston, done in the Ben-Gay technique of one of America's great artists, Roy Lichtenstein. First I drew a frame bordering the rectangular space, then I added a plaque at the bottom in the shape of a comic-strip bubble, suitably inscribed: WHO KNOWS WHAT EVIL LURKS IN THE HEARTS OF MEN. But the symbolism escaped this so-called "art expert."

"What is this?" he complained.

"There is actually less here than meets the eye," I explained patiently. "I drew Lamont Cranston at work as The Shadow." The visiting professor didn't say anything. "I hope this isn't your way of telling me the Famous Artists School thinks that what's popular today isn't art," I said angrily.

"You have a flair," he said, withdrawing a batch of admission forms from his portfolio. "You definitely have the talent. It would be criminal not to do something about it. We have twelve famous artists, men such as Jon Whitcomb and Norman Rockwell, ready to help you become a success. The complete course is only six hundred and twenty-five dollars."

"For that kind of bread, will your school teach me the fundamentals, like how to get Robert and Ethel Scull interested in my work, which are the best galleries to exhibit in, and how to keep my prices up?" The visiting professor's silence was making me suspicious. "What *do* you teach at the Famous Artists School?" I asked.

The visiting professor marked my test B minus. My grades were already so good, I told him, that I didn't see much point in going any further with the Famous Artists School. He had been so unstinting in praise of my ability that I felt like a child prodigy. They had nothing more to teach me.

But I didn't rest on my laurels. While waiting for an inspiration about what to draw, paint, or sculpt, I turned on to something that combined all my talents—underground-film making. I screened the rushes of the home movies I had made over the years. Their slick commercial quality so depressed me that I wrote to Andy Warhol for pointers.

"Everybody's been saying they don't like your painting," began my letter to the old master, "but that you are a great film maker. Would it be possible for me to study the art of cinema with you? I especially want to take your course in shooting out of focus and making double exposures. What I have in mind is a feature based on my novel. I plan to film it by focusing the camera on the pages, beginning with "Chapter One, Page one, Page two, and so forth, without cutting a word. My goal is to make an uncompromising film, one that people will walk out on.

"P.S. I have my own hand-held camera."

The next day, a faculty member from the correspondence music school I'd written to stopped by the house to discuss my lessons in advanced piano and composition. "Do you know Chopin's Opus 3, Number 9?" he asked, as I sat down at the piano.

"I don't play Chopin."

"How about Rachmaninoff, then?"

"I don't play Rachmaninoff." After running through MacDowell, Saint-Saëns and Rossini, I finally made it clear to him that I played only the moderns—more specifically, John Cage, and then only his important work 4'33". "My ambition is to compose serious classical music like that," I explained. "In fact, I've just finished my first piece. May I play *Concerto Sinusoidal Wave on a Frequency of 20,000 Cycles Per Second in A Flat* for you?" I turned the tape recorder on. After a while, I asked, "Well, what's your professional opinion?"

"I didn't hear anything," he finally said, "except a dog howling out in your yard."

"That's the beauty of it. The reason he's howling is that I'm blowing a dog whistle. It's above the threshold of human hearing, of course, but

with repeated listening, you may be able to feel it in your molars. Why
don't you listen to the whole thing again?"

"That won't be necessary," he said. "Is that the only kind of music
you're interested in learning?"

"Well, random sounds also turn me on."

He said he thought I could learn how to do those things myself. I
thanked him for his confidence.

Several days later, the phone rang in my study, where I was composing my *Symphony Number One*, which called for the musicians to sit
idly by their instruments for an hour. I hoped it would be Mr. Warhol
giving me an appointment to take my screen test or advising me to
forget technique and concentrate on getting my first film entered in a
festival. "This is the Fred Astaire Dance School," said a sultry woman's
voice. "We have an important question to ask you. What was the name
of the first President of the United States?"

"Booker T. Washington," I answered.

"That's close enough," she said breathlessly. "You've just won a free
private one-hour dance lesson. This is your chance to learn the modern
dance steps that may have been keeping you from achieving social
success."

"I have a physical handicap."

"I'm so sorry," she said sympathetically. "Forgive me for calling."

"What I mean is I have two left feet. Ever since I was a teen-ager, all
the girls have been saying I'm hopeless. It would take a lifetime of
lessons to teach me how to dance. I know your studio wouldn't want to
get involved in long-term arrangements like that."

"If you can walk," she said, breathing hard, "we can teach you how to
dance. When would you like your free lesson? Any time at your
convenience."

Even a Renaissance man like Leonardo probably did the "in" dances,
such as the tarantella, when he wasn't painting portraits or taking flying
lessons. "I'll be tied up working on my novel, painting, composing my
symphony, and making my film until 11:30 p.m.," I explained. "Why
don't you come over to my place about midnight?"

She said I would have to go to the Fred Astaire Dance Studio nearest
my home to pick up my prize. But I couldn't find the time during the
next few days. What bothered me was how Renaissance men managed

to keep all the arts straight in their minds. In some way, I had to learn
how to organize my spare time, which by now was sheer chaos.

On my way over to the dance studio on the bus a few days later, I
saw an ad in the paper for a kind of famous executive's school, called
Mr. Executive of New York, which claimed to teach bright young men
all the short cuts to the top in the business world, including how to
budget their time effectively. Fortunately, a new course was starting
that night at the Columbia University Club in New York and the ad
offered a free first lesson. At that moment, capital gains seemed more
important than the boogaloo, so I went off to gain administrative
wisdom.

Our teacher—or group leader, as he called himself—explained to the
twenty-four men on their way up that psychologists have proven you
have ten seconds to make a good impression at an interview. That is
certainly true at a party. "At Mr. Executive, we teach you how to look
like an executive, act like an executive, and sound like an executive." I
would need to know all those things when I started talking to the
Rockefellers, the Guggenheims, and the Fords about foundation sub-
sidies to continue my studies in the arts. "While you're up," I'd be able
to say firmly to the man interviewing me, "get me a grant."

The class was divided into "buzz groups" for brain-storming hy-
pothetical problems. The object was to teach us how to freewheel, to
unblock our minds, to think creatively. "At Mr. Executive," the group
leader said enthusiastically, "we learn how to think smarter, not work
harder." I came up with the winning answer on the question of how to
cure lateness at the plant: "Last man in the door blows the whistle."

Everybody also had to make a five-minute speech about himself.
While listening to the other fellows talk about their things, I got to
thinking about the similarities between business and art. Basically, we
were all striving for the same thing: recognition. The faster we got it,
the better. My classmates were all content to work their way up to the
top of big corporations. But I wanted instant recognition. I needed a
*shtick*. Suddenly it came to me: the fruition of my own private renaissance would be to open a *boutique*.

A *boutique* run by a Renaissance man like myself would soon become
a mecca of wit and wisdom, a gathering place for the literary set, the
art set, the television set. What would bring the customers in would be

a massive mixed-media project: I could read aloud from my novel in progress; exhibit my paintings, drawings, and sculpture; show my homemade movie—all at the same time. Even the classical-music crowd would be lured into the store by my John Cage recitals, nonplayed on a seventeenth-century harpsichord.

"Please advise if your firm would be interested in manufacturing the following line of clothes for my shop," I wrote to the president of the Kimberly-Stevens Corporation: "(1) a six-button, double-breasted pinch-back formal dinner jacket with sergeant's stripes and color-coordinated epaulets; (2) a disposable paper mourning suit for use at funerals or other occasions where black is appropriate; (3) a 'blazer,' or whatever less incendiary name the paper-fabric industry would call this type of sports jacket; (4) a business suit—an executive model made out of *Wall Street Journals*—for the man who wants to look like a million bucks; and (5) a raincoat of blotting paper. My *boutique* plans to carry a quality line of merchandise, so the materials should be of high rag content. They shouldn't show footprints and should be water-resistant enough so that a woman might still be able to cry on a man's shoulder."

"For your business suit," answered Claiborn M. Carr, Jr., president of one of the largest paper-fabric corporations, "perhaps the cuffs can be left starkly white for those in the habit of jotting notes; and, for those who don't take shorthand, a more extensive sleeve ranging from wrist to midway between the elbow and the shoulder can be left white."

I tried to find loopholes in my plans for the *boutique*, which I planned to call "The Collected Papers of Marvin Kitman." Should paper suits go out of style, they'd still be useful as potholders, as napkins, or for polishing the sports car. The only obstacle standing in the way of the *boutique's* success seemed to be me. Nobody under thirty would trust me, because of my voice.

IS YOUR SPEECH HOLDING YOU BACK? asked an ad in *The New York Times* the next morning. "Dorothy Sarnoff, famed Broadway and TV star, can give you the speech personality you've always wanted." I went over to her salon on the mezzanine of the Hotel St. Moritz to hear what the beautiful actress could do for me with her Speech Cosmetics Course.

"Say anything you like," she said, putting my voice on tape so we could analyze the problem together. Thinking about her musical-comedy background, the first thing that came to mind was: "The rain in

Spain stays mainly on the plain. . . ." She suggested that I tell a story instead. I told her about my thing. There wasn't a wet eye in the house.

"Your problem is that you don't speak with authority," she explained. "What's missing in your voice is confidence. In the show-business sense, you don't have what we call *sell*."

"That's why I want to learn how to speak with an English accent."

"Noel Coward wouldn't be *you*," she laughed. I agreed with her: a Coward voice would be all right if I wanted to make it with the literati.

"The kind of accent I need to be effective in my *boutique* is a working-class-English accent. Can you teach me the East Liverpool sound?"

"People want to hear the real *you*," she said, shaking her head.

"Couldn't we use electronic amplification sound equipment? The record companies do it all the time with kids from South Philadelphia."

"You'd be a phony."

I looked around to see who was calling me names. Most speech teachers work in drab rooms in office buildings. Miss Sarnoff's salon was filled with mock Louis XIV furniture, glass crystal chandeliers, and mirrors with gold frames made of plaster of Paris. I realized that I could never get a groovy voice surrounded by such bad vibrations; Miss Sarnoff didn't even look like the kind person pictured in her newspaper ads. "I'll ring you up sometime," I said. "Cheery bye."

On my way back to Leonia that day, it struck me that the Kitman *boutique* would never work after all. Running a clothing store, even under such favorable mixed-media circumstances, would mean being face to face with hundreds of people each day; and who ever heard of a brilliant, sensitive artist being able to get along with anyone? Can you imagine one of the greats—Mick Jagger, for instance—asking whether the pants should break a little at the shoe tops, or maybe be without cuffs altogether? Of course not. Well, Kitman wouldn't stoop, either.

But my newly emerging talents were going to waste. Then, suddenly, the vast, rolling, inspirational Jersey Meadows turned me on. Eureka! North Beach! I had found my thing! I whipped out an old Baby Ruth wrapper carried in case of artistic emergency and deftly sketched the first new ad, complete with board of advisers and Connecticut farmhouse. I was ready to announce the first-semester curriculum of the Marvin Kitman Famous Renaissance Man School.

Y OU *are bothered, disturbed. Something, you*
*feel, is vaguely wrong. You are sombre and you*
*don't respond well to others. You have no sense*
*of intimacy. Maybe you are too well-adjusted.*

# Joy Is the Prize: A Trip to the Esalen Institute

*by Leo Litwak*

Big Sur is an eighty-mile stretch of California coast below the Monterey Peninsula. It is approximately midway between Los Angeles and San Francisco and difficult of access from either direction. Before the coastal highway was completed in 1936, the shore was accessible only by foot. The Los Padres National Forest, one of the largest preserves in the country, extends thirty miles inland and is two hundred miles long; it occupies most of the area. Not much land is available for private ownership. There are only three hundred residents. The rugged terrain of Los Padres includes redwood canyons, barren mountain ranges, desert flora, thick forests. It is the province of mountain lions and wild boar.

Stone cliffs rise two thousand feet above the ocean. Beyond a wedge of meadow, the steeply inclined hillside begins. For great distances there is no meadow at all and the serpentine coastal highway hangs on the cliffside. It is a two-lane road, sometimes impassable after heavy rains. The fog bank wavers off shore. When it sweeps in, the traveler faces an uncanny trip, guided entirely by a few white dashes of the center line that are visible. With hairpin turns, sharp rises and declines, the road can be dangerous in bad weather. On clear days when the setting sun ignites dust particles on your windshield you are forced to drive blind for dangerous seconds.

Nonetheless, four thousand people traveled this road last year, in disregard of weather, aimed toward the Esalen Institute, famous until a few years ago under a different name, Big Sur Hot Springs. These are unlikely adventurers. They are doctors, social workers, clinical psychologists, teachers, students, business executives, engineers, housewives— or just fun lovers who have come to take the baths.

Big Sur Hot Springs was originally renowned as the Eden discovered by Henry Miller and Jack Kerouac. Joan Baez once lived there. The springs were purchased in 1910 from a man named Slade by Dr. Henry C. Murphy, of Salinas. It was Dr. Murphy's intention to establish a health spa. In order to use the mineral waters he brought in two bathtubs by fishing sloop. They were hauled up the cliff and placed on the ledge at the source of the springs. But because of their inaccessibility, the springs did not flourish as a spa. Not until Dr. Murphy's grandson, Michael, assumed operation of the property in the mid 1950's did the baths begin to receive attention—attention that has grown with the development of Esalen Institute.

Michael Murphy at thirty-seven appears to be in his early twenties. He is slender and boyish and has a marvelous smile. I took part in a panel discussion at Hot Springs some years ago and I was not impressed either by the topic, my performance, or the audience. I did enjoy the baths. I had misgivings about Murphy's program, yet none about him. He seemed to me generous, charming, innocent, credulous, enthusiastic, and enormously sympathetic. A Stanford alumnus who had done some graduate work in psychology and philosophy, he had recently returned from an eighteen-month study of the art of meditation at the Aurobindo Ashram in Pondicherry, India, and he devoted a considerable part of each day to meditation. I believe he had—and still has—in mind some great mission, based on his Indian experience. I am not quite sure what the scope of his mission is. A friend of his told me: "Mike wants to turn on the world." Esalen Institute is his instrument for doing so. It has come a long way from the shoddy panels of a few years ago. Its spreading impact may seriously affect our methods of therapy and education.

In the course of a year, almost a thousand professional persons—social workers, psychiatrists, clinical psychologists—enroll in Esalen workshops. Close to seven hundred psychotherapists have been trained to administer techniques devised by staff members—Frederick Perls, Virginia Satir, Bernard Gunther, and William Schutz. These techniques have been demonstrated at hospitals, universities, and medical schools. This year Esalen has opened a San Francisco extension which in the first two months of operation has attracted an attendance in excess of ten thousand, offering the same workshops and seminars that are available at Big Sur. Esalen-type communities have begun to appear throughout the country, in Atlanta, Chicago, Los Angeles, Cleveland, La Jolla. One has even appeared in Vancouver, Canada. Murphy offers advice and help, and permits use of his mailing list.

Consider some offerings of the Esalen winter brochure. Seminars led by Alan Watts, the Zen interpreter, and Susan Sontag, the camp interpreter. Workshops for professional therapists conducted by Frederick Perls, an early associate of Freud and Wilhelm Reich and a founder of Gestalt therapy. A lecture panel including the psychologist Carl Rogers and Herman Kahn, the "thinking about the unthinkable" man. Some of the titles are: "Kinetic Theater," "Psycotechnics," "Do You Do It? Or Does It Do You?", "Dante's Way to the Stars," "Creativity and the Daimonic," "On Deepening the Marriage Encounter," "Tibetan Book of the Dead," "Anxiety and Tension Control," "Racial Confrontation as a Transcendental Experience."

What principle guides a mélange that consists of dance workshops, therapy workshops, sensory-awareness experiments, the Tibetan Book of the Dead, Herman Kahn, Carl Rogers, Frederick Perls, and Susan Sontag?

Esalen's vice president, George B. Leonard, has written a general statement of purpose. He says: "We believe that all men somehow possess a divine potentiality; that ways may be worked out—specific, systematic ways—to help, not the few, but the many toward a vastly expanded capacity to learn, to love, to feel deeply, to create. We reject the tired dualism that seeks God and human potentialities by denying the joys of the senses, the immediacy of unpostponed life." The programs, he says, are aimed toward "the joys of the senses."

I had signed up for a workshop led by Dr. William Schutz, a group therapist who has taught at Harvard and the Albert Einstein College of Medicine, among other institutions, and has served on the staff of the

National Training Laboratories Interne Training Program at Bethel, Me. His latest book, *Joy*, was published in 1967 by Grove Press.

In the brochure description of Dr. Schutz's workshop I read a warning that the experience woull be more than verbal: "An encounter workshop with body movements, sensory awareness, fantasy experiments, psychodrama. Developing the ability to experience joy is the workshop's guiding theme."

Joy as the prize of a five-day workshop?

"How can we speak of joy," Leonard has written, "on this dark and suffering planet? How can we speak of anything else? We have heard enough of despair."

It was easy enough to dismiss the language. It seemed naïve to promise so great a reward for so small an investment. Joy for $175 (a five-day workshop) and $3000 (a nine-months course in Esalen techniques) seemed cheap at the price. I did have considerable anxieties that some of those "body movements" might be humiliating. And what precisely was meant by "sensory awareness"?

Esalen has changed considerably since my previous visit. Rows of new cabins are ranged along terraces on the hillside. The lodge is located at the bottom of a steep incline, in a meadow. The meadow is perhaps two hundred yards deep and ends at the cliff edge. The Pacific Ocean is 150 feet below. A staff of fifty operates the kitchen, supervises the baths, cleans the cabins and garden, and works on construction.

I passed hippy laborers, stripped to the waist, long hair flowing, operating with pick and shovel. Dreamy girls in long gowns played flutes near the pool.

I was somewhat put off by what I considered to be an excessive show of affection. Men hugged men. Men hugged women. Women hugged women. These were not hippies, but older folks, like myself, who had come for the workshop. People flew into one another's arms, and it wasn't my style at all.

After dinner, thirty of us met in the gallery for our first session. We began our excursion toward joy at 9 p.m. of a Sunday in a woodsy room on a balmy, starry night.

William Schutz, solidly built, with bald head and muzzle beard, began by telling us that in the course of the workshop we would come to dangerous ground. At such times we ought not to resist entering, for in this area lay our greatest prospect for self-transcendence. He told us to avoid verbal manipulations and to concentrate on our feelings.

We began with exercises. A fat lady in leotards directed us to be absurd. We touched our noses with our tongues. We clutched one another, made faces at one another. Afterward, we gathered in groups of five and were given an ambiguous instruction to discover one another by touching in any way we found agreeable. I crouched in front of a strange-looking young man with an underslung jaw and powerful shoulders. I tried unlocking his legs and he glared at me.

When Shutz asked each group of five to select one couple that seemed least close, the young man with the underslung jaw selected me. The hostile pairs were then requested to stand at opposite diagonals of the room and approach each other. They were to do whatever they felt like doing when they met in the center of the room. A burly middle-aged man marched toward a petite lady. They met, they paused, stared, then suddenly embraced. The next couple, two husky men, both frozen rigid, confronted each other, stared, then also embraced. The young man and I came next. We started at opposite diagonals. We met in the center of the room. I found myself looking into the meanest, coldest eyes I had even seen. He pressed his hands to his sides, and it was clear to me that we were not going to embrace. I reached for his hand to shake it. He jerked free. I put my hand on his shoulder; he shrugged me off. We continued staring and finally returned to our group.

There was a general discussion of this encounter. Some feared we might start fighting. Nothing, of course, was further from my mind. I had gone out, intending to play their game and suddenly found myself staring at a lunatic. He had very mean, cold eyes, a crazy shape to his jaw, lips so grim that his ill-feeling was unmistakable. Back in our group he said to me, in a raspy, shrill voice: "You thought I was going to bat you in the face; that's why you turned away." There was a slurred quality to his speech, and it occurred to me that I might have triggered off a madman. I denied that I had turned away and I was challenged to stare him down. I was annoyed that I had been forced into something so silly.

We proceeded, on the basis of our first impressions, to give one another names, which we kept for the duration of the workshop. My nemesis accepted the name of Rebel. There was a plump, lovely girl we called Kate. A silent, powerful man with spectacles we named Clark. Our fat group leader received the name of Brigitte. A lumpy, solemn man with thick spectacles we named Gary. An elegant, trim middle-aged woman we named Sheba. A buxom, mournful woman with long hair became Joan. A jovial middle-aged pipe smoker with a Jean Hersholt manner we named Hans. A fierce, mustached swaggerer in Bermuda shorts was Daniel. A quiet man with a little boy's face we named Victor. I was named Lionel. We were addressed by these names at all times.

I considered this renaming of ourselves a naïve attempt to create an atmosphere free of any outside reference. Many of the techniques impressed me as naïve. It seemed tactless and obvious to ask so blunt and vague a question as "What are you feeling?" Yet what happened in the course of five days was that the obvious became clarified. Clichés became significant.

I found myself discovering what had always been under my nose. I had not known how my body felt under conditions of tension or fear or grief. I discovered that I was numb. I had all sorts of tricks for avoiding encounter. I didn't particularly like to be touched. I avoided looking strangers in the eye. I took pride in my coolness and trickery. I didn't believe one should give oneself away. It seemed to me a virtue to appear cool, to be relatively immune to feeling, so that I could receive shocks without appearing to. I considered it important to keep up appearances. I'm no longer proud of what I now believe to be an incapacity rather than a talent.

I thought my group rather dull. I saw no great beauty and a great deal of weakness. I felt somewhat superior, since I was there on assignment, not by choice. I hated and feared Reb.

But in the next five days, I became enormously fond of these apparently uninteresting strangers. We encountered one another in violent and intimate ways, and I could no longer dismiss them.

I was convinced that Rebel was insane. He opened our second meeting with gratuitous insults. He referred to me as 'Charley Goodguy." When Brigitte, the leader of our group, told him not to think in stereotypes, he sneered at her. "Why don't you shut up, Fats?" It is difficult to convey the nastiness of his tone—an abrasive, jeering quality.

Daniel exploded. He called Rebel a shark and a rattlesnake. He said he wanted to quit the group because he despised this frightening, violent kid. "You scare me," he told Reb. "It's people like you who are responsible for Vietnam and Auschwitz. You're a monster and you're going to suck up all the energy of this group and it's not worth it. I want to get out."

I told Daniel his response seemed excessive. Vietnam and Auschwitz? "He's a little hostile," I said.

Reb didn't want any favors from me. "Hostile?" he sneered. "Say, I bet I know what you are. You sound to me like a professor. Or a pawnbroker. Which are you, a professor or a pawnbroker?"

Schutz intervened. He said to me and Rebel: "I feel you have something going. Why don't you have it out?" He suggested that we arm wrestle, an innocuous contest, but, under the circumstances, there seemed to be a great deal invested in winning or losing. My arm felt numb, and there was some trembling in my thighs. I feared I might not have all my strength, and Rebel appeared to be a powerful kid.

I pinned him so easily, however, that the group accused him of having quit. Daniel was jubilant: "You're a loser. You're trying to get clobbered."

Rebel was teased into trying again. On the second trial, he pressed my left arm down and demanded a rematch with the right hand. We remained locked together for close to twenty minutes. It was unbearable. I lost all sensation in my hand and arm. I willed my hand not to yield. Finally, I hoped he would press me down and get it over with. It ended when Rebel squirmed around and braced his foot against the wall and the contest was called.

Daniel was delighted by the outcome. He felt as though I had won something for him. Schutz asked: "Why don't you wrestle Reb?" Daniel despised violence. He probably would lose and he didn't want to give that monster the satisfaction of a victory. Violence was right up that shark's alley. He refused to play his games. Nonetheless, Daniel was on the ground with Rebel a moment later, beet red with strain, trembling down to his calves. Rebel raised his elbow, pressed Daniel down, and the match was called off. Daniel leaped to his feet, circled the room. He suddenly charged Rebel, who was seated, and knocked him from his chair. He then rushed at Schutz, yelling: "It's you I hate, you bastard, for making me do this." Schutz did not flinch, and Daniel backed off. I could see that his impulse was histrionic. I felt sorry for Reb, who mumbled: "I copped out. I should have hit him."

Reb later presented a different guise. Far from being an idiot, he was an extremely precocious twenty-year-old computer engineer, self-taught in the humanities. His father had abandoned the family when he was a child. His mother was a cold customer—never a sign of feeling. He didn't know where he stood with her. She taunted him in the same abrasive style which he tried with us.

Reb suffered sexual agonies that had brought him several hundred miles in search of a solution. He considered himself perverse and contemptible, the only impotent twenty-year-old kid in the world. He admitted he found women repugnant as sexual objects, and it was hardly surprising that his crude advances were rebuffed. He admitted that his strategy had been to strike out in hope that someone would strike back so that he might *feel*. He was boyish and affectionate outside the group.

My feeling for him underwent a complete reversal. He began to impress me as an intelligent kid, trying with great courage to repair terrible injuries. The monster I had seen simply vanished.

I never anticipated the effect of these revelations, as one after another of these strangers expressed his grief and was eased. I woke up one night and felt as if everything were changed. I felt as if I were about to weep. The following morning the feeling was even more intense.

Brigitte and I walked down to the cliff edge. We lay beneath a tree. She could see that I was close to weeping. I told her that I'd been thinking about my numbness, which I had traced to the war. I tried to keep the tears down. I felt vulnerable and unguarded. I felt that I was about to lose all my secrets and I was ready to let them go. Not being guarded, I had no need to put anyone down, and I felt what it was to be unarmed. I could look anyone in the eyes and my eyes were open.

That night I said to Daniel: "Why do you keep diverting us with intellectual arguments? I see suffering in your eyes. You give me a

glimpse of it, then you turn it off. Your eyes go dead and the intellectual stuff bores me. I feel that's part of your strategy."

Schutz suggested that the two of us sit in the center of the room and
talk to each other. I told Daniel that I was close to surrender. I wanted
to let go. I felt near to my grief. I wanted to release it and be purged.
Daniel asked about my marriage and my work. Just when he hit a
nerve, bringing me near the release I wanted, he began to speculate on
the tragedy of the human condition. I told him: "You're letting me off
and I don't want to be let off."

Schutz asked if I would be willing to take a fantasy trip.

It was late afternoon and the room was already dark. I lay down,
Schutz beside me, and the group gathered around. I closed my eyes.
Schutz asked me to imagine myself very tiny and to imagine that tiny
self entering my own body. He wanted me to describe the trip.

I saw an enormous statue of myself, lying in a desert, mouth open as
if I were dead. I entered my mouth. I climbed down my gullet,
entering it as if it were a manhole. I climbed into my chest cavity.
Schultz asked me what I saw. "It's empty," I said. "There's nothing
here." I was totally absorbed by the effort to visualize entering myself
and lost all sense of the group. I told Schutz there was no heart in my
body. Suddenly, I felt tremendous pressure in my chest, as if tears were
going to explode. He told me to go to the vicinity of the heart and
report what I saw. There, on a ledge of the chest wall, near where the
heart should have been, I saw a baby-buggy. He asked me to look into
it. I didn't want to, because I feared I might weep, but I looked, and I
saw a doll. He asked me to touch it. I was relieved to discover that it
was only a doll. Schutz asked me if I could bring a heart into my body.
And suddenly there it was, a heart sheathed in slime, hung with blood
vessels. And that heart broke me up. I felt my chest convulse. I exploded. I burst into tears.

I recognized the heart. The incident had occurred more than twenty
years before and had left me cold. I had written about it in a story
published long ago in *Esquire*. The point of the story was that such
events should have affected me but never did. The war in Germany
was about over. We had just taken a German village without resistance.
We had fine billets in German houses. The cellars were loaded with
jams and sausages and wine. I was the aid man with the outfit, and was

usually summoned by the call of "Aid man!" When I heard that call I became numb, and when I was numb I could go anywhere and do anything. I figured the battles were over. It came as a shock when I heard the call this time. There were rifle shots, then: "Aid man!" I ran to the guards and they pointed to bushes ten yards from where they had been posted. They had spotted a German soldier and called to him to surrender. He didn't answer and they fired. I went to the bushes and turned him over. He was a kid about sixteen, blond, his hair strung out in the bushes, still alive. The .30-caliber bullets had scooped out his chest and I saw his heart. It was the same heart I put in my chest twenty-three years later. He was still alive, gray with shock, going fast. He stared up at me—a mournful, little boy's face. He asked: "Why did you shoot? I wanted to surrender." I told him we didn't know.

Now, twenty-three years later, I wailed for that German boy who had never mattered to me and I heaved up my numbness. The trip through my body lasted more than an hour. I found wounds everywhere. I remembered a wounded friend whimpering: "Help me, Leo," which I did—a close friend, yet after he was hit no friend at all, not missed a second after I heard of his death, numb to him as I was to everyone else, preparing for losses by anesthetizing myself. And in the course of that trip through my body I started to feel again, and discovered what I'd missed. I felt wide open, lightened, ready to meet others simply and directly. No need for lies, no need to fear humiliation. I was ready to be a fool. I experienced the joy Schutz had promised to deliver. I'm grateful to him. Not even the offer of love could threaten me.

This was the transformation I underwent in the course of that fantasy trip. The force of the experience began to fade quickly, and now, writing two weeks later, I find that little remains. But I still have a vision of a possibility I had not been aware of—a simple, easy connection with my own feeling and, consequently, with others'.

I had great difficulty emerging from my body. I was pinned against my intestines, pregnant with myself. When I finally began to move and restored all the missing organs and repaired those that were damaged, I feared that all this work was temporary, that if I were to leave, the heart would vanish, the stomach dry up, the intestines be exposed. Schutz asked if there was anyone who could help me get out. I said:

"My daughter." So I invited my daughter to enter my body. She stood near my heart and said: "Come on out, Daddy," and led me out. I ran to a meadow on my chest. I ran through long grass, toward a gate, directly toward the sun. There I lay down and rested.

Occasionally, during my trip, I heard others crying, but I had lost track of the group. I opened my eyes. I had an initial sense of others as darts of candlelight about me. The room seemed to have shifted. It was pitch black outside. Everyone was very close to me—Reb, Daniel, Brigitte, Bill, Joan, Victor, Kate, Clark, Gary, Sheba. Sheba still wept. Brigitte directed us all to lie down and to reach out and touch one another. She turned out the lights and gave us various instructions designed to release us and finally we parted.

It was not easy leaving these people I had met only five days before. Time was distorted and we seemed to have lived years together. It was not easy leaving Big Sur. On the final morning, the entire workshop met to say good-bye. Our group gathered in a tight circle, hugging and kissing, and I found myself hugging everyone, behaving like the idiots I had noticed on first arriving at Esalen. I hugged Rebel. I told him he was a great kid and that a few years from now he might not even recall his present trouble. I told him not to envy his peers. He was probably much better than they.

Schutz ended our last meeting by playing a record from *The Man of La Mancha*, "The Impossible Dream." We were at that point of sentiment where corny lyrics announced truths and we could be illuminated by the wisdom of clichés.

The condition of vulnerability is precious and very fragile. Events and people and old routines and old habits conspire to bring you down. But not all the way down. There is still the recollection of that tingling sense of being wide awake, located in the here and now, feeling freely and entirely, all constraints discarded. It remains a condition to be realized. It could change the way we live.

*A*ND *for the aged ladies and gentlemen (who are also economically stable and reasonably healthy), there is a plan called Terminal Security.*

# D.O.A.?

## by Kathrin Perutz

"You got to pass a physical to get in here," said a small octogenarian at Rossmoor Leisure World. "And they do a financial check on you, too . . ."

"That's because," screamed his rather deaf wife, "they don't want to let in any riff-raff, you see. It's a nice group here . . ."

"Friendliest people in the world," intoned her husband.

"That's right. Friendliest people in the world, so they can't let in any riff-raff."

These friendly people all have a lot in common. They are old, have money and, at least when they enter the shipboard life of a retirement community, are relatively healthy. They are on their last trip, away from children and young people, cradled in security, using up their money like severance pay and leaving behind the inheritance of nothing more than a blessed memory. Like salmon, swimming back through tortuous ways to spawn and die where they were born, America's senior citizens turn back, when society rejects them, to a final infancy before they die. Among activities, hobbies, arts & crafts, fun & games, dances, movies, cocktail parties, they lead the life of a cruise ship, away from time, responsibility and with the least possible awareness of the two shores.

Each of the three New Jersey retirement communities I visited allow the elderly to remove themselves from a society which has already rejected them. At Leisure Village, they can be children, enjoying the moment as it happens, each moment guarded with frivolity. At Meadow Lakes, they can be adolescent, with a newly-acquired independence and even some acknowledgment of the world outside, but still cared for and looked after. At Leisure World, they can be young marrieds, sedate and wrapped up in their own problems. At retirement age, with money, one can choose which former life to recall at the end.

At Rossmoor Leisure World, halfway between New York and Philadelphia, its giant globe looking out on the New Jersey Turnpike at Exit 8A, a down payment of $4,600 will bring you ownership of a $27,000 apartment in forty years, provided you keep up your monthly payments of about $270. The small eighty-four-year-old and his rather deaf wife put down their money a year and a half ago, bought furniture for $2,000, have been living in an apartment since then, hope to move in soon, and can look forward to owning their section of a mock-Colonial house by the time he's 124. At that point, they are free to leave their apartment to whomever they want, provided the association approves.

"I can't take it with me, so what the hell," said the little man, laughing. He and his wife were the only people I saw in the large information building with its velvet-papered walls. They had been waiting an hour and a half to speak to someone about furniture delivery and were delighted to see me. I was equally delighted; this was the second time I had come to Rossmoor and they were the first people I had seen. Though the association claims twenty-four-hour security guards, no one stopped me in the six times I passed the entrance building. The community, of about six hundred residents, maintains the silence that comes after shock. The replica of a New England town (but without stores, hospitals, post office, fire and police departments, cemetery or, of course, schools) lies placid and deteriorating, its lawns turning brown, its undulating stone wall collapsed at every other bend. I remembered Pompeii as I walked through the silence, down winding sidewalks, into large rooms too bare and orderly to maintain even the smell of life. At the end of the information building I finally found a man in an office, but he smiled politely and told me he had nothing to do with Leisure World. He was an assemblyman, he said, who rented a couple of rooms here in order to do his legislative work.

In the large Club House I walked in and out of sumptuous rooms, arsenals of lavish equipment for various crafts. The lapidary machines were covered with plastic; so were the looms, the woodworking machines, ceramic machines; in the enormous Art Room everything was cleaned away, the Darkroom was closed, and the Ladies Room was dark. In Classroom One, vestiges of life remained: the blackboards were scribbled with funny faces and arithmetic ($1 + 1 = 2$ was repeated three times); in Classroom Two a notice on the blackboard reported a house for sale.

The Club House bulletin board announced activities. For that day (April 23) the projects were: 10 a.m. Shopping Trip to Princeton and Advanced Sewing Class; 1 p.m. Beginner's Sewing Class; 1:30 Lamp Shade Making Class; 7:45 Party Bridge and Intermediate Bridge. Most days boasted similar activities, though every Saturday at 7:30 was Fun & Games for Everyone, followed at 8:00 by a dance. For the eleventh of May a concert was announced, featuring Andrzej Bachleda. To arouse interest, a flyleaf was pinned to the board giving newspaper comments on the performer. One, in its entirety, read: "Tenor soloist Andrzej Bachleda in Szymanowski's moving Lullabies—was successfully done by Andrzej Bachleda—St. Petersburg Times." (*Sic* to the whole thing.)

The other end of the Club House contained offices, Multi-Purpose Rooms, and a large Game Room with six pool tables. Later in the day, while ladies were making new lamp shades or rejuvenating old ones with bits of fluff and ribbons, about a dozen men—in polo shirts or sport shirts with string ties—were playing pool. Except for workmen, these were the only active people I saw at Rossmoor, where, according to the brochure, "the living is lively." But, as my octogenarian friend confessed, "I can't do that kind of thing anymore. I'm too old. Those activities aren't for me."

"What do you do, then? You must read."

He smiled patiently. A vintegenarian, like me, has no imagination. "Can't do that. My eyes are too bad."

I then remembered he has enough to do just helping his wife keep house. Since there is no maid service at Leisure World (unless you hire a maid at your own expense, if you can find one), and there is no restaurant on the premises, residents must clean, cook, shop, do laundry, ironing, wash floors and windows, and otherwise emulate those who have not yet earned their right to leisure.

Rossmoor, New Jersey, is one of eight Leisure World communities built by the Rossmoor Corporation, the largest retirement community developers in the world. The New Jersey development was originally planned as a city for up to fifty thousand inhabitants. The site was chosen by drawing a map with New York at one end, Philadelphia at the other and pointing to a spot equidistant between the two. (An Eastern retirement community offers, in place of balmy and predictable climate, an easy proximity to friends, family, and former home.) The Rossmoor Corporation bought up Forsgate Farms and Country Club and guaranteed to the township (Monroe) a large tax-paying unit which would not add to the school burden. Fifty-three hundred acres were bought and plans made for a self-contained community with stores (labeled "ye olde . . ." or "shoppe" in the designs), hospital, restaurants, and all recreational facilities. Originally financed at half a billion dollars, Leisure World soon came into difficulties and the mortgage (taken out by the company with FHA insurance) went up. Not enough buyers were found and the admission age was reduced to fifty-two. Here, as in other retirement communities, a minimum age of fifty-two to fifty-five (though a younger spouse is always admitted) is good business, since the non-retired resident of a retirement village continues to earn money for another ten years and, because he pays mortgage for as long as he lives, relieves the company for a longer time than usual of having to resell. The buyer's advantage is getting his security early, making his last move in the fifties, with the knowledge that the hand he still keeps in the outside world can be retracted at any time. Still, not enough pre-retirees were lured and Rossmoor is now closed to new admissions. No building is done on spec; an entire unit (175–100 apartments) must be sold before building begins. Officials promise that new houses will be started in a month or two, ready for occupancy in early 1969, and that a hospital is still planned.

The model homes range from $12,750 to $34,385, with monthly payments from $155.50 to $310.50, not including electricity, water, or garbage collection. The houses, subdivided into apartments, are flimsily built, perhaps to enable even hard-of-hearing residents to keep up with neighborly goings-on. For $25,000 one can buy a ground-floor apartment with living room, small dining area, kitchen, bathroom, and two bedrooms. For $900 more and a flight of stairs, one gains an extra bathroom and more space in the living area. At all price levels, the upstairs apartments are much better deals. Naturally, they are not very convenient for wheelchairs or people with heart conditions. The principle seems to be that if you're well enough and young enough to climb a replica of old New England stairs, you get your reward on earth. A second bathroom in a ground-floor apartment costs $3,000; but then, if you're not in perfect health after you retire, you must learn to be grateful at all costs.

The cost can be high. Though 80 per cent of medical bills is covered (with an $8.00 deduction on monthly payments for Medicare), this does not include dental treatment, equipment for invalids, or any of the high costs of being seriously ill over a long period of time (nurses, nursing homes, long hospital stays). Naturally, then, retirement communities like Leisure World must reject applicants who are not in relatively good health. Sickness is unpleasant, bad for business (especially death; it tends to discourage the friendly people), and a bad financial risk, since medical bills, if they continue long enough, can use up the financial resources of even quite wealthy people and leave the corporation with a choice of eviction or allowing residents to stay on without contributing their monthly payments, both bad precedents. For those who make their money through old people, there is an unpleasant paradox in modern life. As medical care improves, people live longer, providing a greater potential market for retirement communities. However, they live longer on less money, since they can no longer earn anything and their savings decrease. Even a couple worth half a million dollars at age sixty-five could, through major illness, be penniless twenty years later. Advances in medicine, the growing conquest of killing diseases, are terrible spectres to those who administer housing developments for the old. They want young old people (one out of three Americans at sixty-five has a living parent) who can lead active lives and prefer leading them away from children and other noisy creatures.

At Leisure World there is no noise. Golden silence for the golden years. Widows (40 per cent of the population—in all these places, women outnumber men three to one, and though sometimes two women share an apartment, two men never do) and others in need of solace can climb the twenty stone steps up to Rossmoor's enormous globe, there to stand in tranquillity while surveying the traffic of the Jersey Turnpike and Route 130. This vantage point is, however, deserted. The paint chips on the world, the small community in the valley of the shadow of the globe sits inanimate, a ghost town, a Hollywood set.

At Leisure Village ("where mature adults make the most of their freedom years") in Lakewood, New Jersey, everything bustles in a perpetual cocktail party without dirty or sick jokes. A housing development among a multitude of housing developments for all ages (one called Burnham Woods), Leisure Village offers five different models of one-story apartments, all built to look like houses, ranging from $13,000 to $31,000, of which the best buy is probably Greenbriar, a two-bedroom apartment at $17,000.

I came here directly from Leisure World, where my last encounter had been in front of the mock-Colonial church, a building of utmost whitewashed respectablity from which issued soft strains of organ music. To a lady of about sixty, clad in navy-blue silk, her hair impeccably and firmly arranged on her head, I said that I had been looking around here for an aunt of mine and would now move on to Leisure Village. "Don't go there," she said, taking in my navy-blue suit and white gloves. "It's not the same class. Your aunt would be much happier here, I'm sure. The people . . ." she paused.

"Are more cultured?"

"That's right." She smiled, acknowledging our understanding.

At the entrance to Leisure Village, I was handed a welcome card and directed to Visitors' Parking. There I was met by a happy little man wearing a badge saying HOST and, underneath it, MR. STAUBFANGKERRER. "Hello! You like to see around?"

"Thank you, I'd just like to look. On my own, I mean, if that's all right."

"Sure, sure. But maybe you have questions. I can tell you all about this place. I live here, ya, with my wife. We came two and half years ago, there were maybe 250 people. Now look. Two thousand. We're very happy here."

"You're happy here."

"It's a wonderful place, wonderful. We have a nice house, a garden. I wouldn't want to live anyplace else."

"What do you do all day?"

"Do? I tell you, there's so much to do you don't know where to begin. Golf, there is, shuffleboard, art classes, there's everything. I tell you, these people, they're so busy they don't have time to think what to do."

"But there must be older people, much older than you, who can't do very much."

"Well, well I'm sixty-four. Yes, the older ones—we have a woman here ninety-eight, yes, she can't do very much. Some of our people, they go out to work, many go out to work, they're very busy, everybody's busy here. You want to see? Come, I show you."

Mr. Staubfangkerrer led the way to Community Hall. The large auditorium was, at the moment, a card room where about thirty tables of men were playing bridge.

"They're playing bridge," my guide informed me. "Bridge is very popular game."

"Only men? What about the women?"

"Well, that's interesting. It's like this: the women, they want to play by themselves. They say they don't like when the men smoke. Of course, you know they smoke by themselves, alone."

In the next room, half the size of the auditorium, but still very large, sat twenty tables of women playing cards.

"Men and women don't seem to get on very well here," I remarked—and segregation of the sexes, I later discovered, was a general symptom of retirement communities.

"Ya, you know, they like a rest. They like a rest from each other. The women, they have their talk and the men like to talk to themselves." It was obvious that, with seniority, citizens also acquired prerogatives; social amenities could be ignored and segregation could develop naturally when the sexes no longer held expectations. Women and men, separate but equal, could indulge their separate lusts for gossip and shop talk.

"But they do get together, don't they?"

"Ah, we have dances and, you know, marriages. Three marriages here. Ah, look, no over there. That old man in a wheelchair? He got married here. He had a stroke and his first wife left him, didn't want to be with an invalid or so and he found another wife here. He's happy."

We went through the Arts and Crafts wing, Mr. S. pointing out displays of objects made by residents. Clay birds on clay trees, wire figurines set in driftwood, photographs of blossoming trees, lakes, children, and some charming mosaics of postage stamps. "Ya," said Mr. Staubfangkerrer sadly the third time I commented on these, "Mr. Eberheimer, he passed away last year."

The Art Room was bursting with artistic ladies (no men) working on canvases or small sculptures. In the Photography Room, a zealous Mr. Goldman, who was developing color prints, explained the intricate process and said he'd always been a photographer, now taught photography here, where he lived. He taught part-time, was too busy to do much and, though this occupation didn't make him a millionaire, he liked it. Like Mr. Staubfangkerrer, he had a strong German accent. His eyes were the fake blue of Kodachrome, his hair pepper-and-salt, his body wiry, and he seemed a retirement village resident acceptable only in a wide-screen Hollywood version.

Outside, the shuffleboard courts were full with ladies in slacks or flowered dresses, men in sport clothes or suits with waistcoats. At the boat dock (Leisure Village has three lakes) some young people were fishing. On the streets, people passed each other smiling. "This is the friendliest place in the world," said Mr. S. "All the people are friendly."

"All?"

"Well"—he smiled—"sure, there are crackpots. Everyplace they got crackpots. Here, too."

He took me through the model homes, their walls as flimsy as those of Leisure World. The three (out of five) higher-priced apartments had enclosed porches and garages.

"You pay for your apartment, then you got to pay only your maintenance. You pay electricity, too, then water and sewer and then you got taxes. All in all, I pay eighty-eight bucks. Some pay less, some more. It's a good deal. You say you saw that Leisure World? Not for me, I wouldn't like it. Who wants a forty-year mortgage at this age? You end up paying two, three times what it's worth. And here, you see how they fixed this room up? no, furniture you got to bring yourself—that's for visitors. You can have your child live with you, if he's more than nineteen. We don't got children. Ya, grandchildren come to visit but now they made this rule: no more than two weeks. That's enough. Two weeks and you get tired." We were obstructed by a youngish-elderly couple touring the same model with their Host. "It's like this," the man was saying as we passed, "we live in Brooklyn, so this is great for us, not far from home."

In Leisure Village, as in Leisure World, some medical facilities are available. Here, dentists, doctors, and podiatrists lived in the first houses; at Rossmoor a Medical Center has a doctor and five nurses. Here again, were no stores, no hospital, no maid service, no restaurant. Here, most people owned their apartments and maintenance fees were (perhaps deceptively) lower. In both places, I heard the same claims made for residents: their friendliness, "people from all walks of life—many professionals, we have doctors, lawyers, everything," "people from all parts of the world, from Europe they come here."

Mr. Staubfangkerrer said: "You got all kinds of people here. You do what you want, nobody bothers you. You move in, they give you a party, your neighbors invite you over. If you don't want, you can be alone."

Leisure Village is physically prettier than Leisure World, because of its large lakes, woods to one side, and fields. The architecture is much more utilitarian, however, and the communal rooms much smaller (the Art Room is only a third as large as the one in Leisure World). A major contrast between the two is in the Information Building. At Leisure Village, a large sales staff is busy and professional. A blow-up photograph of a small child hugging an old man has the caption: GRANDPA, I'M GLAD YOU DECIDED TO LIVE SO CLOSE TO US. Plans and models of the community are on display and at a round table are eight telephones which, if picked up, will answer questions like "What kind of people live in Leisure Village?"

Leisure Village is three times the size of Leisure World. A community of two thousand—all adults—should, it would seem, offer shops and services. That a doctor or two reside there is not surprising; in most communities of that size, regardless of age, there would probably be doctors. In this particular one, where the youngest inhabitant is fifty-five and the oldest ninety-eight, complete medical services become at least as essential as a school in another community of the same size. The housing development for old people is a continuation of housing developments generally; within another generation or two it will be possible, if not common, for a person to have spent his entire life in such developments. Since leisure time and unemployment are also general problems, a retirement community exaggerates, merely, aspects of American life.

Still, the old are different from us. They know they will die soon. They have lost the sense of future and know that their abilities or achievements are just a matter of time. They become physically disabled; hearing and vision grow less acute; sports are difficult to pursue; sexual excitement is rare and passion of any kind fades. Living with people of their own age means they can forget or ignore how they differ from the rest of the population. They can escape the normal life of problems, children, commotion.

Retirement communities are only possible when family life has broken down to the point where generations view each other with suspicion. The greatest nightmare for many old people is to depend on their children. Since American children have learned when very young to be economically independent, parents, later on, must learn to expect nothing from them. So the elderly spend their last money—disrupting the traditional middle-class theme of inheritance—to lead a segregated (by age) communal life. Still, they need special attention and services, though neither of the two Leisure communities offer anything much more than the possibility of buying an apartment and having the convenience of recreational facilities nearby. This, however, ignores the main facts about old people: that they are, or will be, in need of medical care and that their financial situation is precarious. The buyers forget these facts themselves, and though they may have $150,000 now and can live on their income, if and when they need major medical care over a protracted period, they will have to go into their capital and will eventually deplete it. Except for the very few really rich, no older person can be financially secure. The "security" they buy in most retirement villages has nothing to do with the security they need.

Meadow Lakes in Hightstown, New Jersey, is an exception: most of the essential services are offered. The monthly service charge—from $258 to $459—includes all meals (at a Stouffer's restaurant), maid service, linens, telephone, and medical fees. As in other places, you must be physically fit to enter (i.e., able to walk to the restaurant). Once you become ill, however, all expenses are undertaken by Meadow Lakes, including nursing home care. The recreational facilities here are like those in the other two, with the additions of a beauty shop, barber, gift shop, snack shop, and actual library. (At the Leisure communities, the libraries are token and not used.) The architecture is pleasing and planned for older people: the entire village is connected by enclosed corridors and bridges, heated or air-conditioned, all level with no rise greater than a half inch. Meadow Lakes residents are socially conscious: they post news from nearby high schools, make clothes for orphanages, donate medications for each other, and are politically active. Most of them vote and last year voted in the first Republican mayor in thirty years. They are socially conscious in other ways, too, and cocktail parties before dinner must now be booked almost a year in advance, though some guests, invariably, will be in no position to turn up. Twenty-five cocktail parties are held each night, in a community of 390 people.

Meadow Lakes, owned and managed by the Presbyterian Homes of the Synod of New Jersey, has many rich residents who travel frequently, some spending a few months each year in Europe. Wherever they are, medical care is completely insured and Meadow Lakes will pay for the plane that brings them back, the ambulance, the hospital. The average age at Meadow Lakes is seventy-five, and people in their sixties are discouraged. The public relations woman told me: "People that age are too young. Last year we had the vice-president of Johnson & Johnson here. He left after six months. We tried to tell him not to come."

This type of discouragement is refreshing after the Leisure communities. Meadow Lakes seems the perfect place for gregarious old people (the only kind to go to retirement villages), but there's a catch: a Capital Fee is required, between $12,500 and $46,500 (depending on the size of your apartment), which is nonreturnable. At your death, the money remains with Meadow Lakes; the apartment (not built like a house but within an apartment house) is not your own; there is no equity. Whatever advantages may come to a resident of Meadow Lakes, the nonreturnable fee is an unequivocal rejection of children's claims.

Not all residents are rich; some have scraped together the Capital Fee somehow (probably through insurance money collected at the onset of widowhood) and now live as economically as possible. Those who make their own breakfasts get a deduction of $8.25 a month, and the local grocer told me: "Most of them, if they want white bread, they ask for Pepperidge Farm, 37 cents. But some, they say, send me the 21 cents bread, the cheapest. And other things, they ask how much this costs and how much is that, and they want whatever costs least." He continued, unsolicited, to give his opinion of the place: "I go down there sometimes for medical treatment. It's depressing there. You know, about 85 per cent of those people have something wrong with them. There's Mrs. L., she has cataracts, she can't see. So she won't go out of her apartment, she never leaves it. When I say, 'Mrs. L., it's beautiful outside, don't you want to go out?' she says no, she won't go. And when I say, 'How about it, Mrs. L.? When I finish work I'll come by with the car and take you for a drive.' But she won't go, she's afraid to leave her apartment. It's depressing there, I tell you. You know it when you come with deliveries and you ring the bell and wait five minutes till somebody comes. And you know the old lady took all that time just walking to the door, with her two canes like this." He demonstrated.

"Still, it's better than those Leisure places. At least it gives all medical care."

"Why? Leisure World you buy your own place. What's wrong? I'd even get a house there. But you know what's wrong? People don't live with their parents anymore. My mother, she lived with us till she died. She did the cooking and sometimes the marketing by phone—just so she'd feel useful. All around here you can see the old houses, with an annex built on for the old people. That's how they used to do it. Now the old people have no place to go."

Two evenings earlier I had spoken to the architect of Meadow Lakes, Leonard Groome, who told me he was building annexes for parents onto Princeton houses. But he was having difficulties, since if he built a kitchen or kitchenette in the annex, it would be considered a two-family house and these are illegal in Princeton. I asked why, since this was a question bothering me throughout my visits to retirement communities, don't old people who can afford it go away—to a Greek island, or Italy, and live there with a few servants for the same price as living in one of these developments?

His answer was obvious: "They don't want to go so far from home. They want to live near their families, near where they used to live."

And yet at Leisure World I met a couple who had just come from Norway. They had bought a $17,500 home here and were going through the model with an interior decorator, planning drapes. Their reasons were that they had always wanted to come to America, winters in Norway were getting too cold for them, and now, after his fourth heart attack, they had decided to make their last move to this mock village off the turnpike.

All retirement communities offer the shipboard life: no responsibilities, organized activities, dances, fun and sociability. In Leisure Village, you go Tourist Class, in frank frivolity. In Leisure World, you go Cabin Class, that deadly middle-ground without the fun of Tourist or the elegance of First, where pretensions have kept you away from the former and finances away from the latter. In Meadow Lakes, you're in First Class, with the services and luxury. On the ship of death, most would prefer to travel First, though some still choose, and some must settle for, their own canoe.

*So you're headed for the Golden West because you want to see how Los Angeles and its suburbs are the Future Landscape of America—an entire state governed by a different set of rules from the rest of the country, a whole tribe living carefree and topless.*

# Topless

by *Richard M. Elman*

Something had definitely gone all wrong in Compton. It was as if the whole town had a belly-ache from too much ice cream. Everybody was cross with everybody else. A whole town turned sour. Everybody feeling as if they'd been "had."

As soon as I got there, the torpor set in. If you've ever been had—had so that it really makes your ears burn—you feel like you would simply like to hide somewhere. Any place. I felt that way, and so I began to stay rather close to Noni's, which didn't help me very much. At the Sycamore, people were having one another regularly, and they called it, at best, lovemaking. Later, there were the usual recriminations:

"I'm glad for you. I really am."

"So next time, maybe we'll try it my way?"

"Every time we try it like that my leg just goes to sleep on me. I'm all pins and needles right now."

Human beings do a poor job of making love to one another. They flail about ineffectually, and are always busy conceptualizing. The "erect swaggering waddle" prior to coitus, which Bingham observed in the male chimpanzee and called the "sex dance," has no relationship whatsoever to the manner in which Noni's guests would meander up to her registration desk to inquire about rooms. In fact, I sometimes wondered if these all-too-ephemeral visitors were ever motivated by

anything other than a perverse willfulness, a desire to have done with it
so that each could be alone with his miserable self again. The same old
monotony forever rebeginning. Strip away all the hoary beards and
superstitions, the taboos, the snide little secrets, and what have you? A
pair of rather inefficient engines at work upon each other. No wonder it
makes the schoolboys snicker. In Compton, the teen-agers swayed like
cattails to a cynical new pop group called the Loving Spoonful, while
their white elders wrinkled their brows over Negroes.

For there was, of course, the race question—but which race question?—and what did it have to do with such things as mass transit,
pollution, higher taxes, or how to spend your leisure time? Who killed
Kennedy? Are you for or against smog or police brutality? When there
is dishonesty in high places and crime on the streets, where *do* you find
decent sales help? Then there was the reading problem, and the
population explosion, and the rise in water rates, and what to do about
all those mothers on welfare, and why so many divorces, and the high
cost of living. It was the kids, if you were an adult. It was adults, if you
were a kid. Worst of all, things were so much better than ever. This was
going to be the Great Society. But just how long would that last? And
what would happen to all of us then? In the end, it was all the frayed
ends of things, those numerous gaudy distractions, which drove everybody, including myself, to back away from thinking about mass mur-
der. At the tip of our fingers was that self-inflicted wound called
Vietnam. We'd stuck it just where it shouldn't have been. We said we
didn't want to, but we did it anyway, and now it was infected, but not
so sore that we were willing to go to the doctor for radical surgery. It
hurts them as much as it hurts us. They're just bound to give up sooner
or later.

"My son is with the First Cav at Iadrang," a man down the block
from Noni's greeted me one day, proudly, from his garden fence.

About all I could say was, "Wonderful!"

"Do you know what the boys drink in the First Cav?"

I didn't have the foggiest idea, and I said so.

The man announced, "Would you believe beer and tomato juice?"

"Beer and tomato juice?"

"I'm not kidding," he said. "I saw it on the TV."

Television, according to some moralists, is a form of escape, but in

Compton one escaped through TV to LBJ, Bobby Kennedy, Mark Lane, and beer and tomato juice. Occasionally, there were also U.S. soldiers burning down Vietnamese villages, but whoever bargained for that? It was as if we'd gone to bed with a pain in the finger, and awakened with a sty.

And then everybody turned cynical and sour, or else they went topless.

I use topless here, in its most general sense, to mean no dignity! No risks! No class! For that's about what it amounts to. The old lower middle classes pulling off their shirts and saying, "Why not? Everybody else is getting away with it, so why the hell not? I don't have to worry about my neighbors. Look! They're all sitting there in the audience!"

When radicals used to believe that the shirtless classes could some day seize power through a redemptionist act of the corporate will, rhetoric still held the masses of men in its sway, and there was one set of rules for public life and another for private life. But what happens when all the old public *petit-bourgeois* high seriousness vanishes, and suddenly exists only in the mind? When your enemies are you, not *they*? When your public morality and your private parts are supposed to mesh? When the spread of affluence is so incredible that the shirtless classes begin to merge with the topless classes?

Ah then, a specter will still linger to haunt us, but it will be that of a naked woman with a light bulb in her belly button: The Tropical Fish! The Topless A Go Go! The Titillator! Or perhaps the Box! No matter which way one drove through Compton, eventually he had to run into such places: The Gam Room! The Sacred Triangle! The Nut Club! It was as if, having banished forever certain kinds of lower middle class caution and shame, the residents of that part of the "Southland" were now intent upon making everybody around them aware of their marvelous candor.

"Would you believe TOPLESS?" a faded sign, somewhere near Pepperdine on the road to Watts, perorated. Imagine, too, nakedness as pluralism: every race, class, caste, and ethnic order represented, a mulligan stew of naked breasts, buttocks, and legs and arms dispensing food and drinks. Near Gardena, where the topless girls were all Oriental, one place advertised chow mein family dinners. Toward Watts, topless took on a shabby negritude; I saw one place decorated with spears and African masks. A number of shabby Mexican joints were spattered through East Los Angeles. Of the Caucasians who'd started the ball rolling to begin with, one saw them topless just about every place else: decked out for the visiting firemen along Sunset Strip, or topless with freckles in Long Beach, Hollywood, San Bernardino. Once, caught in a taffy pull of downtown freeways, I wandered by mistake into a topless drive-in and was served a rare hamburger and a chocolate frosted at my window by a pretty young blonde in short shorts, white boots, and a transparent plastic halter.

In Compton, one of the customers told me, "I'm just finding it harder and harder to bear down like I used to . . .

"Oh, I know what you're thinking," he added, "a man like me with a wife and a kid in college and responsibilities. Well, that's just it. I don't begrudge anybody anything, but even my doctor says I should take it a little easier." When I asked him what he did, he snapped: "Vending machines . . .

"Between here and Boyle Heights, I got 150 machines," the man said, "and I tell you sometimes it just gets to be too much for me. I mean, I have to see each one personally a couple of times a week, just like you would with a real person because sometimes they break down, and even if I could get it, I can't afford any help. *You want to know why?* Sure I'll tell you. What the customers don't steal, they would . . .

"So when it's getting to be like this I just come here and sit awhile and have a drink and watch the show and maybe I talk to the girls and maybe I don't. Why not? It's all perfectly innocent."

And perhaps it was except that when one went off to the men's room, there were all those self-advertisements scribbled on the stalls:

*Ring and valve jobs done . . . while you wait!*
*Need your tube flushed? Call Amy.*
CARTE BLANCHE—DINER'S CLUB—OR CASH—
CALL PATRICIA—READY CASH

And sometimes there were more elusive things scratched into the tables:

*If you like fresh fish, try Venice.*
COME *to the Century Plaza Hotel.*

Or even:

> *Help. I'm a nymphomaniac.*

And there would be a telephone number. Occasionally, too, there would be political notes:

MAO TSE-TUNG SUCKS.

Or:

> *Mother fuckers! Big white pricks!*
> *Here's to Watts 66!*

Or even:

> *Ronald Reagan has a cute ass.*

And once:

> *From Santa Barbara to the Saltan Sea, guess who is taking over?*

And everybody looked and giggled and said it wasn't anything, nothing very much there at all, just as they stared at the wiggling fannies and wobbling breasts and that, too, wasn't anything. Hardly worth looking at! Just there! Another part of the landscape. Perfectly innocent.

Which it was, I suspect, because none of the working men who entered and left such places at lunch time, coffee break, or dinner seemed as if they were staggering through an erotic stupor. Nor did I find any evidence that this prickly heat of topless bars, supper clubs, snooker joints, and beaneries was having even the slightest effect on production quotas at the nearby North American plant. In Compton's divorce court—which I attended for many hours at a stretch—men and women haggled over support payments and tiny scraps of community property, but nobody ever called the other a bitch or a greedy frigid two-timer. But the clients were very nearly topless. Some just wore slacks and T-shirts. Or the women wore sun dresses and even pedal pushers. With all of Compton in various stages of dishabille, why not go the whole hog?

For myself, I always found it rather disconcerting to have a woman lean over to serve me beer, topless. Yet I came to appreciate the charm of the thing. If this was supposed to be a lower-middle-class Garden of Eden before the Fall, there had to be places where you could simulate original nature. It was also as if the entire state of California had been set aside for the frivolous, to be governed, perhaps, by a different set of rules than the rest of the country, or at very least, by those rules laid down solely by climate. It was just a trifle Levantinized, as they say in Israel, and that is not to refer to the "race question." It was in the way people looked—black or white, middle class or poor. Once, in a topless joint near Venice, I came across a grandmotherly woman knitting a sweater. "It's for my boy in Vietnam," she explained. "I don't know whether he needs it or not, but I just think maybe he ought to have one over there."

Others have commented on the dry jewel-like opulence of Southern California, the way an entire landscape seems to be bragging about its liberation from necessity of any kind, even though some people here are working just as hard, if not harder, than elsewhere, but when you "make it" under such circumstances—I mean really "make it"—what do you do? Once, driving south near the Long Beach freeway, I passed a billboard which was decorated in the form of a greeting card. A prominent local businessman had purchased the space to send felicitations to his wife on their wedding anniversary. Clearly, it wasn't simply that he had prospered and wanted the whole vehicular world between Los Angeles and San Diego to know about his good fortune, which he attributed, in part, to a faithful mate. Nor was this simply a self-advertisement that would inevitably redound to his credit, be good for business. Perhaps the man had sounded himself, found his feelings genuine, and then decided that, after all, happy marriages in California are few and far between and why not bang the drums a little, make a little publicity. Besides, the wife—or perhaps one of her friends—driving by would just have to see the way he felt. You couldn't miss it. So, likewise, as one girl put it, "If you've got nice breasts, why hide them?"

Yet many of the girls were quite homely. Still others had been so depilated and cosmeticized that they no longer resembled flesh and blood at all, but were like plastic mannikins—abstractions again! And sometimes there were just as many women as men customers in the place. Was this simply more of the same cynicism and abstraction?

When one gets cynical about sex and nudity, there is not much left. Perhaps we shall all go shopping topless some day on mildly heated sidewalks that move so that the breasts wobble a little, but not so much that they make an unpleasing picture. Then, shall we also go to work topless? Obviously, some Californians already are.

One needs only to enter any of the supermarket drugstores serving the residents of Watts or Willowbrook to have the point driven home with a vengeance. Along with all the old so-called "necessities" of family life, one finds marked-down martini shakers, picnic baskets, tiny alice bathing briefs for men, topless suits, "No-Doze" pills, and fruit-flavored wines (as if grape-flavored wine were distasteful), and it is difficult to browse through such stores with a set of shopping priorities in mind. Perhaps that explains why so many of them were burned and looted in August of 1965. Although a variety of sophisticated psychosocial mechanisms have been cooked up to describe the resentments of the poor which, ultimately, might have exploded in looting, it seems reasonable to suppose that once law and order broke down in Watts, all the old artificial distinctions about private property also broke down. The looters didn't feel barred from having *things* by their poverty or their enforced "leisure." Indeed, living in opulent California, topless now just like everyone else, was it wrong for them to suppose that they had been encouraged to feel a little less than cautious?

The latest and most vicious trend in the long process which denudes you even as it enriches is the no-minimum-balance regular unlimited checking account. Whenever I drove up toward central LA through the residential streets, I was exhorted on the car radio by jingles and homiletics that Security First National (or, perhaps, some other set of abstractions meant to imply a "financial institution") was willing to write me all the checks I cared to write, no balance necessary, if I would call a certain number at once, and none of them would ever bounce. A whole nation "hanging" checks on one another! If I lived in Watts or Compton, it would certainly sound a lot better to me than Welfare, or even, even twenty dollars a week plus welfare in a "work-orientation program" of the War on Poverty.

# About the Editor

JOEL LIEBER is the author of two novels, *Move!* (1968) and *How the Fishes Live* (1967). His new novel, *The Chair*, will be published early in 1969. A free-lance writer, Mr. Lieber lives in New York with his wife, two children, and two dogs.

# About the Contributors

GOODMAN ACE and his wife Jane were on the radio fourteen years as "The Easy Aces." Mr. Ace's most recent book was *The Fine Art of Hypochondria* (1966). Currently, his column, "Top of My Head," appears weekly in *Saturday Review,* and his radio essays are broadcast over WPAT in the New York area.

BOB ELLIOT and RAY GOULDING have two of the best-known voices in radio and TV history. In addition to their zany radio routines on NBC and local New York stations, Bob and Ray were for years the voices of Bert and Harry Piels. Currently, the pair are regulars on the "Today Show" and they produce a variety of commercials.

RICHARD M. ELMAN, born in Brooklyn, has been a writer for National Educational Television, a public affairs director for WBAI-FM in New York, and an English teacher at Bennington College. His nonfiction books include *The Poorhouse State, Ill-At-Ease in Compton,* and *Charles Booth's London,* a collection of which he was co-editor. Mr. Elman is the author of two novels: *The 28th Day of Elul* (1967) and *Lilo's Diary* (1968).

HERBERT GOLD, whose most recent success was *Fathers* (1967), has held many literary honors, including a Guggenheim Fellowship and a National Institute of Arts and Letters award. Among his well-known works are *Salt, Therefore Be Bold,* and *The Man Who Was Not With It.*

CHAUNCEY HOWELL, columnist and features writer for *Women's Wear Daily*, was born in Easton, Pa., where his family has lived since 1740. A Greek major at Amherst College, Mr. Howell has been driving BMW and Harley-Davidson motorcycles around New York City for ten years, with but one accident in all that time.

MARVIN KITMAN, once editor of *Monocle*, lives in Leonia, N. J., scene of many of his essays and journalistic reports. His reviews and articles appear in *The New York Times* and *Playboy*, and his most recent book was *The Number One Best-Seller* (1966).

WILLIAM KLOMAN, a free-lance writer, has written for the *Saturday Evening Post* and *The New York Times*. He did not, as a result of his investigations in the Catskills, get married.

LEO LITWAK, born in Detroit, now lives in San Francisco, where he teaches at San Francisco State College. A novel, *To the Hanging Gardens*, was published in 1964. His stories and articles have been published in *Esquire, Partisan Review, The New York Times*, and other publications.

KATHRIN PERUTZ, New York–born and a Barnard College graduate, presently lives in Philadelphia. She has published four novels: *The Garden, A House on the Sound, The Ghosts*, and most recently *Mother is a Country* (1968).

JOHN FRANCIS PUTNAM is a regular contributor to *The Realist* and an editor at *Mad Magazine*. One of Mr. Putnam's long-standing ambitions is to produce and star in a dirty movie about President Warren G. Harding.

RALPH SCHOENSTEIN has written articles for *Playboy, New York*, and *McCall's*. He is the author of two books, *The Block* (1960) and *Time Lurches On* (1965), and has done TV essays for CBS and NBC. Most recently, he has published a new book, *With T-Shirts and Beer Mugs for All* (1968), and written the book for a musical show.

GENE SHALIT, a former *Look* Magazine staff writer, lives in New Jersey. Presently, he is a free-lance writer and public relations counsel.

CALVIN TRILLIN was born in Kansas City, Mo., and educated at Yale University. A *New Yorker* staff writer, he has written numerous "Reporter at Large" articles for that magazine, one of which has been published as a book, *An Education in Georgia*. Recently, he has criss-crossed the country for a *New Yorker* series called "U.S. Journal."

DAN WAKEFIELD was born and raised in Indianapolis and is a graduate of Columbia University. His books include *Island in the City, Revolt in the South, The Addict,* and *Between the Lines*. His latest is *Supernation at Peace and War* (1968).

CHRIS WELLES was born in Boston and graduated from Princeton University in 1959. After three years as a Naval officer aboard an aircraft carrier, he joined the staff of *Life*. That magazine's entertainment editor, he wrote many articles for *Life* on subjects ranging from business to modern jazz and politics. Currently Mr. Welles is a free-lance writer.

TOM WOLFE, who Walt Kelly has called "the great reporter of our time," is the author of two collections, *The Kandy-Kolored Tangerine-Flake Streamline Baby* and *The Pump House Gang*. His latest book, *The Electric Kool-Aid Acid Test* (1968) is a study of the psychedelic phenomenon.

VIVIAN YUDKIN, a Washington *Post* staff member, writes frequently for that paper's weekend *Potomac* Magazine. She has lived in England, Australia, and the Midwest, and is presently completing a book about her early life in pre-war East End, London. She reports that once, for a while, she was fat.